Lost World
England 1933–1936

Dorothy Hartley in Essex, taken at about the time of these articles.

Lost World
England 1933–1936

Dispatches to the *Daily Sketch*

Dorothy Hartley

Foreword by Lucy Worsley
Selected and introduced by Adrian Bailey

PROSPECT BOOKS

2012

First published in this form in 2012 by Prospect Books,
Allaleigh House, Blackawton, Totnes, Devon TQ9 7DL.

© 2012 text and photographs, the Estate of Dorothy Hartley.
© 2012 foreword, Lucy Worsley.
© 2012 introduction, Adrian Bailey.

The articles printed here were first published in the columns of the
Daily Sketch, 1933–1936. Some of the material was re-used by Dorothy
Hartley in her book *Here's England* (Rich & Cowan Ltd, 1934).

BRITISH LIBRARY CATALOGUING IN PUBLICATION DATA:
A catalogue entry of this book is available from the British Library.

ISBN 978-1-903018-97-2
Typeset in Adobe Garamond by Lemuel Dix and Tom Jaine.

Printed and bound by the Gutenberg Press, Malta.

Contents

CONTENTS

CONTENTS

Rock samphire.

Publisher's note

This book would not exist were it not for the production of a television documentary, *The Lost World of Dorothy Hartley*, by David Parker of Available Light Productions in Bristol, presented by Lucy Worsley. I am extremely grateful to David Parker for the original suggestion and impetus to action, to Lucy Worsley for her foreword, to John Littman on behalf of the Estate of Dorothy Hartley, and to Adrian Bailey for his selection of the articles and his introduction.

The text I have printed is that of the original pieces in the *Daily Sketch*. I have taken some liberties with the sub-editors' contributions of headlines and paragraphing but otherwise left the spelling, capitalization and other features as I found them.

I am especially grateful to Adrian Bailey for access to some of Dorothy Hartley's own photographs which she took on her travels and then pasted up into albums with short captions or explanatory notes. The pictures printed in the *Sketch* itself were not of sufficient quality to bear reproduction, but we are fortunate to have a few of the originals of those, as well as others that illustrate her subjects. The photographs themselves are small (82 x 55 mm) and the focus often less than crisp, but we have done what we could to make them acceptable. I regret that we have none of her drawings, the unmistakable hallmark of Hartley's work.

I might here draw attention to the fact that 1933 was an uncommonly hot summer, that a drought ran from spring 1933 to autumn 1934, that snow fell in October 1934 and again, heavily, in May 1935 (though the winter as a whole was warmer than usual), and that autumn 1935 was extremely wet with extensive flooding. King George V's silver jubilee was celebrated on 6 May 1935.

Tom Jaine

Foreword

For the last ten years, I've been the happy occupant of an office in Apartment 25 of Hampton Court Palace. When the wind's in the right direction, I can smell the smoke of the fire lit daily for our visitors to enjoy in the palace's great Tudor kitchens.

My work as a curator at Historic Royal Palaces is just as much about the social history as it is about royal history, because palaces were homes to servants as well as kings and queens. I've always been interested in the texture of ordinary people's lives, starting with what they ate. So a firm fixture on my office bookshelf is a well-thumbed copy of *Food in England*, published in 1954 by Dorothy Hartley.

Dorothy Hartley's *magnum opus* on the history of English cooking makes a wonderful starting-point for everyone interested in the history of food. Speak to any historical re-enactor or live interpreter, and they'll recommend their own top recipe or sketch from the book. The drawing of a section through a fireplace or the instructions for making a 'Medieval Pressure Cooker' are usually firm favourites. Despite its publication date, though, much of the content of *Food in England* was recycled from the series of early articles re-published here, originally written by Dorothy between the wars for the *Daily Sketch*.

Food in England is a classic, and has legions of fans. Yet if you speak to a historian, you'll often get a slightly cooler response, and here I must make an admission. I'd always been a bit snooty about Miss Hartley. My problem was her lack of footnotes and the enthusiastic, almost messianic, excitement she has for the ways of the past. Where, I used to wonder, was the probing question, the record of sources checked, the rigour of the reliable historian?

Well, you won't find it in Dorothy Hartley's work. What you will find instead, though, is a gift for communication, a humorous, generous spirit of enquiry, and a dedication to reigniting the romance of the past that goes beyond all reason.

In my case, it was only when I was invited to make a BBC TV programme about Dorothy's life that I really began to appreciate how richly eccentric she was, and where the value of her work really lies.

Dorothy Rosaman Hartley, born in 1893, was the daughter of a headmaster of a boy's school in Skipton, Yorkshire, whose family later moved to comfortable rectory in Nottinghamshire. She found work as an illustrator and a teacher of art, but never really settled down, either to marriage or to steady employment. She became a journalist and author, with subjects including the Tudor agricultural writer Thomas Tusser, customs, food, costume and geography. She produced many of her later books at her home in the Welsh village of Froncysylltau, where she ended her life and was buried in 1985.

Once you understand that Dorothy had been an art teacher, you appreciate the way her prose searches out colour and detail, and the way she simplifies, enthuses, brings her subjects to life for us as if we are her pupils. And yet she also has a sly, dry wit that means she's never patronizing.

For me, Dorothy Hartley is a slightly crazy but utterly admirable figure, who broke free of a solidly middle-class background to become a roving reporter for rural England. To research her books and articles, she travelled the country, interviewing country folk who still just about did things 'the old way' before mass production and industrialization and mechanization changed farming beyond recognition. Her lifespan witnessed cataclysmic change in the countryside, and she conceived it as her life's work to drink up the dregs of the old ways. For her the old ways were the right ways, and she has been criticized for failing to engage in the modern world. She paints the past in rosy colours: rural workers are always busy, happy and slightly implausibly satisfied with life in Dorothy's vision of England.

Certainly there's something of a dilettante about her, and certainly she had solid family wealth behind her. This was chiefly the property owned by her mother's family in the Welsh village of Fron. But the money was tied up, and did not translate into an easy or lavish life-style. In fact, Dorothy always seemed rather hard-up, and proud of it. She liked living simply, solitarily, travelling from place to place, sometimes sleeping in the hedge, and eating meals provided by the kindness of strangers (noting down afterwards exactly the food had been prepared). Much to her mother's and her friends' frustration, she never married, or had children, and she essentially ignored all the rules for how the daughters of respectable schoolmasters were supposed to live their lives.

Dorothy's *Daily Sketch* articles share something with the contemporary 'Mrs Miniver' series by Jan Struther, which similarly take a rich relish in the tiny, happy details of daily life. You won't find any hint, here, of the great problems of the inter-war period: class division, discontent, depression and world upheaval.

Instead, though, you'll find playfulness and joyfulness. Read them to learn bizarre facts about daily life in the past, and to hear the distinctive voice of an extraordinary woman.

Lucy Worsley
Hampton Court, August 2012

Introduction

From 1933 to 1936, the historian Dorothy Hartley wrote 150 weekly articles for the tabloid *Daily Sketch*, the series being entitled 'In England Now'. A selection of these richly diverse and entertaining pieces forms the contents of this book. The title, *Lost World*, refers to the decades between two world wars that witnessed a significant shift in modern society, during which the slow-moving rural world of yesterday, where long-established practices were cherished, could no longer keep pace with industrialization and many occupations were lost forever.

When her first article appeared, in Monday's issue of 10 April 1933, she was an established illustrator, a travel writer, journalist, photographer, teacher, cook, and a meticulous chronicler of the countryside and the passing seasons. She had a profound knowledge of crafts and trades and rural customs, which she shared with her readers.

Throughout her long, eventful life Dorothy Hartley was a remarkable, unstoppable source of creative energy and resolve; at times travelling around the country with a billycan and sketchbooks, pen and brush, by bike or on foot, sleeping rough under the stars, and on one occasion in a snowdrift under a hedge. A friend of Gypsies and tinkers, about whom she writes with sympathy and humour, she was also acquainted with tramps and wayfarers, who greeted her as a fellow-traveller.

We follow her footprints in the snow en route to Canterbury: 'I was freezing on the Pilgrims' Way, my fingers were claw curled with cold inside my gauntlets. The east side of my face was stiffly frozen and my mind was numb. Almost I could hear the ghosts of Chaucer's riders … their horse bells tinkling down the path like melting ice.' She finds a woodman's hut in a spinney and gradually thaws out by his fire, by which time she has coaxed the woodman to reveal the meanings of woodland lore.

From the beginning of her career at the end of the First World War until her death in 1985 at the age of 92, she was to write more than a dozen books. Most notable was her great, all-encompassing *Food in England*, published in 1954 and the result – like most of her works – of ten years' research (although she later admitted, following publication, that she'd been composing it since 1939). *Food in England* remains in print and has become a classic of its kind.

From the opening lines it is easy to see where her heart lay. 'English cooking is old-fashioned, because we like it that way.' And yet the book for which she would prefer to be remembered was her study of the sixteenth century Essex farmer-poet Thomas Tusser, whose *Five Hundred Pointes of Good Husbandrie* is an instruction manual and calendar for the Tudor farmer.

What drove her to identify herself with a farmer of the late Middle Ages is hard to fathom, but she is finely tuned to Tusser's earthy style, 'where his flowers are cabbages' and he 'gloats on manure'. It is the rustic poetry that grabs her attention, and ours too, and she makes the old farmer come alive. 'If there be earth magic through a quill it is here. Between the uncouth lines we hear the years pass, as you heard it. Hear the crackling of the breaking frost, the silence of winter snow, the lapping of the floods.'

In *Thomas Tusser* (1931) we can see the influences on her later works, *Here's England* (1934), *Made in England* (1939), and *Food in England*, for in Tusser she gives recipes. A blueprint, in fact, for the Hartley editorial style where the text is skilfully combined with her own fine illustrations, often with recipes, a formula she employed in these articles for the *Sketch*. A word here, too, on the relation between her journalism and her published books. Fact-finding expeditions and excursions often resulted in several outings in print. Thus *Here's England* is a compilation of some of these *Sketch* articles, and echoes of a single adventure may be heard in many subsequent works. She was too intelligent to let a good story go to waste. So who was this paragon of creative energy?

Dorothy Rosaman Hartley was born on 4 October 1893 at Skipton Grammar School for Boys where her father, Edward Tomson Hartley, was the ordained headmaster. Later in life, when his eyesight was failing, Edward Hartley was instituted as rector of Rempstone in Nottinghamshire. Dorothy's mother, Amy Lucy Hartley, a music teacher, came from Froncysyllte or Froncysylltau (more usually referred to as 'Fron' or 'Vron') near Llangollen in north Wales.

Dorothy was the youngest of three children. Her brother Walter Tomson Hartley was born in 1878, her sister Enid Myfanwy in 1884. Dorothy and Enid were educated by the nuns at St Monica's Convent in Skipton and at Loughborough High School, although later she often complained of her lack of education. However, it seems not to have thwarted her ambitions, for the Hartleys were dedicated to the pursuit of academic study and the arts.

Future careers and ways of life are of course invariably determined in childhood. Dorothy's mother and her aunt were amateur painters and from them Dorothy may have inherited her skill at drawing. The family had sufficient musical talent to form a band of its members. We find photographs showing Pater playing the 'cello, Walter and Enid violins (Enid also played the 'cello, the piano and could sing), Mater the piano (she was the music teacher at Skipton Grammar), and Dorothy on double bass, an accomplishment she later fails to mention.

Yet although Edward Hartley was a beneficed clergyman, there seemed to be little emphasis on religion in the home. Above all, it was important to be intellectually fulfilled, to be active and occupied, and teaching was a family tradition. Enid obliged by becoming a schoolteacher. The creative drive and pedagogy seems to have impeded the maternal instinct, for both Enid and Dorothy failed to form lasting relationships with men. Indeed, Dorothy had an ongoing and unresolved conflict with her mother who, quite reasonably, sought to encourage her errant daughter to find the right man and settle down to married life.

This, remember, was the 1920s, and getting married was what respectable middle-class girls were expected to do, or at least be seen to make the effort. She remained, however, a spinster, though not because she'd failed to attract suitors (she'd had several proposals), but because she seems to have decided to exchange married life for a career. In short, she didn't have time for the needs of men or the demands of a family. She briefly entertained a certain Mr Barham, who proposed to her by letter. She replied, treating him to a long discourse on Viking burial customs. 'That'll see him off!' she declared confidently. Dorothy paid a heavy price for her freedom and autonomy, for she frequently complained of loneliness, of acute homesickness when away and, when she reached the age of retirement, she longed to be surrounded by children.

Yet it is difficult to reconcile her complaints of loneliness with the following entry in her diary in 1935 when she was 42. She wrote, 'I have spent weeks in a half-buried, deserted hut on a sand dune, absolutely alone, seeing no one, hearing nothing but the cry of the gulls or the clamour of oyster catchers along the shore.' This self-imposed isolation became a lifelong habit, which suited the solitary nature of the dedicated researcher. She moved to London where she rented a room at 5, Coptic Street opposite the British Museum. Here she would spend months under the dome of the Reading Room, that splendid book-lined arena of scholarly pursuit and learning where she could study medieval manuscripts.

Her education at Loughborough and Nottingham Art School was interrupted by the First World War when Dorothy worked in a munitions factory in Nottingham, an experience that provoked and underpinned her strong right-wing views (her fellow workers, she opined, were idle and corrupt). At the end of the war, she went on to the Regent Street Polytechnic in London. She was highly commended for 'an exceptional ability at drawing', prompting one publisher later to say, 'Damn all artists, but that leggy female certainly can draw!' Once qualified, Dorothy continued to teach through much of her life, first at the Nottingham School of Art, then at the Regent Street Poly and, after the Second World War, sometimes domestic economy, presumably at schools, and lecturing at University College and Goldsmiths' College in London.

Dorothy Hartley was essentially an illustrator rather than an academic painter, whose style in the 1930s was inevitably influenced by William Morris and the Arts and Crafts Movement, and particularly by the distant echoes of medieval subjects popular among the Pre-Raphaelites and in the fairy and folklore world of Arthur Rackham. In a letter to a friend she writes, 'All I want is to get on with my own work in the fourteenth century. I'd not survive this century if I could not bolt out into the fourteenth and forget it!'

The fourteenth century was of course the period of Chaucer and Langland's Piers Plowman and it is very likely that Dorothy had been influenced by her father's love of Chaucer. As well as the poetic *splendeurs* there were the *misères* of the Black Death and the Hundred Years War, but the two extremes were embraced by Hartley who found emotional and intellectual security by identifying herself and her work with past centuries.

******

I first encountered Dorothy Hartley in the late 1960s when she was in her mid-seventies. At the time I was researching the life of Florence White, also a journalist, travel writer, artist and cook, and a friend of Dorothy's. My diary records my meeting with Dee, as her friends and family called her: 'Most hospitable but house difficult to find. Living on a pittance. Served lamb chops. Very proud and independent. Folk historian of rural life. English eccentric and a national treasure.'

Tall and slender, with long legs and a discerning sense of fashion ('I foresee I shall have to slide into greys and blues this autumn'), she remained a remarkable source of creative and physical energy: a visitor recalls her hostess at the age of 80, 'very elegantly dressed, with a beautiful bone structure and that kind of chic that one associated with French women, and who could read without glasses, and strode ahead so quickly that I had a job keeping up with her.'

She took care to remind others of her unmarried status by signing her letters 'D. Hartley (Miss)', which she continued to do even when our own acquaintance blossomed into a more lasting friendship. She also urged me to bear in mind that she lived, for the most part, in the Middle Ages and once, when I rang her at home, she picked up the phone and snapped, 'I can't talk to you now. I'm in the fourteenth century!' and promptly put the receiver down.

Her domestic affairs were always haphazard. Rather than continuing to live in the spacious, eight-bedroom family home at Fron, she chose to stay, with her four hundred books and four cats, in one of the six cottages on her land. There she resided for over twenty years. She fought developers, wayward tenants, the local council (who were planning to drive a road through her garden), rogue dealers, loneliness, ill health and old age. And yet, at the age of 70, D. Hartley (Miss), applied to a hospital in Africa to help work with lepers.

Her application was politely rejected on the grounds of her lack of experience. Undeterred, she applied instead for a teaching post in the eastern Caribbean, and boarded a banana boat bound for St Vincent. (It turned out that because of an administrative blunder, the job had been wrongly advertised and she had to return to England.) She never stopped working however and, during the mid-1970s, when she was over 80, she was petitioning me to find a publisher for her medieval romance *The Tournament of Tottenham*.

The pieces she had written for the *Sketch*, some 40 years earlier, well reflect her passion for English medieval history and her love for English rural life. We are not talking here of dry-as-dust historical facts, but of the author's intimate involvement with the land and its people, as when she writes, 'It's really serious to miss the tree blossom in England. The wild cherry comes first. The soft, loose blossoms sway in sudden laughter among the grey-brown trees in the spinneys.'

Her abiding interest in traditional country foods that led eventually to *Food in England* was well represented in the *Sketch* articles. Cider and clotted cream from the West Country, cherries and hops from Kent, shrimp teas and haver bread from Yorkshire, watercress from Hampshire, smokies and mutton hams from Scotland, bilberries and laver from Wales, blackberries from the Midland wolds.

She tempts us with her description of Yorkshire appetites, and the 'white cloth spread' of a big Yorkshire high tea: 'There was always a white jar of potted fish, or potted meat on the table. Of course there would be the usual chops or steaks, and game pie, and ham, and a cold round of beef, and apple tart, and pie and pikelets, and a slab of parkin, and boiled eggs, and hot tea cakes, and jam (two sorts, red and yellow), and plum cake, and cheese, and all the *usual* things one had for one's tea in Yorkshire, but you always left space for the potted meat, and salt butter, and watercress, and home-made loaves, because they were *good*.'

Readers of the *Sketch* were rewarded with country recipes, and I've included the majority in this book: ways with blackberries, and field mushrooms, damsons and sloes. She tells us that country cooks used to make a suet pudding from shreds of boiled bacon and hawthorn buds or watercress, and did you know that there are regional types of toffee apple? Dorothy Hartley admits to eating six 'in exasperated research' while identifying 'The Cambrian', 'The Cockney Standard' and the 'Oil-slab halo' types, just as she identifies different styles of thatching, employing five types of straw and regional varieties of reed and rush.

We learn that in the Scottish highlands they use marrum grass and ling (they still do). She finds haystacks 'extraordinarily interesting', in their variety and regional design: 'Put me on a haystack' she declares, 'and I'll tell you where I am.' She treats the reader to a lesson in ploughing, but the modern reader must take into account that this was in the days when the plough was pulled by a team of shire horses. She chides us for calling a scythe a scythe, for she is able to demonstrate that there are several types, but we are left secure in the knowledge that the pitchfork has remained unchanged for centuries – how reassuring! Here and there she drops in passages of medieval English or Anglicized French 'to amuse the scholarly reader'; the *Sketch* had a middle-class and largely conservative readership.

Dorothy Hartley identifies with her subjects and her readers alike. Very little escapes her close attention, and her sharp eye captures every detail, especially when in pursuit of facts, the more arcane the better. 'Can you find out', she writes to a friend in East Anglia 'if they still strew rushes in Norfolk churches on certain days?' which she follows with, 'I've just located the eleventh century gauge for the height at which to cut the corn off the straw…'

Highly personal, but with a wonderfully direct and fresh style; idiosyncratic, eccentric even, as when she talks to turnips, chats to scarecrows, or sympathizes with sheep and shepherds alike. I would confidently argue that only Dorothy Hartley could have written this: 'There is a tilt to the end of a Welsh phrase as if a laugh had caught its foot on the Border doorstep that runs from Caerwys to Ludlow'. Or when she writes to a friend, 'I am slumped in the big chair in front of a log fire, drifting blue smoke over flames like gold tulip's ghosts. It is Hiawatha that says the rainbow is where the ghost flowers are.' A little dotty perhaps? Yes, here and there maybe, but only where her writing strays into the territory normally occupied by folklorists.

'In England *now*, within 50 miles of London lives a charcoal burner, dwelling in a little hut in a green wood full of bluebells complete with nightingale. (With water nymphs in moonlight pools, and a magic frog who gives him three guesses thrown in.)' But then she goes on to tell us that he drove a car, and sat in his hut listening to the wireless. Her job, as she saw it, was to record the ways of the countryside, in the hope of preserving what remained of rural life, in particular the ancient crafts and agricultural methods soon to be overtaken by advanced techniques and demands for increased productivity.

Other travel writers of the time, such as Harold Massingham, A.G. Street, H.V. Morton and Harry Batsford, were similarly engaged in recording the rapidly changing world of the English countryside, brought about by improved public transport, better roads and the ready availability of the motor car. Readers able to fork out less than £200 could now buy an Austin Seven say, or a Morris Minor, straight off the production line. In 1933 an advertisement appeared inviting motorists to 'change up' from the hugely popular Austin Seven to the roomier Austin Ten. Weekend motorists could 'go for a spin', and explore unknown rural Britain, having read Dorothy Hartley's column at the breakfast table.

Much of the appeal of these pieces lies in her own nostalgia, 'So old, and so constant, is small green England, so unchanging, that many a time, between a whiff of wood smoke, and the crackle of faded yellow parchment, I've gone back far away, dreaming down the old centuries, the lost years passing by…' and the impression that, like the journalist she was, filing her copy from the field, dictating to the *Sketch* sub-editors from a 'phone box in a remote village among blue remembered hills.

I wondered if she had ever bumped into George Orwell in 'small green England', or crossed the path of J.B. Priestley. Both writers were exploring social conditions in England during the Depression, upholding socialist values that naturally mapped different, stonier routes than the leafy lanes followed by Dorothy Hartley. Where Orwell saw only desperate poverty and deprivation among the mining community of Wigan, Hartley described the Wigan miner's cosy kitchen where the family sat down to Lancashire hotpot and the stuffed chicken dish known as 'Hindle Wakes'. Nor was she averse to

Dorothy Hartley's bicycle, at rest before the farmhouse pump.

giving her pieces a bit of spin, as when, for example, she introduced her readers to some of the 'jolliest workers in England', the tent-peg makers of the Buckinghamshire beech woods. She found them busily shaping their pegs where 'the white cherry blossom blows down drifts of snow and the wind rustles the crisp, brown beech leaves'. These were the dark woods around Stokenchurch and Turville, where the lawyer and dramatist John Mortimer roamed as a teenager. He remembered not tent-peg makers but wood-turners or 'bodgers' who turned chair legs on primitive lathes for pitifully low wages over long hours, and were regularly exploited by the furniture factories of High Wycombe. Not so jolly, then.

Many of the *Sketch* pieces were extended notes taken from diaries and memoranda, or from memory. When we read about Dorothy on the threshold of her long career, striding down a mountain to explore Smoo Cave on the far edge of the Scottish Highlands, it was something she recalled from fifteen years before, during the winter of 1918. She was just 25, and she describes herself as 'young, carefree and happy as a queen.'

She had been walking for two days from the rail terminus at Lairg, as there was no connecting transport in those days except for the weekly mail cart pulled by six little shaggy ponies. She'd waded across an icy burn, but now her long legs were striding past the snow-capped conical summit of Ben Stack, on her way to Durness. 'I must have looked a tattered boggart,' she writes, 'for my woollen cap had been cut in two and used to pad the wrists of my dripping mittens, a long pair of worsted stockings were pulled on outside my shoes to keep the snow from working down inside; the hem was torn from my already brief tweed skirt, and my oilskin covered with fish scales off a herring boat!'

In her backpack there were the essential diary, sketchbook, pen and ink to record the details of her travels. Later, she would add a box camera and in due course became a skilled photographer, processing and printing her own negatives and holding exhibitions of her work. She extended the boundaries of her world by learning to drive and took delivery of an Austin Seven open tourer. This gave her the freedom to travel around Ireland along the route once taken by the twelfth-century prelate, historian and diplomat Giraldus Cambrensis, which resulted in her *Irish Holiday*, eventually published in 1938 (echoes of this trip are in the piece 'Inishbofin', below).

However, without doubt the most inspiring, indeed thrilling period of her life was her trip to Africa, where she motored with a couple of friends from the Cape to Kenya, thence by 'plane to Cairo, in 1931 when she was 38. This was the Africa of other, notable pioneer women, Karen Blixen and the aviatrix Beryl Markham. It produced some of her most passionate and singular prose, and she fell in love with the land and its people. She writes home to Mater: 'I want to go on and on and on, and never stop seeing this happy world that is so beautiful! How can I tell you a line of how wonderful it all is – but the sky this evening, all clear apple green and lovely. I can't paint it clear enough. I can't sing it, nor write it, nor dance it, and yet I want to tell you so much it is burning apple green flames inside me!'

The solitary way of life that she chose to follow could be endlessly indulged in the African bush where, 'all I'll ever need is a blanket and a gun', but it would remain an indulgence she could ill afford. 'I must come back and work to repay the £150 I owe you,' she wrote to Mater, who had been funding her daughter's adventure with regular payments by cheque to poste restante collection-points along her route. Furthermore she had a career to pursue: her book on Thomas Tusser had been published by Country Life on the day that she arrived in Dar-es-Salaam, homeward bound.

It would turn out to be a sad homecoming. Her mother, the beloved Mater, died shortly after her return. 'I just fell out of everything', she recalled years later in a letter to me, 'travelling around the country, subduing my misery'. This was in fact a period of intense creative energy, and she put her restless wanderings to good effect in these pieces for the *Sketch*.

One can be assured that less has changed in Africa's 'apple green' world than has changed in Dorothy Hartley's 'small green England'. In the 1930s, and well within living memory, life in the country, and to some extent the towns, was Spartan by modern standards. While there might be up to three or four postal deliveries a day, country bus services were few and far between, some buses might run only on market days. If you didn't have a bike, you walked.

Few homes had electricity, for the National Grid was only founded in 1933, and wasn't fully up and running until the late 1930s, which meant that many homes relied on coal gas for lighting, cooking and heating. Dorothy Hartley's cottage had oil lamps, a coal fire, and a gas fire in her bedroom, which she describes in a letter to a distant friend. 'A pretty, small room, white walls, white simple furniture, blue quilt on the bed, a bunch of pink roses in an old blue Delft jar, and green towels, dark oak floorboards and one rug'. Today it would feature on the cover of *Good Housekeeping*.

You would have been hard-pressed to find a cottage with a bathroom, and terraced houses in poorer districts had their lavatories in the yard 'out the back'. Washing day, traditionally on a Monday, saw the housewife in the scullery with its stone sink, boiling the weekly wash in the copper embedded in a brick structure and heated by a coal fire beneath. Washed clothes would be put through a mangle and dried on the washing line. If you needed a bath (and you probably did) you sat in a large tin bath filled with hot water from a kettle heated on the coal-fired range or on a gas ring. Dorothy had no hot water in her cottage because, 'the plumber can't get the right sort of boiler. I'm still washing in the tub before the fire in my bedroom.'

Women knitted and sewed and made clothes for the family, and in the evening they might sit around a coal fire in the winter, listening to the battery-powered radio or wireless. A 1933 report on the nation's health noted that we still had slums, a bad diet, and polluted milk and water. Slum clearance was a major political issue when Aldous Huxley published his *Brave New World*, and H.G. Wells *The Shape of*

Things to Come. It would take twenty years before electricity reached more or less every home in the land, ushering in the brave new world that we now take for granted, the world of vacuum cleaners, washing machines, dryers, dishwashers, refrigerators, television and record players.

While some trades and lifestyles have managed to weather and survive globalization and the rapid strides of technological progress, more profound changes have taken place in agriculture over the past fifty years than over the previous two centuries. The traditional crafts recorded by Hartley could not compete with mass-production and standardized manufacture of components, while farming methods have been radically updated with the onset of mechanization.

And so Dorothy's friend the charcoal burner has switched off his radio and quit the little hut in the bluebell wood. The nightingale sings unheard, for the charcoal manufacturer now has a steel kiln, a website video, and supplies supermarkets with bags of fuel for barbecues. When she explored Smoo Cave along the wilder shores of Sutherland in 1918, Dorothy observed that 'few know of it.' Today the cave too has a website, plus a hotel, a youth hostel and car park, and welcomes 40,000 visitors a year.

Does anything remain unchanged and unregulated, and unreported by the Internet, of Dorothy Hartley's rural England? The few lingering beechwood bodgers turned out their last tent pegs and chair legs some time during the 1960s and there are none left today, although a documentary film of the bodger's skills can be viewed in the Wycombe Museum.

With their passing, so went the flint gatherers, once regular visitors to the pebble beaches of Dungeness in Kent. Hartley photographed these men, whose task it was to sort and fill baskets with flint pebbles for the potteries in the Five Towns. The selected pebbles were those free of iron (contaminated pebbles bore reddish streaks), and were eventually pulverized and ground to a fine powder in ball mills in Stoke-on-Trent, to be mixed with pottery clay, the silica in the flint giving added strength to the finished pot. Today, the silica is obtained in the form of mineral sand and quarried extensively in Cheshire.

The labour-intensive trade of the pebble pickers has gone, alas, and remains merely a curiosity of industrial history. Furthermore, you are advised against collecting pebbles from the shingle these days, for the area is a protected environment. The beaches from Dymchurch around to Rye are among the largest in the world and are home to a distinctive flora and fauna.

In the late springtime, beyond Lydd, you'll see acres of brilliant blue viper's-bugloss and, where the marshes give way to the ocean of pebbles, islands of (edible) sea kale and the white-flowering sea campion. I was told by a resident at Lydd that the entire beach is constantly on the move. It is an unstable environment of marching shingle that at one time supported a unique method of locomotion, slip-on footwear designed by locals, who knew them as 'back-stays'.

These wooden 'skis' enabled the wearer to skim effortlessly over the shingle. Dorothy Hartley was encouraged to try on a pair, and found that a day of slip-sliding over the pebbles gave her 'an awful appetite'. They were regularly worn by the women who helped push the Dungeness lifeboat across the beach, the 'lady launchers', whom Hartley would certainly have met, and whose noble efforts were eventually replaced by tractor power in the 1950s.

Perhaps there is a lone, ghost figure that still 'back-stays' his or her way home in this strange, stony world, but in reality the remaining few pairs of the original footwear may be seen in the fine little museum in Lydd. While these local museums can preserve the past through artefacts, exhibits and photographs of rural crafts and country ways, certain skills and products are inevitably and irretrievably lost. 'Well is this series called "In England Now",' declared its author, 'for time and time again I find old jobs done in new ways, and new jobs proving as old as the hills.' She might have added 'some jobs and skills disappearing forever', jobs which she lovingly recorded.

Although we may decry past changes and inevitable extinctions, there are plenty of cheering instances of resilience and innovation. Up in Yorkshire, bakers used to make haver or oat bread, a batter of fine oatmeal, yeast and water thrown with a practised flick of the wrist on to a hot griddle or bakestone to spread out like a pancake. Champion among the haver bakers was James Leach of Skipton, where Dorothy Hartley was born. Oat bread fell out of favour when varied packets of oatcakes appeared on the supermarket shelves, and all that remains of this local delicacy is a business card that Dorothy gave me years ago, and is in front of me as I write. It says:

ESTABLISHED IN 1858

J. Leach

OAT BREAD BAKER
HAND-MADE THIN OAT-BREAD MADE TO ORDER FROM
THE BEST OF OATMEAL, AND GUARANTEED FREE FROM
THIRDS, SHARPS, OR ANY ADULTERATION WHATEVER

Hardcastle's Yard, High Street
SKIPTON

But Yorkshire traditions are stoutly defended, and while oat bread is lost forever, curd cakes, parkin, gingerbread and Yorkshire fat rascals are protected species widely enjoyed in teashops, and there's still a healthy demand for 'reet good clogs' from workers in foundries and glassworks, and from the fashion industry, while the clog makers maintain a thriving export market, particularly to Spain.

In the countryside, marketing has helped to make domestic ends meet. Hartley's world of 'sad little country markets', or pannier markets, has really taken on a new dimension with the spread of farm shops and the so-called farmers' markets. She wrote, eighty years ago, of the farm women who sit neglected with their fresh butter, home-made cakes and eggs, and wait patiently all day until towards evening when they will sell their little stock for less than its value, rather than carry it back the weary road home. 'Here, in these farmers markets, you find honesty and real worth', she says. 'Go and look for them, lovers of England.' Today, you won't have far to look at all.

The cheese industry, too, has grown from a mere dozen listed varieties in the 1960s to more than 700 according to the British Cheese Board. In fact, there has always existed a sub-culture of rustic cheeses in Britain, not acknowledged by the Cheese Board, a product of outlying farms and smallholdings. I remember being given a cheese made in a bothy in Aberdeenshire, and being told that it didn't have a name. It was simply 'cheese'. Hartley is proud to tell us that the majority of our national cheeses are as varied as England itself, and she writes of saffron cheese and a bright, ginger-coloured goat's milk cheese made in the hills of Flint, and rogue blue-veined cheeses made in remote Dale farms. 'Yes – cheeses have character,' she declares, and with patriotic zeal adds, 'and English cheeses are best for English people,' even though we now export Cheddar cheese to France.

Perhaps farming has been more alert to innovation than any industry. Profit drives the engine of change in the highest of gears. Tradition is often sacrificed to expediency. The haystacks I remember as a lad are now baled in huge wheels vacuum-packed in black plastic to gently ferment as silage for cattle feed. Even the fine art of thatching roofs has been influenced by market forces: the water reed used by thatchers right across the country is now imported in bulk from Turkey, from Poland and, of course, from China. But even here the lost world of Dorothy Hartley is sometimes being reclaimed and rediscovered, particularly where our growing affluence combines with social change to create new demands. Local councils, much to their credit, in areas where thatching is long established, insist that in every new housing development at least two houses have thatched roofs. Most councils are well aware of the need to preserve our rural heritage, and you can't even replace a pane of glass in the windows of listed buildings without approval.

Another example is her first *Sketch* article, 'Thinking Mutton'. This features a utilitarian product once staple throughout Britain. In *Food in England* she devotes no fewer than twenty-nine pages to the subject. But it was a meat in vertiginous decline. The arrival of frozen lamb from New Zealand, the greater convenience of small lamb joints, and the extra tenderness offered by young animals meant that butchers turned away from mutton. But having said that, and mindful of our heritage combined with our natural inclination to rescue lost causes, there has been a 'Mutton Renaissance', spearheaded by no less a personage than the Prince of Wales, to help sheep farmers realize a decent price for their ewes after they become too old to breed. Furthermore – and here's where social change discovers new markets – Britain's Muslim community has greatly increased the sale of mutton, offering a helping hand in the struggle to make ends meet. The butchers and bakers, the hop-pickers and pebble-pickers, the woodman, the bodgers and the charcoal burners, the haymakers and thatchers, the Gypsies and the tinkers, the shepherds and hill farmers, even the ghosts of Chaucer's riders, all feature in the following articles and have their brief say, which Dorothy Hartley the historian so lovingly and dutifully recorded.

She was enough of a pragmatist to welcome innovation. I last saw her in the year that she died. She was in bed, in Fron House, a cat curled asleep at her feet. 'If everything I possess vanished suddenly, I'd be sorry; but I value things unpossessed – the wind and the trees and sky and running water and kind thoughts much more.' And she added, 'What a poetic old party, eh?'

Adrian Bailey,
Bath, August 2012

Dorothy Hartley's articles
in the *Daily Sketch*,
selected from the series
'In England Now',
1933–1936

Thinking mutton

He was respectable and elderly, he had grey side whiskers and ought to have been a pillar of the church, and he lay on his back half-way through a blocked-up sheep hole. His face was turned to the sky and his eyes were shut. The stones he lay on were knobbly and he grunted painfully as he oozed through. Afterwards he picked himself up slowly, replaced a stone in the gap hole, readjusted his galluses and tie and, turning round, saw me.

I coughed. He coughed. The sheep at the other side of the wall said 'Baa-a-a-a' (the sound only made the silence louder). He said, 'I've coomed under't dyke.' I said 'Yes' and waited.

There was a perfectly good stile a few yards farther down the road and I looked at it audibly. 'I've give 'em the slip,' he said. 'They were following me,' he added. 'What for?' I asked. 'Hay,' he said.

Wildly I looked round for the other March hare, and the sheep said 'Baa-a-a-a' again loudly. The man grinned sheepishly. 'They *would* follow me,' he said, 'five old 'uns. *Ewes.*' My brain cleared a little and we fell into step.

'They be *old* ewes, the other won't be lambing until April' (i.e., the old sheep have their lambs earliest – and many contented old ladies are lying in the sun in the lower meadows now, watching their lambs racing about).

'The old 'uns like to get around the house,' he said; 'they get knowing where the hay comes from, and the kids fuss 'em with bits of bread and sweet.'

We were walking along the cart track now, longside the wall. I could hear the sheep running to keep up with our footsteps at the other side. Earlier in the day I'd watched a shepherd and his dogs out working along the upper hillside – they were high up above the valley road, but I could pick them up and lose them for miles, as they crossed the patches of white snow and disappeared against the dark, withered ling. Later, I'd seen the dog, gently bringing a special few sheep downwards towards the farm pastures. Our Northern sheep are hardy and often have their lambs on the mountain, but, especially in bad, snowy weather, they are brought down to the warmer levels and the luxury of shelter.

These old ewes had come down with the man and dog to a welcome armful of hay and the remains of a sandwich lunch, and had then refused to be left behind in their little field! Three times he had started out for the farm and tea and three times they had leaped the wall and out after him! Hence his undignified exit by the sheep hole.

'But why don't they jump the wall now?' I asked (for your black-faced sheep will clear seven-foot with a running jump).

'They'll not think on't,' he replied – 'they'll hang around the hole where I've come out,' he nodded his experienced head, 'I'd have left the dog to bid them,' he explained, 'but I wanted him for some more work up yonder, and they ewes won't follow me now, they'll watch that hole' (my side of our road ran nearest the dyke, and I thought I heard a hurried breathing along the other side of it, but said nothing).

'Yes, they breed very tame some of the old 'uns. Cunning? Yes, they are that; they'll find their way home miles if they get lost on the road.'

'No, not worth much if too old. I had one ewe I thought too old to breed. I only had the offer of 15s. standing for her (i.e., as she stood, for meat), and that weren't worth taking, so I killed her for ourselves, and we have mutton three weeks off her and there's eight of us, not much wrong with that.'

I asked about mutton hams, for they used to be made locally. He said a few farms made one if they were 'stook' with mutton, but 'nowadays the women don't seem too keen and now the buses run too easy to get fresh meat, and bacon, too. We do mostly keep our own bacon, some of the top farms lay in good supply, but it's none too easy to kill for ourselves.'

'Why?'

'Well, it's got to be done in proper slaughter house, or prove reason for not. Of course, if you get all straight, you can kill on your own premises, but the writing comes difficult for some of the top farmers, they don't manage to read the forms very easy.'

'What about sheep that break their legs or any sick animals?' I asked.

'Oh, you may kill them out of hand, so you can prove it saves suffering, and it's sometimes there's a few animals gets killed to save their lives, as you might say, and it's no matter what you do with your *own*; but you mustn't "offer for sale" unless you can prove it's fit for human consumption.'

I remembered a horrible description of a 14th century method of making Brasy mutton edible. It's written in Anglicised French – as queer and bad as the mutton!

I give this; it may amuse some scholar to puzzle it out:

Si une berlyz murge sudergnement il methent le char en ewe aulant de hure com e entre mydi noune e pus le pendant su e kant le ewe est escule le front saler e pus ben secher.

And I mentally gave thanks for some modern innovations.

Lesson of the Eggs

'It seems a pity, though, that you don't use your own animals oftener,' I suggested; 'it would save buying from the butcher.'

'Well, and then he'd be grumbling, and we'd get less choice,' was the reply. 'And whiles, when there's a snow down, we get heartily sick of the same mutton by the time it's all done.'

'Still,' with a twinkle in his eye, 'it's better than Capt. So-and-so I heard of.'

'Why?' 'Oh, *he* set up an incubator and it went wrong first day.'

'Well?' I asked. 'Oh, then they had to eat one hundred and forty-four hard-boiled eggs straight off,' he chuckled. 'Well, here I turn down to my tea, and if you want the bridge you keep round to the left. Good-night.' 'Good-night.'

I had caught the muffled hammer of little hooves on grass at the far side of the stone wall for the last quarter of a mile, and now, as I turned down to the bridge and he turned home through the farm gate, I saw five blackfaced ewes, all rather short of breath, neatly jump the end of the stone dyke and trot in after him.

Monday, 10 April 1933

Pedigree and mousetrap

There are two sorts of cheese. Pedigree and Mousetrap. The last is not made. It usually happens in wedges. In London, landladies put it on square dishes under pot catafalques, and you will always know it's 'mousetrap' because they say, 'I've brought chew a nice bit of cheese.'

I know of one such cheese wedge that lay untouched so long that it glued itself on to its slab by a sort of gummy secretion through its own pores, and my friend, who was an artist, touched it up with colours and gave the whole a coat of varnish and hung it up for another 'h'ornament' between a china cat and two shells and a ship on a plush plate.

Born in the Round

It hung there for years, and the next lodger said that, in his time, it had wrinkled a bit, and he always thought it was a view of Morecambe Bay. That's 'mousetrap.'

Pedigree cheeses are apart, and are born in the round. They live on round stands in country houses and hotels, and in wooden bowls in cottages and inns. These cheeses always have napkins wrapped round them, to show they are properly taken care of. No, this is not for appearance; it's to prevent the too-sudden change of temperature from the cold larder to the over-heated dining-room or kitchen. Any dairymaid will tell you that a cheese is all as sensitive as a baby; that's why old thick-walled farmhouses can store cheeses – 'natural like.' (They used to keep them under the beds quite often.)

'Evill to Dygest'

Whole volumes could be written on the pedigree cheeses of England. Centuries-old manuscripts tell of their virtuous diversity. There were

Bringing milk.

Un-moulding.

A man 'face lifting' the surface of a Stilton. It has to be smoothed over very carefully.

snowy soft and cool milk cheeses, and cream cheeses, and some that were coloured pale green, with sap of green herbs; it's likely the Roman nettles and docks massed so closely around old farms were purposeful, because many cheeses had nettle juice to sharpen them, and were laid on dock leaves.

Some cheeses even in those days were 'Hot and dry and evill to dygest.' Of Suffolk cheese it was said: –

Those that made me were uncivil
For they made me harder than the devil
Knives won't cut me, fire won't sweat me
Dogs bark at me, but can't bite me.

But the majority of English cheeses are good, and varied as England.

When East Anglia was a golden land of wheat, a saffron cheese was made, so that on the East you ate white bread and golden cheese: and on the West, in Devon and Cornwall, golden saffron bread and white cream cheese.

All the smaller districts have their own make of cheese, varied as the climate, pasturage, breed of animal, and customs of the people. Goats, ewes, cows all varied, and all milk was used, but in each district the characteristic cheese of that district developed by natural competition, so that the finest qualities *of its kind* were brought up to perfection, and the *differences* accentuated.

A few characteristic old English cheeses survive, old branches of the once flourishing family tree. Cheshire cheese is still large and red, like a harvest moon or carrots (and partakes of the nature of both). In old times they cut a circle out of the top, poured in a tankard of sack, and bunged it up and left it 'to digest itself' – a similar treatment often improves modern Cheshire cheese, which is apt to be dry and stolid. (Like a Cheshire farmer, they both warm and soften under the influence of drink.) Still, it's a good sensible, serviceable cheese is Cheshire.

K.O. Cheese

There is a variety of Goat Milk cheese that used to be made in Flint, up on the hills and on the waste lands by the coast. It was bright ginger-red and knocked you down at one whiff (if it still exists it ought to figure in the disarmament conference).

There is a delicious white milk cheese sold by the country women in the Oswestry and North Welsh markets. (If it is with this cheese the blackberry-eyed Welsh 'birdies' made overtures to the English warriors on guard in the marches, I don't wonder the breed is so mixed along the border!) This milk cheese is cold, and deliciously fresh, slightly salt, is decorated with primroses and served on snowy cheese cloths. If you find such a cheese for sale on a grey green cabbage leaf, buy it, for it's probably come from one of the old top farms, 'Pen-y-Pass' or 'Pen-y-Craig' – where they still use three-pronged forks and where the cow's milk is rich and the dairies are scoured with spring water and white sand.

Sometimes on these hills, at very remote farms, you can get a curd cheese that 'blue-moulds' in the most wonderful way – the country folk believe it is because the cows grazed by the old copper mine streams – and point out that using an old-fashioned copper wire curd-breaker had the same effect – but this is non-proven to me – there may be something in it – it's a pleasant cheese and rare to find.

But, Stranger! Beware of the 'Welsh Cheese of the Beauty Spots.' I met old Mrs. Jones, who had just sold off one of her milk cheeses, now green and rotten with age, to an American antiquarian for a shilling.

Indeed to Badness

Said I: 'Now, Mrs. Jones, have you no shame to do so to a poor, unsuspecting foreigner? Those cheeses are *6d. fresh* at the market on Wednesdays – *4d.* by Saturday, and that one was four weeks old and gone *bad*. O! shame on you, Mrs. Jones.'

'Well, well, and yes indeed, it wass too bad; it was very wrong ass you say' (the Welsh always take the wind out of one's moral sails), 'but, indeed, the poor lady wass all for the old things and wanted something with a real old flavour, and would have nothing of the cheese the smell of it she could not bear, and she did give me a shilling, and how would I be so rude as dispute with her, and she a visitor?'

North Wales has suffered more than any district from this 'beauty spot' mania and the influx of smart young business men and dealers (with oily hair and hooked noses), who sadly misuse the honesty and simplicity of the country women.

Wednesday, 12 April 1933

More about cheese

If you want the genuine thing when you are in North Wales you must go up into the mountains, or find the sad little forgotten country markets.

Thereabouts the farm women sit, patient and neglected, with their fresh butter and home-made cakes; and eggs and dressed poultry. (So carefully 'dressed,' with their livers under one wing and neat parsley button-holes on their bosoms.) They have no idea of salesmanship and will sell their little stock for less than its value rather than carry it back the weary road home. There, in these 'pannier' markets, you will find honesty and real worth. Go and look for them, visitor to England.

But to return to England and Cheese! Cheddar has a fine peppery cheese. A ripe Cheddar with a good 'bite' to it takes a lot of beating and it's a good cheese to go with ale and exercise.

Stilton is ancestral – it belongs to family portraits and gout. It has an atmosphere of country houses and 'About Town,' and at the club the waiter dates by it – 'when we finished that Stilton, sir.' At Christmas time, Stiltons go out to homesick Englishmen all over the globe. Soldered up into a tin, and packed in wooden crates, and nailed, and dispatched, a Stilton cheese costs all of £5 before it reaches some Rhodesian outpost! Yet an Australian cheese can reach England at 4*d.* a pound. Something queer about our transport!

There are Leicester, and Lancashire, and Cumberland, and Wiltshire cheeses that are good, but the most thoroughly English cheese is the Wensleydale. It's a little like Stilton, but the process varies slightly. Delicate as the Dales' colouring, and yet sturdy; and with an 'honesty' about it (I do not know any other word for the quality I want to describe). Something of the limestone that has preserved in the Dalesman his subtle child-like quality, seems to be in this

Dalesman's cheese (for cheeses are characteristic). This cheese has lost repute sometimes by its rarity, for rather than leave an order unfilled, between March and June, they will send up a Hay cheese – i.e., a cheese made while the cows are on the lower pastures or being partly fed with hay. The Wensleydale cheese made then is dead white, does not 'blue,' and is soft in texture. A fair amount is made and has a ready sale locally, and in Lancashire, chiefly because it cooks best! The Dales folk themselves often break it up with a fork and add milk and eggs and make delicious cheese cakes (very like curd cakes) and they used to have a dish in which thin slices of bread were fried in the breakfast bacon fat, bedabbled with the cheese or crisped in the oven – (I can't think why innkeepers don't use it more now, to supplement their excellent, but eternal, eggs and bacon). This 'Hay cheese' is a good dull cheese, but it is not best Wensleydale.

A good Wensleydale cheese made in late spring when the cows are at grass is perfect. It is a pale cream, fine textured, and it breaks a little crumblingly, there are faint blue-grey veins in it, and it tastes of blue-grey moorland grass and cold moorland streams, and has the faint aroma of wet alder wood. The country folk will tell you the milk from the high pastures is best, and also when, in Spring, the cows get the fresh quick grass, with a scrunchy mouthful of blown snow on it. Our dale cows are no hot-house-fed byre dwellers. They are sent out nearly all the year and the milk is carried down from the sheds in pails on the backs of the milkers. Perhaps the fresh flavour is something to do with the cleanness of the limewashed dairies and white scoured oaken cheese pots, for the Dales farms are the cleanest in the world. Sun and wind, and scouring rain and snow of the wind-swept moorlands!

'Although the lower meddowes doe abound in the plenty of grasse, yet the higher ground even beareth the sweeter grasse, and it is a rule amongst Husbandmen that the low meddowes doe fill, but the high meddowes do feede. The low are for the stable, but the high are for the

Cattle, that [grass] *which is long will maintaine life, but that which is short will breede milk.'*

So mind you get a fresh spring grass cheese from a high farm; for after a delicate nutty Wensleydale all other cheeses seem blatant and rough.

Yes – cheeses have character, and English cheeses are best for English people. Foreign cheeses are sold in England. Parmesan and Gorgonzola belong to Soho and Hammersmith, Gruyere is holy soap and Camembert pure temperament. Roquefort and Pont l'Eveque are modernistic, and there is a strong Dutch School, but if you are a peaceable sort of chap, who likes simple things that are really good – you will like Wensleydale. There's a sweet reasonableness about a Wensleydale cheese.

Thursday, 13 April 1933

Reet good clogs

Now here is something that needs understanding. Clogs are going out – as a mass production. Following the closing of many pits, and the decline of work, and change in the mills, the clog trade is definitely becoming smaller, but there is, and always will be, a definite demand for a certain number of clogs.

Dairy farm workers, clattering about over the swilled floors, need clogs. The rough, wet cement and tiles wear out anything else.

Workers standing on slats (the wood and iron draining-boards before machines) need clogs. This does not appear so at first glance, but try standing on an uneven surface for a whole day's work, and you will realise the need for the smooth wooden sole; cobbles have the same effect underfoot.

Yard workers, whether on the hill farms or in the dray-horse sheds of some manufacturing town, need clogs. Any wet, hard, rough footing needs clogs for comfort – they are characteristically a 'stone,' not a 'sand' shoe.

For Small Boys

There is still a steady demand for children's clogs – small boys' especially – and I should think you'd get a more freely grown foot, with the instep less injured, than when children use close-fitting boots and shoes, which are squeezed on longer than they should be because they are more expensive to replace.

The great mass production of standard clogs that clattered by hundreds and thousands to the mills in the early morning as the whistles blew is passed, but there is, and seems likely to remain, a fair number of clogs still in hard use. And while mass production produced ever cheaper and quicker clogs, the clog itself deteriorated – it was still serviceable, but standardised out of all individuality.

Now there are fewer clogs sold the quality is finer, and, except where economic pressure is very heavy, the wearer of clogs can afford to get a 'reet good clog.'

Bernadette's Sabots

To digress, for a small true story of the comprehension of clogs.

A small community of French nuns settled in a remote Yorkshire district near us. Any women more different from the rough, kind, materialistic and bluntly honest Yorkshire women had, suddenly, to rely upon each other!

Little Kitchen-Sister Bernadette, tiny, Breton, and lonely, wept and retired to bed.

The blunt, friendly gardener could not persuade her to come down to the kailyard. The nuns and the priest scolded and exhorted in vain, and then the rawboned Yorkshire charwoman came up to do the rooms.

'Twas wet after the rain, and she'd brought her lassie's grown-out clogs to lend to the 'littlest Sister'.

Sister Bernadette took one look. 'O la! les bons sabots!' She clattered down the garden path; she saw the apple blossom pink and cool and wet! She and the Yorkshire woman embraced each other, damply; thereafter they were inseparable companions – but heaven knows what language they talked between them! It was often drowned in the clatter of clogs!

Incidentally, Yorkshire, Westmorland and Lancashire clogs all vary slightly, but firmly, and the Leicestershire and South Country clogs vary in pattern. You see, to clog connoisseurs there are many points understood and appreciated that the ordinary (especially the Southern) mortal never knows exist. You've got to wear clogs from a child to acquire the grace and skill of the lassies who will spin you a dance on a wet, slippery pavement. A workless chap going off down a long road in search of a job knows many things about a clog-iron, and – you've got to have 'summat to sit on' while you're waiting!

Birth of a Clog

So let us view the industrial clog. Take the first view of clogs, down by the waterside, in a remote river valley full of bird song, and the clop, clop of an axe on new wood. Alder is the best. It doesn't split and stands the wet well. (Oak? You make a sole of oak and it will split under your foot the first time you stamp on a stone!)

The gipsies used to monopolise the clog-sole trade, cutting the blocks (rough shapes) and selling to the finisher. Sometimes the gipsy sold direct, and sometimes the clog-maker bought the trees and commissioned the gipsy to do the cutting. In those cases you will find a scrap of bark-rind left on each clog shape to show the owner the gipsy had not cut down *smaller* than he need, like the 'tell-tale' a lathe hand leaves when he roughs out work.

This rind proved the clog-maker had cut skilfully, and also that he had located the 'pair by the grain,' so that the shrinkage in drying out was uniform.

The white square piles by the river side and the blue camp smoke are seldom found now. I know where there may be a few, soon; but – well, *you* might not be the sort of person who'd eat a grilled trout that could 'look you in the face' (i.e., its mouth *not* torn by a fly-hook!)

For the leather you can range the hillsides or the Argentine – always provided you take good strong pieces, and cut to the weathering, and locality, and fashion – but the iron sole of the clog is its life, and your comfort.

There is a length for sole and instep, and a separate piece for the heel. The heel piece is simple but there's subtlety in the foot plate. You see a clog is unbendable (there's a *spring*; 'O, Ah'd not say it was *immovable*'), but in walking, the curve must be given by the iron, and the iron must grip the ground and protect the toe.

If the iron is plain nailed on the heads of the nails wear off and the iron clatters loose, so the strips must be pierced and a sunk pocket made for the nail head, and around it the ridge that will protect the head and strengthen the pierced iron.

The part under the foot must be thickened. A chap that's much to do in water needs a good height to keep the wood above the wet, and for slats of iron they sometimes fix another iron to prevent wedging, and an old hand will not only get this height adjusted, but will adjust the length of this extra thickness to his own step.

For Tall and Short

A tall chap with a fair stride likes a level 'reach' to his toe, and a little chap likes a 'more rounded rocking.' But the less nailing the better; like horseshoes, it's the shape. Originally the nails were made by little groups of older men, working around a small central forge, each at his own small anvil. *These are the old anvil stones – pierced with square holes for the nail anvils, outside many old 'works'* (that is something to find).

The nails had many names ('sparrow bills' was one), and a clog-iron 'shop' usually had its own nail-making section kept busy. (Later they used cutland studs from Leeds way and serrated bills from Belgium.) There were a few old nail makers left for years, because brush makers needed a nail with square base and round neck under its head. An old hand could do it 'quicker than you could see.'

A 'good nail and few.' It destroys the sole to be 'nail rid.'

Yes, they are clamped through, like horseshoe nails. They'll not come out till the iron wears, and the iron will wear thin as a razor before it gives out, and will cleave to the sole to the last. And the flattened turn is steady and level at the toe, because – well, you've got to have a clear end for sitting down on while you are waiting for work these days!

Friday, 21 April 1933

The jolly tent peggers

Less than an hour out of London, find a country bus; get off at exactly the right corner, and walk half a mile down the country lane, turn out of the lane and clamber up a wooded hillside, and you will find some of the jolliest workers in England. The Tent Peg Makers.

Under the trees the wood violets grow thick, and the white cherry blossom blows down in drifts of snow. The hedges and bushes are full of quick-flying birds busy with their nests – a little wind laughs up from the river, and rustles the crisp brown beech leaves.

On the day I was there last week swift scurries of rain and sunlight chased each other through the trees. The Tent Peg Makers had moved to a new pitch; they have only been in their new place a few days, yet already there are traces to find them by if you know where to look, a curl of wood shaving blown over the violets, a chip of new white wood in the mud off a boot by the stile – a V mark on a tree.

All traces to track down old friends, or, best of all, a whiff of their wood smoke among the cherry blossom!

I caught the first whiff of wood smoke and saw the first shaver of wood simultaneously, and a few breaths farther on was their shed. As a triumphant welcome came the sudden chu-chow, chu-chow of their long saw, slicing up the beech.

The sawyer spotted me first, and I waited until the cut was through before I took a picture of him, measuring up for the next length. He is holding the standard peg against the log to measure for the next cut. The grey, thin beech bark shines smooth as silk, and the wood is creamy white and cuts like cheese. It is now full of sap. Exactly like cheeses are the smooth, round sections of beech tree, each a scrap longer than the finished pegs will be.

Comfort or Chaos

To the unknowing, tent pegs are insignificant wooden hooks that fasten down tents. To the traveller, and a man of camps, they are rooted security, the firm peg upon which hangs his comfort. Are they small things to fuss over? Remove all the collar studs at a city banquet, and picture the effect! Remove the tent pegs of an army under canvas, and await chaos! Now, there are a thousand miles of experience behind my knowledge of tent pegs. I have made them, and proved them, under many conditions.

Where Wood Wins

Iron pegs drive in easily, but are heavy to carry, and in queer climates quickly rust the rope. Lighter metals may bend or snap against the shock of a hidden rock. Cracking frost or hot sun change them (let a weary day on the edge of the desert 100 degrees in the shade testify to this!) – also a very real trouble with all metal pegs in all grounds – they make a hole, wear it smoothly larger, and come out as easily as they slide in. (Let a horrible night under pelting northern sleet and rain testify to this!)

Now, wood swells and dries with the ground, and wedges itself tighter. For experienced comfort I have found wood reliable, but that wood must be properly made up.

Have the Best

The cheapest sawn tent pegs look all right; and for a couple of days gentle picnic may last, but one good whack, and they lose their heads (a thing one must never do under canvas), and in damp they will split atwain! Also, the rough edges of sawn wood will fray through a half-inch rope in one night. No one who has not lived under canvas can believe the sheer wear of a flapping, tugging tent, especially in wet weather when one is obliged to slack the guy ropes.

In camp, through months of daily use, a set of light, strong tent pegs can become known as individuals!

In a life of crime I remember most guiltily one cold wet camp when I burnt three spare tent pegs! There was not scrap of fuel on a stony wet desert and we were so tired that it really seemed that without a drink of hot coffee we should not survive to drive another peg anyhow! So the sacrifice was made.

Haunted by Pegs!

Never did tent pegs die more carefully. One was shredded to paper fineness – one split to spillikins, and one was the log, breathed upon with prayer, and it produced a boiling billy-can! Revived, we went forward, and the four regular pegs on duty, realising that now all depended upon them, stiffened up to their responsibilities and lasted out, but somehow those three little innocent tent pegs have haunted me. Let true travellers commend this – no others will understand the feeling!

But to return to the English beechwoods. There was a time not long ago when the woods were full of chair makers, beautiful chairs, all turned with an old pole lathe. A cherry tree chair, turned in the woods, was a wedding present dear to any English woman (and would solve the problem of many a wife now, could she get one!).

The scent in the wood was faint, delicious, and never faded. It was stronger in damp weather. One of the workers told me he had made a set of 12 chairs for his own wedding.

Now in the woods, over the brown, rustling leaves and the violets, the tent pegs of a nation were coming into being at the rate of 800 to 600 a day, or more. A million were bought by the Government last year from one firm, and each of that million was well and truly split with the grain, shaped by the grain, and would, therefore, drive in Straight, hold Steady, and Stay Firm. Truly British tent pegs.

Grandpa and the Shavers

They are being piled into hollow battlements, four square to the dry-ing wind. They will be well dried out and seasoned before selling.

Building the pile — 25+25+25+25: 100 to the pile.

Sacks of tent pegs;
Bucks beechwoods.

There were strong, thick grandfather tent pegs, all of 36 inches long! fit to uphold pavilions of state, or marquees at a garden party, and there were tiny four-inch shavers that looked too young to leave their mothers, but would support some hiker's home, or peg down a frivolous tennis net, gladly enough. Large or small, they faced their responsibilities no less firmly for their size, for each size peg is cut out of the tree to its own measurement, and each has the same careful work expended upon it.

Better Than Machines

It is skilful work. The workers have an almost uncanny hereditary knowledge of the wood under their fingers, a knowledge that splits and shapes wood with swift, sure skill.

The tools are primitive in their simplicity – a block, angle bill, mallet and spoke shave, and the simple, wooden foot-vice used by all country woodmen, all hand tools, but they can do what no machine can do – they can think, and no machine has yet made a better tent peg than those made in the beech woods under the cherry trees in England now.

Tuesday, 2 May 1933

Smoo cave

Up in the Far North, at the Western Point by Cape Wrath, is Smoo Cave. To the right of Durness it lies, and few know of it. Fifteen years ago the only way to reach Durness was by Robbie's pony mail cart. Four or six sturdy little shaggy ponies and a high, iron-wheeled cart, and Robbie, and the Cullan Dhu, all those long miles to the Cape from Laing, where the rail ended.

There was a house halfway – a rough stone inn where the ponies were changed and one stretched cramped legs and sometimes spent the night en route.

Ponies to the Rescue

Robbie told me, two years later, of the entry of the first motor-lorry that ultimately replaced him. It took six stages to get to the Cape!

It got the first day as far as the burn, and they had to widen the bridge (and the ponies took the mail off her), and then they drove as far as the lower pass, and 'she would no take the curve,' so they had to cut back the road (and the ponies took the mail off her). Then she got to the top of the pass, and the radiator boiled dry (and the ponies took the mail off her), and then she came down the other side and went into the loch – and that was a long job (and the ponies took the mail off her), and so it went on!

I wish I could remember all the sequence, but by the new bridge and the broken wall and the battered lorry I knew he spoke true words. But there was no mail lorry when I'm writing of, only the ponies.

I had lost my way and waded through a marshy burn earlier that day before I suddenly tilted down over Ben Stack, and reached Laxford Bridge and the roadway over to Durness. My soaked clothes stiffened and dried while waiting for the mail cart.

Fish-scale Trimmings

I must have looked a tattered boggart, for my woollen cap had been cut in two and used to pad the wrists of my dripping mittens, a long pair of worsted stockings were pulled on outside my shoes to keep the snow from working down inside; the hem was torn from my already brief tweed skirt, and my oilskin covered with fish scales off a herring boat!

But one was young, and warm, and carefree in those days, and, happy as a queen, I sat behind the ponies as we rattled down the last mile into Durness.

Shared With the Gulls

Mrs. Robbie took me in herself, and well pleased I was to reach her friendly arms and welcome, for I was tired out, and I had had nothing since the day before except a dried 'oatie,' the half of which I had thrown to the loch gulls for the joy of seeing them tilting down from the sky to the snow, white against the blue, blue against the white.

It was dark as Robbie and I and his meeting labourers floundered stiffly over the snow laden with packages along the way to the house, and there was sudden warmth of fire and hot broth and the big, wide blanket that Mrs. Robbie wrapped me into. The warmth of the welcome and the broth made the whole world swim out into a mist of red gold and hot ache – and, hardly awake, Mrs. Robbie put me to bed in the cupboard bed facing the firelight in the kitchen, and the last sounds I heard were the clumping of footsteps going up the wooden staircase over my head and the steady, monotonous sound of Robbie's brother reading the Bible in the next room.

I woke deliciously late in the night, as one does after the first sleep of utter weariness has worn off. The peace of thousand years was around me, the leather deerskin curtains that hung before the bed screening it off had been looped back, and a wee glimmer of lamplight left for me, as one would leave a nightlight for a child in a strange room.

Companions of the Night

The kitchen was small and warm and full of quiet sleep. On the low wooden table lay a pool of light under the lamp; underneath, in the dark, on the stretcher below, a long row of little, short-legged hens crowded close together; every now and then one of them would give a sleepy 'croon,' and the others would shuffle a little and set to sleep again. The old sheep, who had been part of the furniture when I came in, had been turned out into the passage, and I could hear her breathing under the door.

The old sheepdog got up slowly from under the dresser against the wall and walked quietly to the fireplace. Feeling my open eyes, he turned and came across, and stood a moment by my bed, and dropped a friendly cold nose into my hand lying open on the bed; he sighed reassuringly, gave a contented look around to note that all was well and quiet, then walked back to bed again; around and around and a flop and a long sigh —

Peace of 1,000 Years

He woke at intervals all through the night, just to do his quiet round; he walked to the fireplace, across to the door to listen to the old sheep, the friendly pause by my bed to see if I was sleeping, and the contented return to his own. And all night long upon the hearth the soft trail of smoke rose up from the peats, slowly and steadily, weaving the endless, soft-told story of peace that is a thousand years old.

Next day I went to find the cave. Follow the river, but do not follow it too far – for it goes down into the earth, and below, in the lashing wet, dark and cold lies Smoo Cave.

It's just a cave (what did you expect to find?) Outside on the ledges broken driftwood lies splintered, and after a storm dead dogfish lie strewn about.

Danger in the Dark

There is a deep lake inside, and the weed hangs limp and clammy and dark, great heavy masses of weed. Anything might be concealed in that cave. Many boats have hidden.

A queer, dangerous place in the dark of a winter's evening with the rising tide. My feet slipped on the treacherous weed, and I flung my arms upwards, clutching against the rock. My hands sank wrist deep under the green, slimy weed, and my fingers unexpectedly closed around a thick, strong iron mooring ring. It was driven into the rock. It was old, disused and rusted, and it hung now, completely hidden by the dripping weed, but – the staple of the ring bolt had been nearly worn through!

Friday, 5 May 1933

A village wedding

Blodwin is getting married to-morrow. The village is rather pleased about it. My mother is giving her the crockery for the new house. She is getting one of the Council houses first, but hoping to move nearer to Bill's quarry (Bill works in the limestone quarries) when one of the top houses falls vacant. 'Ty Ucha,' the top, is likely to be empty soon, and it's a nice house, and the garden's right for Bill.

The Council houses *have* gardens, but they are only builder's rubbish and, besides the gardens to all those, is in the middle of the circle, under *all* the eighteen other houses' windows; and it's no fun gardening when everybody sees each bean before you put it in, and can know they'll get kale if they come, 'cause they've seen you cut it; besides, she'll get her own water, and the Davis's was always used to that, being from Tyn y Pystill way.

Water Laid On
O yes, Council houses have water laid *on* when it isn't *off* at the main, and when I was at Mrs. Jones No. 4, you could hear Mrs. Jones No. 6 tap go 'weedle, weedle, weedle,' and Mrs. Jones 4 says, 'That's Mrs. Jones 6, she must be going to the whist drive to-night, because if it was the pictures, she'd not be bothering to wash her neck, because it's dark in pictures and they put a new step-down up last week, and never said, and Mrs. Roberts Ty y Craig stepped over it and came down on her eggs.'

It's not the same as having your own spring, because your own spring water keeps your butter lovely and cool, and Bill will build her a little well-house over it, same as mother has, and to wash feathers, and such like, you can tie them down in the water and leave it to run, but tap water gets measured.

How to use a Bath

Mrs. Jones she put her ham legs to soak in the bath and left the tap running while she went to chapel, and when they got heavy they sat down at the bottom on the waste hole and the water came over the top of the bath, and that brought down the two ceilings in the room below, where she'd left the supper laid, and it took them a week to dig out the plaster, and then they couldn't eat the mutton, which shows you've got to be careful how you use a bath.

O yes, the ham was all right, but the water doesn't seem the same when its *harassed* so, before you get it, nor it doesn't seem wholesome lying so long in anybody's tubing before it reaches you....

But to return to the wedding—

Blodwin chose the pottery and kitchen things because her own mother was giving her the bedding. My mother always gives them the choice of bedding or crocks or household things, and it shows her very sympathetic understanding, for she says, 'My dear, young ones want to spend their money on looking nice and making the house pretty. No young wife wants to spend 'first earnings' on dull dish-pots and towels that a man never notices; so if I set them up well for the beginning, they'll be comfortable for the first few years anyhow; and by then they'll have learnt sense!'

My mother is the only woman I know who has a waiting list of maids, waiting to come to her. She's been booked up three in advance before now! They come and stay till they get married and usually teach the next one and show her the 'ways' before they go.

The Old Far-Off Days

In the old, far-off days, when we had eight girls, their average time was ten to fourteen years. And copper kettles (the traditional copper kettle after seven years' service still holds good with us county folk) were a matter of course. One girl who came straight from school got three kettles before she married! And my mother was torn between her anxiety lest the child (then 36!) would never 'get settled' and her dread of never having another cook who could 'make such poetical soufflés as Jinny; and your father *does* enjoy them so.'

Three Years Average

Now mother is alone and has only one maid, and so the average is three years. 'Just long enough,' as an earlier Blodwin remarked, 'to make up your mind and do the sewing.' Actually, *this* Blodwin, who is getting married to-morrow, was six years, and so the village was – well, not *anxious* exactly, but it was felt that she really ought to make up her mind. You see, they got used to the butcher's cart stopping up the lane outside our house for fifteen minutes, or the baker's cart stopping up the lower lane for fifteen minutes, *or* the milk-float stopping up the top lane for fifteen minutes – but when all three got held up simultaneously, and they all used to glare at each other on the high road – well – it was felt that Blodwin ought to consider the community and fix it!

And *then* the minx went and got a boy from right the other side of the valley! And the bread, and the meat, and the milk were simultaneously delivered on time! And my gentle little mater had to agree to the two 'afternoons off' being rolled into one 'early-lunch-day,' so that there was time to cycle over so far to see Bill's mother.

The Wedding Cake

Blodwin's been at home a month now and she's made her wedding-cake all ready for to-morrow. The first of the wedding present things to be used were the icing sets and the exciting box of silver balls and cake ornaments. The wedding-cake is three tiers high and on top is a little silver 'bird' vase full of *real* orange blossom! (Mater! Is that tiny silver vase really kitchenware? Well, you know my dear, Blodwin liked it – because it was always extra polished, and the child hadn't anything just right to hold her orange blossom that the gardener at the hall gave her.)

The cake is made from our old manuscript recipe, written in

our old yellow book. The cake has got rum and mace and nutmegs and almonds in it, and it's all weighed in egg weights. The recipe is given to *Our* Blodwins only, who guard it as a sacred secret and win all the chapel cake competitions with it for miles around. We had none of us realised the secret sacredness of this recipe book till a migratory charwoman had the audacity to ask for it. Blodwin, pink with indignation, brought the old book from the kitchen drawer and secreted it firmly in my writing desk, with request to keep it locked up in future.

'Did I want *our* recipe – your great-grandmother's *own* recipe – to be made – and badly made – at a brick works?' I realised the seriousness of the position, and now none of the recipes that Blodwin and Co. have considered specially 'ours' is broadcast, but considered as exclusive 'family' possessions and *used* exclusively, too!

Some dishes belong to some occasions. Why, the rector must always have apple pie and the visiting football team boiled bacon and trimmings. I don't know – but I was warned that 'we' shouldn't win if they didn't. Once when I put my foot down and the visiting team got cold beef, 'we' didn't win, and I felt dreadfully guilty; and Blodwin put us on a tapioca diet for nearly a week.

And – and now Blodwin is getting married to-morrow, and, as the village says, 'she ought to be happy; she's taken long enough to make up her mind.' And as Blodwin says, 'As bride, she'll be wearing pale blue, because, though I always *did* intend pink, Bill likes me in blue best, and you'd best give in to a man when you *can*, because there's many a time where a married woman's got to hold her own, and we'll not be living far off when we are at "Ty Ucha," and Bill says he'll come over and fix your cellar steps for you as soon's ever we comes back; because being a quarryman, he can always pinch you a bit of cement from our works, as you know his boss. So it's all in the family.'

With which spirit of happy compromise in the air, Our Blodwin is getting married to-morrow.

Monday, 8 May 1933

Flint for the Five Towns

Clip! Chup! Crack! Scrabble, scrabble, and crunch: Clip! Chup! What on earth is that noise? It came over the sandy barrier between the wash of the sea, louder or fainter as the wind blew. At first, hearing it half asleep, among the humming reeds and singing sand, I thought it was sea gulls breaking shell fish on the rock, the cracks were as loud and as sharp.

Have you ever watched them? Lying on your tummy on the warm rocks watching them long, lazy afternoons? Just as the thrush has his convenient slaughter stone in a quiet corner of your garden, so the same gulls come again and again to the same spot for a peaceful fish dinner.

They will take a cockle high in the air and then drop it – crack! – and swoop! and 'next, please.' And the queer thing is that, just as a crow refuses to build with a dropped stick (he evidently think there's something wrong with the stick, for he will fly back a mile to fetch another sooner than pick up the fallen one), so these gulls will go to no end of trouble flopping off after a bounced shell, rather than pick up and drop another one!

But to come back to this persistent cracking noise that sounded across the dunes: it pierced my lazy dream, and presented such a picture of interminable, continuous, cockle-gulping, that my reason woke me into inquiring protest! Besides, there weren't any rocks!

There were about twenty men, scattered about on the beach, just above the wave lines, where the wet, dark shingle turned white as it dried.

They were picking up that endless mountainous world of rounded stones and putting it into baskets *one at a time*. These few men were trying to shift ten miles of solid beach in their fingers and carrying it off in hand-baskets!

These few men are trying to shift ten miles of solid beach in their fingers.

English Weather

Cautiously I approach and inquired about the weather (that's always soothing and reassuring to the English; high or low, rich or poor, we can all say what we think about our own weather; politicians cannot take it from us). It was beginning to rain; they said 'It looked like it was going to be wet.' So we were sane on the weather, anyhow.

Then a curious phenomenon; as the rain came down and the wind-dried shingle turned from powdery white to glistening varnished wet, they all moved up nearer the roadway; but still they continued to fill their baskets carefully, by hand, one or two stones at a time, and trundle them away as rapidly as possible.

It was reasonable, they might be mending a roadway? or embankment? or doing some building? But in that case, why not a shovel and cart? 'Why do you pick each stone up by hand?' I

Wet *shingle.*

asked. 'Fur glass,' said one. 'Pots,' elucidated another. 'Stone-ware,' completed the third… 'Jumping Jupiter! I thought you were shifting the beach!'

I suppose it was my idiotic indiarubber face that finished them, because suddenly we were all laughing, and an advancing wave caught us while we were still helpless.

For the Potteries

A grey-bearded man came from the next group, and half a dozen lads returning with empty perambulators and boxes stopped to hear what we were laughing at; between them they explained. These special flints are used in the Potteries, and at intervals the Five Towns send down a special truck train to fetch the supply of flints.

'Not any flint will do, they have to be these black rounded ones – see?' – they showed me dark, rough eggs of dull black, varying in size from a walnut to a man's fist.

'They mustn't have any white streaks on them.' 'The white won't fuse,' they tell me.

'We can spot them quicker where it's wet, they show dark, that's why we moved up the beach after it rained,' said one. 'I thought you shifted a bit nervous when I passed you with the barrow!'

'You'll find our first pile on the roadway,' they told me. I went; and found it half a mile farther down.

A circular pile of rounded, highly-polished loose flint eggs on a smooth slope are about as manageable as a peck of marbles on a shovelboard.

'That's why,' the picker explained, 'we are trundling them straight to the truck-side now and put 'em in direct.' He scooped back a few cwt. that were joyously rolling towards the rural constable as he spoke.

Heavy Work

My companion continued to talk with a watchful eye on his end of the restless pile. 'It's heavy work,' he told me, 'we couldn't do it continuous, but coming as it does just now we're glad enough to lay into it for a spell. One pad (basket) weighs about 7st., and by the time you've done 27 baskets you can call it a day. Powerful machines it takes to crush up these stones.' (His end of the pile of flints heaved, shuddered and cascaded down over our toes.)

'We're expecting the lorry back any minute,' he told me, gripping his shovel (with a gurgle of laughter the other end of the pile of flints toppled down endways to greet it), 'and when we've shovelled it in and it's off to the Potteries it's finished for,' he said, plying the shovel vigorously. (A fear took the flints and they spread sideways in trembling hops away from him.)

The lorry hove in sight and drew up by the pile, and the two shovellers set to work to scoop up the load of rolling flints and fling it on board. The crashing of their shovelfuls drowned all discourse, and I returned to the pickers, who were resting on the stone wall.

Monday, 15 May 1933

Don back-stays and off we go

'If we are going to walk, I'll have to borrow you a pair of stays.' I demurred that I'd never worn them.

'Oh, that's all right! You'll probably split them or they'll fly off you, but it's five miles, so you'd better have them.'

Reader! Did you know there was a place in England where they ski daily as a matter of course? Not ski in the *longest* sense of the word, because they are only about 18in. long, but ski they are, and you shoot along very conveniently once you get the hang of it.

Acres of Stone

You'd never suspect, from the completely care-free appearance of the town, that the people kept a secret sport like that behind their daily life. The streets, the church, the shops, the pubs are all peaceful and unsuspecting. The sea is heard faintly in the distance, the grass lands lie level to the sun, the gorse is molten gold, and the crying of seabirds and the bleating of lambs blow to and fro between the summer winds.

But beyond the rim of the green lands lie the lands of the back-stay, grey acres of stone, sea-cleansed grey shingle, laced with lines of drift-weed and starred with tiny flowers.

Not for Lovers

It is a quiet, undisturbed world. Sea borne clouds blow in across the sky and trail blue shadows over the downs. Inland, in the smoke-scented evenings, the young new moon rises in rainbow silver over the marshes.

I can only think of one disadvantage to the inhabitants: lovers could not linger by the ripples in the twilight, whispering sweet nothings, because you can't hear yourself think wearing back-stays!

(Still, there's room for two people sitting close on four back-stays.)

A back-stay is of wood, 18in. by 8in., has one strap of leather that you put over your foot, is tar and mud and lumps and scratches of reminiscent use on the top side, and underneath is white as bone.

Dungeness back-stays

Drawing by Adrian Bailey.

Putting on the back-stays.

Coming downhill is splendid fun.

Two Nasty Tricks

My guide, an expert, started me off on the level. Back-stays are easy as pie on the levels, and we rantled along at a fine pace – left, right, rutt–rutt–rutt–rutt, but once off the levels, and start speeding downhill, the back-stays either leave you and go on ahead, or fly up behind and hit you in the neck.

On this account, beginners are permitted (nay, admonished!) to belay the crossbar of leather to their bootlaces, because 20 feet is a fair fly for a back-stay, given a good start and a wind blowing.

Downhill, put in your heels and scoot. Up-hill dig in your toes and plod, and for goodness' sake don't look as if you were doing anything out of the ordinary. I tell you, *everyone* does it here.

The children back-stay to school, the baker boy props his bicycle against the high-road hedge and back-stays to the back door. When the fisher boats are sighted over the billows, the sailor's bride gives a pat to her permanent wave, pops on her back-stays and slips down to greet him. The gardener back-stays, the doctor back-stays. We met the curate back-staying to Sunday school class, and the scholars back-stayed to greet him. I suppose even the truants (we did not see any) back-stayed away (or would you call this back-sliding?). When I tell you that a perfectly good old-established inn with an excellent brew can only be reached by back-staying, need I say more?

Runt! runt! runt! runt! It has many adaptations, this life on the shingle. Its health statistics are marvellous. All rubbish is eliminated. Every scrap of burnt ash is wanted for the garden, and even tins are pounded out of existence.

Below the hollows of the shingle clear water gurgles. Scoop down a few feet and below the loose, dry stones there it is, sparkling clear and cold. The goats know of it, and so does the purple-branching seakale.

The most astonishing thing at the end of that barren, stony wild was finding a colony of bees and 'honey for sale!' Then one realised that there were acres of tiny aromatic herbs netting their way among the stones, tiny leaves that smelled like incense, sage and thyme flowers, and the green rosettes of coming purple fox-gloves, and, like the promised land, the gold of gorse against the skyline. The fragrance rose as a rainbow from a newly-opened pot of that strange honey. The bee-master herself hardly knows wherefrom the little workers gather, but seemingly, if that is the first real English honey the Romans found, I don't wonder that they came back for more (same as me!).

The terns have a colony beyond, and we walked wet-foot awhile on the shingle, and the terns, of the tiny black heads, slender wings and tiny scarlet feet, tilt up and down the wind with troubled, anxious little cries.

A Procession

Inland, as we crashed back through the twilight, we found smooth places where the stones were marked with a shadow line that showed silvery like watered silk. The hares made them.

Lie down flat, chin on the shingle, with the silver streak against the skyline, and by and by you will see the procession go past, or if you are lucky, as I was, you may see an astonished brown gentleman sitting bolt upright, two ears twitched up tight on top of his head and his whiskers fairly spinning around, within a yard of you! Then you will see nothing but a single shingle slipping down the silver road trackway and the grey sea mist sliding up over the marshes.

Then rise up with a crash and a clatter, hitch up your back-stays, and set out – runt! runt! and rattle! – for home, and arrive down the High-street with your back-stays, string slung, clattering behind your back and an awful appetite inside you.

Tuesday, 30 May 1933

This is the way we bake our bread

Down at our Stores on a Saturday night, they sell 7-lb. loaves of bread; the little mountain ponies come down to fetch it, and are well balanced, with the loaf on one side, and can of paraffin on the other, and all the bundles and the baby in the middle – then back they go, picking their neat foot-tracks up the steep hill sides, where none but the little mountain pony could find a footing.

They Know

We rather pride ourselves on our bread in our parts. You see, We have Our Mill! It is no picturesque ruin of the beauty spots, but a real, honest-to-goodness working mill, and a miller, white as dust, with a golden thumb. He can tell what wheat is good by one rub, and 'twas said his grandfather could tell, on which side of the shadowed hills the corn was grown, 'by the feel of the colour of it!'

Now, that was impressive! My grand-dad could tell which side of the mountain his mutton came off, but that was easy, because a lot more wild thyme grows on some sides of the hills than on others, and it is the thyme makes our mutton so tasty.

So our flour is good, and our ovens are adequate, and we nearly all 'bake.'

Just Right

There is no need to say what – just, 'we bake.' 'Do you bake?' 'She bakes,' 'He *has* baked,' and in all the valley I think that Miss Jamie's bread is just a little the best. It is so fine and close and fresh smelling, and the outside crust is just right. When you come up from the farm with an armful of bread, all warm and brown, and wrapped up in a linen cloth, you know you have got something good.

She begins to bake overnight, when the lad brings in the 3ft. logs of dry wood, and Miss Jamie takes the week-before-last's newspaper from under the settle cushion and builds the fire in the brick oven. Next morning it is lit early.

Come Into the Oven

Have you ever seen a beehive oven alight? Ours is 4ft. across and rounded, and fits into a bulge in the outer wall. The logs are burned inside it.

I sometimes wonder if a white bread loaf, in the brick oven, was the beginning of the Phœnix nest? Open the oven door when the flames have died down and see. Inside is a circle of white-hot ash, and then the logs, that have burnt themselves into a nest; round as any bird could build it; and all to the middle of the oven, is a pulsing scarlet purple flame, that fans, and breathes gold and purple breaths; like a bird of fire beating its wings.

An iron rake goes in, and scrape, scrape, then; w-o-o-f! Down fall the charred logs, dying out in black and grey ash upon the stone floor. But for half an hour more, the tiny blue flames still run about them, up and down, like tiny blue woodlice, whining and weeping, because the fun is over.

But Miss Jamie, she grips a firm damp mop, and swishes round inside that oven – souse! till the bricks go dark, and the oven door breathes steam. Then she puts one little brown hand inside; tilts her head for one moment; and says 'Right, Janie!' and, in go the loaves. 'Slide them right to the back.' 'No; shove in there.' 'Give *me* the bat.' 'There; what did I tell you?' 'So,' and the oven door is shut tight, and everyone sighs and says, 'That was a nice bit of wood,' or 'It will be out about 3 o'clock!' or 'You can come and clear now, Tom,' according to what they are thinking of; and *the* baking is over for another fortnight or a month. (Yes, the bread keeps moist as long as that.)

Proper Loaves

Our loaves are what we call 'proper loaves,' because they sit down upon themselves. We secretly rather depreciate a loaf that has to be supported by a tin, though we always run-a-few-tins, when there's a 'tea' on, or parties, because 'they are so good to cut.' But, I don't think we have any feeling *against* tin loaves – they are most sensible.

In industrial districts where the English mechanic lives, his rectilinear loaf probably feels the same aloofness to ours.

(N.B., in Africa, near the mines, we found English tin loaves baked in had-been-half-petrol-tins. They had ghostly trade marks upon them, and every second loaf had a wart, where the stopper used to be! It is little things like that that bind our Empire!)

Some tin loaves try to compromise, by being filled very full and bulging over. These are sometimes called 'Church-and-chapel' loaves, but the completely tinned loaf that comes out a suppressed square; well, when we feel lenient, we say 'it's good for sandwiches,' but we all feel it is rather ultra-modern in design!

There used to be Lancashire loaves, baked in jam-pots, that came out like Gothic mushrooms. They were convenient, because your man got the stalk with cheese, and the children got the top with jam. Elsewhere, there are 'cobs,' Coburgs, rollers, rounds, and punches, but 'long' bread only grows naturally in the Midlands or East Anglia, where the French settlers came. In the South, under bake-pots you get flattish 'pot loaves,' and all the mountain districts and some sea coasts have 'bake-stones.'

Scottish and English 'bake-stones' are quite different; and there is a solid flat Welsh 'bake-stone,' barely ½in. thick, which split and buttered is jolly good. Scottish 'baps' are bake-stones gone to heaven. They have become ethereal and 1½in. thick, and are snowy white. Of brown breads there is little room to speak now, but the Welsh sturdy 'barra brieth' is worth finding.

Tea-cakes are not bread, but verge onto it. Yorkshire tea-cakes have dimples in their middles, where they used to be threaded on cord. They are split, and internally toasted, and no Yorkshire tea-table feels decent without them (one for each person). Nottinghamshire has a super-tea-cake, baked in saucers, with a soupçon of candied peel. They are served hot from the oven.

Muffins, pikelets and crumpets, and such-all are not bread. Scones are definitely where bread stops being bread, so I have but lightly sketched the round and quartered scones, found in all colours and most localities of England. Oat-cakes must be separately reviewed, but 'pan bread,' i.e., baked over the fire and turned twice, and boiled 'Boston-bread' are both to be found in country places.

This last is worth consideration by camp cooks, as it is the nearest substitute for a genuine-to-goodness loaf. It's simply bread, boiled and boiled and boiled, and, when done, rolled out damp on to oatmeal and dried to a finish before the fire. This gives it a sort of 'crust.' If you are clever you wrap it in netting before boiling, when it comes out very fancifully. But you have got to be clever to guess just how much it is going to swell, and once I experimented and it swelled till it took the string bag bodily inside itself and had to be hung up for the tomtits, and even then mater said she was afraid they would catch their feet when they were pecking!…

But come back to the oven door; the bread has been turned and is out now. The pies are going in, and some stone jars of stewed fruit are standing ready. Afterwards the paper bags full of feathers that are hanging from the ceiling will go in and stay in overnight, so that not a scrap of heat is wasted, and, as I go off hugging my new crusty loaf, I am wishing all people knew how interesting bread is, and that more baked their own, in England now.

Tuesday, 6 June 1933

The village wakes up

My Mistress; is Master; Here, re, re, re!
So She is; Here, re, re, re!
So She is; Every Where, re, re, re, re!

A cock crows under my window. He says, 'My Mistress is Master: Hereee!' Two fields away his son and heir braces his claws against the half-door and levels his head for the time-honoured reply: 'So she is: Hereeee!' and then across the valley from a hidden farm comes the distant comment 'So, She is Everywhereeee!'

There has been a faint squeaking of ivy leaves on wet glass window panes all through the night, and now the glistening leaves shiver and spill little cascades of wet as I shove open wide the window, and a starling, who had been sheltering under the eaves overhead, starts out with a crash and a splatter of cold raindrops over my head as I lean out.

Damp 'Slices of Bread'

It's a morning such as you only get on a little island, a morning in England in July. A clear, cool morning after rain. A white sky across which trails the wind-fretted silver of the blown rainstorms. No sun, only a clear whiteness in the east and blue shadows ghostly on whitened grass.

Below my window the slate roofs of the village turn every tilt of grey and silver wetness to the sky. The long grasses are heavy with a load of windblown trembling crystal. The torn, woolly cobwebs along the hedge are grey as pearl, and the rank, green elder bushes that crowd between the houses, holding up their thick 'slices of bread' drenched with wet.

First Ducks, Then Kettles

The bird chorus flows on like a waterfall, over and under the quiet cooing of the wood-pigeons.

The hills are singing with the wet. Below, by the low bridge, the moss is purring and soaking down to the bog.

There breaks out a quacking and spluttering as Mrs. Postle's white ducks go splashing joyously across into the stream to gurgle and chuckle in the delicious, cold, juicy wet mud, and paddle over the scurrying sand. Simultaneously with their release comes the clank of a bucket and the complaining grunts of a pump; then the filling of a kettle (running up a little scale with a satisfying staccato click to put the lid on).

The blue smoke of dry wood begins to curl out of chimney pots, the door mats are shaken vigorously and flung over the yard walls.

The rattle of a dog chain comes from a kennel, and cats, appearing from nowhere (as is the magic of cats), come out and blink disparagingly at the light, stretch like elastic, and then selecting the driest spot available (usually on the mats) place their four paws carefully, yawn, and sit down to wait for the milk.

As it's Monday and likely to be a wash day, quite a number of small chimneys above lean-to's or small outhouses are smoking up, too. These are the poor little off-hand chimneys that 'only get a mouthful of smoke once a week,' as the saying goes.

Several little black and white figures have come out of the cottages and had a look at the sky, and wherever two such little figures come out simultaneously, they drift together, by a curious capillary attraction, and together regard the sky inquiringly. And since rain before seven, fine before eleven, is our safest prophecy, usually nod their heads, and toddle in again, and two more blue boiler chimney smokes start up.

As a sort of bravado a few strong kitchen chairs appear in the open, and some white clothes-lines with their fork-nosed line props are spearing defiance against the wind.

The church tower looks down on the early morning smoke.

Indoors, muffled calls and occasional squeals pronounce that early rising is being inculcated into the reluctant young, and a few nightshirted babies regard the day from doorsteps.

A thump and bang of wooden doors mixes with men's voices, and the ring of lumpy iron horseshoes on cobbles, as one after another the big, gentle farm horses are let loose, and make their way across the yards down to the pond. There comes a lowing of cows, halting reluctantly as they pass the calf sheds.

The village is thoroughly awake now, and there is a continuous quiet coming and going. Postie has just gone past, cycling up the lane to fetch his pony that takes the mail cart. He'll only have to peddle one way, for the pony will tow him back free-wheeling at the end of the hitching-rope.

Little Bill Thomas has made off inconspicuously along the hedge to the old pigeon cote, where he has kept his Angora rabbits ever since his big brother jestingly threatened to run the safety razor over them, because their continual moulting gave him hay fever.

All Getting Busy

The children who 'do-the-milks before school' are drifting down to the sheds, and the ones that have forgotten to bring their cans are going back to fetch them.

Mrs. Ruttles has gone by up the hill to do the schools. She turns down to speak to Mr. Echob. That's so that Mr. Echob is to come and help her shift the desks after school to-night ready for the Institute meeting. (So they are going to have it in the schools after all.)

The funny U-shaped thing in the bottom of that garden is old Jimmy Boxer (he used to be a ring attendant, hence the surname) bending to see if his vegetable marrows are setting.

Little Tommy Gardner has just come down from the allotments. With six curling cucumbers sticking out of his pockets, three on each side, so that he looks like an earwig with green legs. That means his week-end visitors are going back to-day. They'd take flowers, but it is too wet to gather them.

Just now Mrs. Stubbs went down her garden and peered into the empty pig-pen, and now she's taken the rector's old lawn mower and cider mat and barricaded up the door, so her Rhode Island hen *is* sitting. They found the old lady (the hen, I mean, not Mrs. Stubbs) on 16 eggs inside the hay tosser when they went to fetch it out, and she drew blood off three of them before they could shift her, so the eggs must be hard set. Wonder how long she'll be? It's funny, come to think of it, hens lay their eggs different times, yet they all arrange to hatch out nearly the same day ...

Suddenly a shout and crash, and rattle of loose stones, and the

milk float comes clattering loose hoof down the lane, and there are greeting voices and calls and the crash and bump of heavy milk churns being dumped out and in.

There is always something adventurous about early-morning milk. Is it the speeding spirit of the urban milk lorries that has infected us, or the dash of the Roman chariot in the construction of the milk float?

Even the Donkey Raced

I've known places where the milk comes down to the highway on a sledge. In another district, where several milk floats forgather to one depot, there's some really smart racing, with the rural constable disarmingly invited to 'Have a shilling on it each way with the engine-driver of the 6.45.' Even one tiny holding that sent one churn on a donkey cart, that donkey (ordinarily a sober animal) would catch the infection.

I believe the unearthly yodel with which the town milkman greets the bottled dawn is just the overflowing exhilaration of his 'good morning' ancestry.

The frenzied departure of our milk float marks the end of early morning in the village.

Now between the opening and shutting of a door comes the sizzle of frying bacon and the rattle of teacups. Children and kittens make hopefully for back doors, and Mrs. Wadkins and Mrs. Postle are planning the day's work under my window. Their voices rise up.

Strawberry Jam

'Good morning, Mrs. Postle. It's been a nice drop of rain we've had?'

'Well, it do seem to have come down, that's certain.'

Mrs. Wadkin straddles meteorologically over a puddle. 'My dad won't be half pleased, because they wanted to cut lower four acres last night and he stuck them out this was going to come.'

'They'll leave it over till next week now.'

'They prophesy it's always fine for East Wymeswold Choir Outing.'

'Good morning, Mrs. Hallam. We was just saying it do seem to have come down in the night.'

'I was minded to jam to-day, but them strawberries'll be too wet to gather. There's a tidy few ought to be got, too – the birds get that audacious if they're left.'

Which reminds me there is only one month in the year in England when you can eat all the strawberries you want before breakfast. What's the office motto? Do It Now! – er – good morning!

Tuesday, 4 July 1933

Ever been to a sheep-shearing?

When you went to the sheep washing were you invited to the shearing? Time was, not so long ago, when you would have been dancing under the summer moon at the week-end of sheep-shearing. Very neat footed some of those shepherd lads could be when they were in their slippers.

Old folks say, big sheep-shearing parties went out when machine clippers came in. While the sheep were done by hand, with hand shears, and the flocks ran to thousands, it was 'all hands to the shearing,' and there would be a regular set-to at each farm in turn; and you'd meet foreigners from fifty mile away, and 'folk that you had not seen since – last shearing!'

Sandwiches and Treacle

Up the dales, I remember, huge rounds of beef would be roasted for the hands. It would be slowly roasted and covered closely till it was cold, then next day the womenfolk would stand in a row, and one would cut even slices of the close farmhouse bread, another spread it thick with salty butter, yellow as gold, the next would lay on a slice of brown and white beef, one would give a good sprinkling of salt and clap the other slice down, and then lay it atop the piles resting on white board cloths in the big basket, and each basket had a little jar of new mustard, with a long bone spoon tied to the handle.

Those plainly-cut sandwiches *were* good; the beer was in glass jugs, a clear golden-reddish colour, with the foam slowly sliding down outside.

There was parkin and cheese for tea, and cheesecakes, and, for us children, treacle – lovely stuff. It wasn't black nor refined 'silver,' it was transparent dark amber, and came in kits (i.e., small tubs), and all the farm animals got a mugful when they were sick.

Doggie Friends

Treacle was cheaper than jam in those days (except rhubarb), and wholesome, and it swam beautifully and perilously off the oatcake, and stuck to things, dogs especially, and there were always lots of dogs at shearing.

Contrary to the general idea, the white-tipped sheepdog had a natural flair for childhood. Quite genuinely and without sentiment, these dogs would adopt child friends, and used to 'act reet saft,' as the shepherds would say, for a game of tag or catchball with some children. I had several working friends who would race down the steep fells for a quick greeting lick and a reluctant dash back to duty. No sheepdog would ever fight with another when among the sheep, but they would cut each other out shamelessly on the farms and cadge in the kitchen for beef bones. They enjoyed sheep-shearing week immensely.

The real reason for the dance was that the big barns standing empty before the corn harvest were cleared and swept for the shearers, and made a perfect dance-room. Some sacks well stuffed with hay, one for each shearer to rest upon, were thrown down (but a lot of our own chaps used stools for the sheep).

Have you ever seen a sheep clipped? Even with the newest shearing machines (which are a beautiful mésalliance between a dentist's drill and a safety razor) the procedure is something the same.

The sheep is caught and held on its back while the neck and chest are done first, and down the belly to the tail. While the sheep is thus up-ended, the shepherd often takes the opportunity to examine the hoofs. It looks funny to see a silly sheep lying back in the shearer's arms like a fat old lady swooning, with the shepherd kneeling down, gravely manicuring her toes.

They trot whole flocks through a curative footbath sometimes to cure cracks and chapping. It smarts rather, like some of our dressings, but it cures the hurt, though, as a shepherd remarked, 'The sheep don't know that, and they stand looking at you.'

[85]

A month of poor food or illness in the sheep would make a thin place in the length of the wool. With old ewes who have lambed, often their fleece drops and 'raggeds' of itself; youngsters have strong, woolly fleece, and the first time it is cut comes off a bit differently. There is a great deal to learn in the shearing sheds.

The fleece is snow-white inside with a lovely silvery sheen, and as soon as it comes off the sheep a worker (it used to be a woman) takes it, lays it out flat, skin side down, trims it, putting any loose locks into the middle, folds over the two sides into the centre, and then, beginning at the tail end, rolls it up tight.

When they get to the neck end they put a knee on it and then, pulling out the neck wool into a long rope, they twist it round the fleece and tuck the end in and carry it away in a neat, round, shining white bundle. There is nothing prettier than a newly-shorn fleece, unless it is very thick thistle-down, with the sun on it.

The farm I knew best, they would put away in a low, oak-floored room, with the shutters to, and the sunlight would come through the shutters in long, silver spears and the white fleeces would gleam and shine in the dark. When all was done they were covered up with a cloth to wait for the wool buyer, because the shepherds will tell you wool is a live thing, and goes on living a little after it leaves the sheep's back.

The Woolsack

Everyone knows that in the House of Lords the Lord Chancellor sits on a woolsack, but few realise that huge, smooth mattress was the regular packing of wool done by two labourers in the barn.

The great strongly-woven linen sacks were slung from the roof of the barns so that the lower side just swam the floor. A line of the white fleece bundles was laid along inside it and another on top of the first, so there was a layer just as long and as wide as the completed side of the wool pack would be, and two men then got inside the bag (the open edge just reached their necks) and then they walked up and down, stamping down the wool and forcing it into the corners with their toes. Another layer was handed in and they trampled down that, and so on, packing evenly and firmly till by and by they were walking along the swaying top of a wall of wool four or five feet high, and had to steady themselves against extra ropes hung from the ceiling while they trod down the last few layers of wool.

The minute they jumped out the assistants closed in on the sack, securing the open mouth from side to side, and it had to be sewn up at once before the elastic wool burst up and boiled over the top. When it was done, the new wool sack was stood against the wall, where it swelled and stiffened itself until it seemed as it really must burst. It was a special job weaving the cloth for the woolsack.

Plucked Sheep

Up in the North and on the islands, the sheep aren't shorn, they are plucked! And between the plucking in the North and the expeditious shearing in the South is every sort of form and method in sheep-shearing.

I expressed astonishment because some sheep were being shorn unwashed, and the old shepherd laughed. 'Six years ago,' he said, 'they would have been washed. That's a fac'. This is the only time I've every knowed to get money for dut (dirt).'

Though comparing their creamy Downsland fleeces with some of our peat-stained, weather-worn Northern fleeces, I could not see any dirt at all. In the North the youngsters are clipped before washing sometimes, but then the dates are all different, for our Northern lambs are about arriving when some of the Southern lambs are living with mint-sauce.

Tuesday, 11 July 1933

This week we'll thatch

And...rain upon the loft
Mixed with the murmuring wind; much like the sound
Of bees aswarm, did cast him in a swoon.

Lots admire thatched cottages, few know how that thatch is put on, and only those who have lived under thatch appreciate its advantages. There are many advantages.

I've known cottages become uninhabitable when the old thatch roof was removed and replaced by tiles. The sun beating through made the low rooms unbearably hot, and whereas the thatch, setting well out, had protected the walls the newly exposed upper plaster simply soaked up the rain like blotting paper. Also (and this is a matter for cottages set back from a roadway) the noise of the traffic, that used to be deadened by the thatch, became unbearable under a light metal roof.

Warming Up for Winter

There is also the question of heat and cold. The thick wooden covering of a thatch is much warmer in winter and cooler in summer than anything else. Once you get a thatched house warmed through it will stay warm all winter, and it will be the end of the summer before the thatch is hot, and then a thunder-storm and a blow of wind will cool it down again.

A bedroom under thick thatch is always cool and most curiously quiet. Even noises in the house itself seemed to be absorbed and deadened. Yet tiny sounds are delicately clear. It would be interesting to know if some forms of deafness find any difference under thatch.

By the same token thatch under which I lived myself; they raised the walls and put a tiled roof over it, and the starlings breaking through into the thatch roof and the house martins building underneath the tiled one kept things musical.

Hard-Boiled Eggs

There were two centrally-heated sites round the chimney stack; and each was fiercely contended for by both camps every year. I believe the birds used to use the chimney for a private incubator – it used to get really hot on baking days, so I suppose they liked hard-boiled eggs.

But returning to thatch. The main different varieties in England are reed, straw, ling, rush, bavin, turf. (That's not counting turf, rick, hay, and corn stack work.) Each of these main divisions is subdivided again into many others. Straw may be either rye, oat, wheat, Somersetshire or Wiltshire reed (which isn't reed at all) and many compromises.

Rye was considered best and grown specially for thatching. Round straw specially hand reaped *is* best, and was grown for the purpose long after threshing machines and mowing machines (that cracked and broke the straw) came into use. I've known them use cracked straw when they can't get any other, but all agree it's not much use.

'In Somersetshire…they do shear their wheat very low and all the wheat straw that they purpose to make thacke of, they do not thresshe it, but cut off the ears and bind it in sheaves and call it reed, and therewith they thatch their houses.'

Reed thatching may be Norfolk, Suffolk, or Kent reeds, or Welsh and northern border reeds, which are not reeds at all, but rushes. Norfolk reed is terrible strong, and will last 50 years well tended. It weathers with a grey iridescent sheen, like a pigeon's neck, and it matches the flint work perfectly.

Kent reed is very like it, but stands to be thicker set.

Down Devon way 'tis very thick and soft straw thatch.

Oxfordshire thatch is thick, but closer and less exuberant than the west, and there's a strong concise school beyond Tewkesbury.

Some of the South Down thatch has the very curve of the chalk over it, sweeping almost down to the ground and bending up and over the gable ends.

Some districts in Buckinghamshire have thatched walls and thatched houses very beautifully done, and a few Leicester thatches that I know have an extra line of thatch run round below the windows and over the porch as if the rim of the house's straw hat had split and slid down over its eyes. In some districts the thatch rises in heavy eyebrows over the windows. (These usually are very high-pitched roofs.) Some lower-pitched cottages seem to pull the thatch well down over their ears.

Up North we thatch less; preferring slabs of stone, in which we agree with Gloucester and the Cotswolds. But we use ling thatch very successfully. This is darker work and you can't 'show off' with trimming and fancy pattern like you can with reed or straw; but it's enduring (ah! it is that!).

This thatch is frequently roped down against the wind. Sometimes the ends of the rope are tied to rocks, or a log of driftwood or pegged into the houses themselves. In winter, out in the windy islands, I have seen cottages with their thatches so wrapped that they look like parcels more than anything else.

A Bit of All Sorts

One variety of roofing (but I hesitate to class it as thatch) occurs near the harbours. You see, we fling our old fishing nets over the top, and peg them down, and then we tar over the top of that, and chuck up some pebbles, and, 'well it's a bit of all sorts as you might say.'

The structural basis upon which the thatch is fastened varies as much as the thatch. The roof ridge must be roughly a right angle. It's usually more – say about 60 degrees, that allows the thatch to slope down it pretty thickly. The main scaffolding of beams fit from the eaves to the ridge pole, and between them the horizontal strips are fastened according to the thatch.

The work begins at the eaves and bundle after bundle is raised, each very slightly overlapping, and fastened and tied on to the horizontal strips, with ties of willow, string, rush, or wedged with wooden pegs, till the ridge pole is reached, when the last sheaves must go over, on either side. (It is here that the fancy work comes in.) Straw gets 'combed down,' reed gets 'beaten up.'

Where houses are reeded, as houses have need,
Go pare off the moss and beat in the reed.

Weather and frost tend to 'lift' reed a little, like frost lifts the soil, especially when the thatch is new, so it is wise to drive it in and down tightly in the spring, and remove moss, which would hold the damp and cause it to rot.

The season for thatching has always varied. Theoretically it is best to do it after corn harvest in the autumn, when the straw is dry but not brittle, but needs must be kept till the green outer leaves wither off. 'We stack till they drooporpham,' one reed thatcher explained.

On the other hand, if you are going to have half your roof off, you'd best do it in the summer! and it's pleasanter working in summer, and, as a charming writer in 1641 remarks, 'it will not get a man a heat in a frosty morning sitting on the top of a house, where the wind cometh to him on every side!'

Actually, we try to get it done if there's a slack moment before the hay harvest, and if it isn't done then it has to wait till the busy time is over, so you will see straw thatched cottages, a handsome piebald pattern both spring and autumn.

Tuesday, 18 July 1933

A craft as old as England

Over the sand dunes by the sea, where the white sand blows in the wind, grows the marrum grass, grey as dreams and strong as a promise given. And there lives still one of the oldest industries of England. Old probably when Cæsar came.

It has nearly died out many times, but always there have been a few faithful country people to go down and carry on, often more for the sake of the meeting, and the custom and use of it, than for the little money it barely earned. It is a craft that deserves to survive and develop, this old skilful enduring work of the marrum grass. They cut the grass in the late summer, when the deep sand is warmed through and the grass, long and pliant, lies in swathes of silk before the wind.

Sad Old Women

Perhaps there will be a party of 20 or 40 people down there, laughing and calling to each other, and twelve or more knives will be hacking vigorously. Perhaps only four or five old women will be there, alone among the dunes. Very sad are these little lost parties that sit down to rest and tea among the shifting, blowing sand dunes. For times are difficult and few country children can afford to stay at home on the land, and the old people are lonely and feel sad and forgotten.

Once, far away in the West, I came upon one old woman sitting solitary; by her was a pile of fresh cuttings, her blue eyes were looking away and away out to sea through the wavering grass – and as I came close to her, silent foot through the sand, she looked through me and smiled and spoke softly to me, as if I were a lost shadow that she had been thinking of. Behind her, across the smooth sand dunes, the track of her old footsteps went, lonely, back to the cottage; the tired footsteps were very slow and close together, and there were little ruffled places where she had stopped to rest.

Marrum grass set to 'win' in shining cones.

Sixty years she had come she told me, to cut the grasses, and as the blue shadows slid across the summer sea, and the dreams came and went in her eyes, she told me stories of parties long ago – where whole villages had come to the marrum cutting and the sledges had gone home high-laden with grass, and there had been laughter and songs and long evenings in the barns sorting the grasses – but – that was long ago – the lads had all gone abroad, the girls had gone into factories, and 'the men had gone to wars'; and 'it was dull without the young ones to make us laugh.'

Very different was a jolly party I found. They are still going strong on that sand dune! And good luck and more power to them. They deserve it! I wish you could see them setting out – word goes round the village one fine morning, and then off they go! stringing out in a long, laughing, panting line over the sand dunes to forgather at teatime, sunburnt and hot. 'It's warm work swinging that cutter; you try it!'

The dunes where the grey grass grows.

Cutting.

The knives are specially made – an old scythe; 'a nice bit of old hand-forged "cutting-iron," if you can find it in some barn indeed, that is the best,' 'the blacksmith he will make you a good one, if you tell him what it's for.'

'See, it must be heavy at the top end, for it goes deep through the sand, so – to cut down to the roots' – and clop! clop! clop! clop! and the grass is laid in swathes. The late, level sun, catching the flying sand, makes crystals, wheels of light spun out against the sky, but the real skill is in the stacking movement.

Whir-r-r! Clip

Quick as lightning they whip together a strand of grass rope, take a huge armful of slipping, glossy grass and, whir-r-r–clip!! it's spread through all the conic sections and left – a glistening cone of green silk with a neat knot at its top! (I want to see this done in slow motion!) The cones are left to 'win' and then carted home. Afterwards it's made up. Plain twist, double twist, weaving, plaiting, and a dozen exciting skilful tricks they showed me, laughing and thoroughly amused at my bewilderment.

I tried to get one of the cleverest to do the movement slowly for me to make diagrams, but it only showed an unexpected factor. *The grass is springy, and the speed of the working fingers is timed to catch the spring back of the plait with its own bending,* so that the marrum grass *itself* seems alive; and you have the pixie look of a live grass creature *making itself,* while a laughing old lady tickles its whiskers!

But the greatest fun was when I asked to see the mats, for presently, down the empty white roadway, came slowly and independent five large flapping *pancakes!* – each with two funny little human boots poking out, and trotting along on the under-side. You see, a mat is 10 feet across, and if you put the middle on your head it just touches the ground all around, and you can peek through the crevices and – so flap! flap! here we come along! The round mats are 'special' order – square is the usual make – and sold for hay-stack covers.

Hay will never heat through these covers, nor any rain beat through. They can be used by gardeners to stop frost on early fruit, or to lay on store shelves, or over the ground in the open. The marrum grass is perfectly waterproof and rotproof – the fibre has grown thus through hundreds of years, to withstand driving rain, and salt spray, and the wear of the grinding, polishing sands – and it's of this the mats are woven, and with it they are sewn.

And Lots of Things

Mats, bags, anything! The village chapels have hassocks of it. Do you want a garden seat or a chair cover or a footstool? Do you want a broom for swilling the yard or sweeping the hearth or a brush for whitewashing the house?

Come and find the marrum grass workers and have a cup of tea and a new laid egg to it and butter from a round wooden mould (with a fine cow carved on it!) and home-made bread, and afterwards, see if you can persuade some friendly old eyes to twinkle and laugh, and some skilful old hands to twist you a hollow-bodied bird, with a waving grass tail; or a green-rush and white-pebble musical-box that looks as if the Little People themselves had woven it for some changeling baby.

And *then* – you will have found the marrum grass workers-and a craft that is as old and as young as England now.

Tuesday, 25 July 1933

A lesson in haymaking

'Seldom is leisure found to thatch stacks as long as there is corn to carry.' So says a book a hundred years old, before reapers, binders and mechanical harvesters took over the field work. Even now, in the North, when making the hay and singling (i.e., thinning out) the turnips overlap, it is always a scramble to get both done. Down South it is easier, for the hay comes under earlier.

A Good Year

This has been an exceptional year for nearly all districts. The hay has come to time, and last week every stacker in the South seemed to be on his ladder working overtime. It averages 1s. 10d. per 100ft. stacking – not excessive, for only those men-of-straw, born and bred to the job, can get on quickly enough to do a complete top in one day. One or two fields were caught by the wet week and had heated and had to be burnt off, but on the average the hay crop is exceptionally good this year.

Now, will country readers forgive me while I just run through the hay field, to show the town ones what you are driving at?

These hayfields in January were looked over carefully. The old English 'meddoes' used to be what we now call water meadows, that is, land flooded under water in the spring. The fine silt deposited made this grass lush, and for years it was the staple fodder. For years farms have been importing and experimenting with overseas flowery grasses and trefoil mixtures to enrich the English hay, and new grass-seed mixtures were carefully sorted and tried according to fields and climate – but I believe the *Anthoxanthum odoratum* grass and the short, woolly grass that makes our hay smell so sweet are natives.

Yes – centuries of thought and care have gone into the grasses of our hayfield.

In winter the fields are first raked with a horse-drawn comb-harrow that claws up the moss, knocks down mole-hills and lumps, removes strangled weeds, and leaves the surface scratched up and loosened a little. A good man then goes over the ground with care, filling up holes, chucking off stones and bits of stick, and he usually has a poke full of grass seed for any thin places. (That is, supposing it is meadow already.) Early in spring, if the meadow is not a water meadow, manure is often spread.

The chain harrow or brush harrow are often run over after this, and the last brushing takes place about April and leaves the fields lying up and down smooth as striped silk, the gate is shut tight; and don't you go walking about that field any more.

The time before the grass is ripe for cutting is very technical. If you see a farmer cutting early and calling it 'seeds,' don't you call it hay. Hay is the mature grass and this main crop comes later. The exact moment when the grass is full and not yet begun to wither and become woody and is not yet too sappy to dry well, is a date taking years of experience to appreciate, and there is the awful compromise with the weather, to complicate matters, for you *must* have a spell of dry weather for hay.

Hayfield Hustle

The general rule is that the sooner after the grass is cut down, it's dried and 'got in,' the better, but if it rains on cut hay it half revives (like cut flowers that are put into water), and if you've ever smelt vase water that has not been changed, you will know what happens in sodden grass. Also, grass that has been wet from the outside, lying horizontally, it takes much longer to dry than grass which is only wet with its own sap on the inside.

Nowadays, in the hayfields, the new tossers and mechanical pick-ups sweep around, and as soon as the hay is dry and won (not quite the same thing), it is whipped up and off the field and into the stack quick as lightning. It is these new field loaders and the good weather

Thatching a stack.

between them that have set all the thatchers atop of their ladders this week.

From hay wain to stack they often fix up a pulley and tackle, and with a horse to draw the rope away, the grapplefuls go aloft as quick as the stack man can shake it into place. Even this is not an unskilled job. Notice how a good field worker, with an almost instinctive movement, shakes the sun-bleached over-dry forkfuls over darker, damper patches, and tosses the soft, loose, unmanageable stuff so that the strands lie downwards, sloping from the inside of the stack outwards to the edge. The men change places and move about the swaying, rocky stack, shifting their weight and strength, and building with even tightness throughout. Now you have got your haystack and the thatcher has gone up to cover it.

This is a common hillside stack method. The men being mounted on the stack, bundles of straw are handed to them one by one, as needed, and the bundle being retained in its place by a graip, i.e., pointed stake driven deep into the hay. The straw is first placed over the eaves, and handful after handful upwards from the eaves to the top are added until the thatch is laid in a wide, smooth strip. As the two men meet on top the straw is laid *along* the ridge, rather more thickly, for it supports the weight of the grass ropes that go across from side to side of the thatch.

When the first strip is laid, it is switched lightly with a willow wand, or combed out with a wide-toothed thatcher's comb. Then the first length ropes are laid across, one near the top, one about three foot down and one about one foot above the eaves.

The ends are fastened securely into the stack and brought across the smooth straw, and pegged down by a stake driven through into the stack. The horizontal lines of rope are carried once around each of the upright cross ropes as they pass them (exactly as if stringing up a parcel) and, as each fresh strip of straw is laid on the coil of ropes is unwound just far enough to cross it, tie round the cross ropes and be pegged down again. So the workers travel along the stack weaving a square mesh-net of roping. Final ropes are run along the ridge and each eave and secured to stakes or pegs driven deep into the ends of the stacks.

They used to put fine straw birds with spreading tails at the gable ends of the stacks, pointing north and south. One said it was the trade mark to show 'what stacker had done the stack.'

A friend in the field, who twisted me up the last straw bird that I have seen this many a long day, smiled shyly: 'Well,' he said, 'it was a bit of all sorts, but they *were* handsome birds and no mistake, and I never heard complaints of them stealing the corn!'

Tuesday, 1 August 1933

Many are the uses of watercress

Watercress deserves honourable mention. It is one of our oldest English salads. I can't guarantee you that Caedmon had it for breakfast, but I don't see why not – it's good for breakfasts.

Watercress is one of the few wild things that are really better grown in cultivated beds than on their wild loose. The clear chalk and limestone streams do grow delicious cress, but when the streams meander through sheep walks and cow pastures, it's not good.

Thick and Fast

In any long stream, you get small snails and fresh water shrimps and fishy visitors among your cress, but the cultivated beds of cress are shallow cement and stone pools, cleared out at intervals and cleaned as carefully as a swimming bath before replanting, and the water in the best ones rushes up clear and absolutely pure from artesian wells.

You see the pipe heads sticking up, and the fountain of icy cold crystal clear water bubbling and splashing down among the cress. It is water that has come clear and untouched and pure from miles below the snow-white chalk. The cress does not have to toughen up and fight, but can grow thick and tender, and as fast as it likes.

It is essentially English – watercress to tea. You get it everywhere. I've had it in country cottages, on the railways, and even in the British Museum. It's characteristic that the North and Yorkshire, that country that appreciates tea, were among the first and still are the chief customers of the watercress beds.

'Tons we send North!' a cress grower told me, 'and they know a good cress, too. It doesn't do to send them none that's run to stalk; the brown cress, now, is what the restaurants like to go with game and cheese and such all.'

Clearing around edges of beds

Nearer to the coast it's 'Shrimps and watercress!' and if you see a white-clothed barrow bumping along over the stones I tell you it makes a nice fresh patch of colour in a grey Northern street, especially if he puts a row of oranges and lemons around the barrow to attract the children.

Yorkshire tea is just about six o'clock (those were schooldays, just the right age to do it justice). There'd be a white cloth spread, and there'd be cold pie at one end and cold round of beef at the other, and a ham on one side, and a deep dish of potted fish paste opposite. And an apple pie and a jug of cream, and cheesecakes (by a slab of parkin) and cheese, and two sorts of jam, red and yellow, in a married glass dish, with a criss-cross handle, and a bowl of watercress all fresh and crisp. The Potteries make a special dish for cress, a holey bowl on top, over a dish below to catch the drips, for it must be served fresh and wet. Then there'd be oatcake and salt butter to eat it with, and, of course, tea cakes, one to each place (and pikelets in the winter). Well! I mean, it puts you on your mettle sitting down to a table like that.

I've known young boys straight off the field come in and sit down and – well, it would take them quite an hour before they had really made any impression; and then they'd get up, looking all peaceful and good, as if butter wouldn't melt in their mouths. Yes, Yorkshire people understand a meal. (You don't get anything until breakfast next day and you never get indigestion.)

Good for Doctoring

Yes, watercress was, and is, and let's hope it will always be, well favoured in England, though its accustomed home is the limestone and chalk, yet you find it everywhere. It's been naturalised in U.S.A. and Canada and introduced to the West Indies and South America. It's a real colonial!

In Leicestershire they reckon it's a good thing to eat in the spring. They prophesy it purifies the blood.

The clever French-descended Nottingham folk use it medically. For eczema they used to beat the cress, armfuls of it, to pulp and plaster it over the skin and bathe with the crushed fresh juice (running it through the mangle in a linen cloth till the bandage was all wet and green), and they'd eat it in large quantities.

In Scarborough an old woman (a sea-doctor) who lived in a tiny cottage used quantities; the fisher folk used to go to her with the ugly scratches and 'festers' that they'd got from sharp fish bones, and they swore by it. She made a green ointment from the cress, the golden broom flowers and clear black hog's lard. The cress gave her oil of sulphur and the broom flowers were used as scab cure for sheep long before tar came in (it's 'spoil a good *sheep* for a ha'porth of tar,' not a ship), but I don't know why the hog had to be black, except they say, it's whitest lard. She sold pounds of the ointment and had grateful patients who came miles for it. Her assistant used to chop the cress fine with a wooden stick and pack it into stone jars, and stand them in the oven till it was 'spinach looking,' and her patients had to take a spoonful of it on their biscuit, to keep their blood pure while they were at sea. When fresh fruit and vegetables were seldom had on the boats, I should think it had real value. Anyhow, on the boats 'Green Salve' and 'Dutch Drops' between them seem to cure all the ills that the 'fish' is heir to!

Tighter the Better
The cress is picked with knives by men wobbling carefully about in waders, picking the youngest and keeping a good stream clear round the edges. The closer it's packed the better it travels, so they pick it in handfuls tight, and tie it into bundles tighter; and compress it into flat baskets tightest of all. It's incredible how tight they pack it! I once put a basket of cress on a chair, and had just cut the strings when I was called away – when I returned the chair was invisible, and a fountain of cress was springing up and curling out across the floor to greet me.

Clearing the Beds
Just now the cress beds are being cleared out, and sad, yellow, leggy trails festoon the banks and men are plodding about with spades and shovels, and the baskets are being 'gone over' to see which can be repaired and how many more must be remade before the next season. But a few beds still go on, and by intercropping you can still get all the cress you want, though country people 'reckon the cress is resting till the twelfth, ready for the birds and sandwiches.'

Keeping It Fresh
By the way, when you get cress don't submerge it in standing water, let it float and let the tap run, or hang it up loosely in a wet cloth. A towel sagging over a bucketful of water in a cool cellar is capital, because the cress breathes through its leaves so fast that it needs a lot of air to keep it crisp, and the colder the water the better. Slip a small piece of ice into the pail if you can. Watercress is so fresh and wholesome, it's worth serving daintily.

Tuesday, 8 August 1933

Mushroom-time

They are up! Nice white, exciting things – mushrooms! There's nothing quite so joyous in early morning as waking up and going out after mushrooms.

That's, of course, if you know where to look! When it's a country you know, you go to certain 'places' where you can be certain of walking to the spot and finding the pretty pinky and white things waiting for you. If you are a visitor it is more uncertain and you will mostly come upon them by chance. The best mascot is *not* to take a basket, then if you have no possible way of carrying them you will probably find plenty.

I remember going out to pay calls with an aunt, never thinking of mushrooms, and, looking over the hedge, there they were! Simply shoving each other out of the field! Well, something had to be done. I found an old rain-rusted tin in the hedge, lined it with grass and filled it and put a neat pile of grass and mushrooms into my hat, and then (I still believe I was an ingenious child, though others often called it more unpleasant names) I blarneyed the aunt out of her stiff silk skirt – it was one of those striped frilled affairs.

A Wash-basketful of Mushrooms

I tied up the narrow end, packed the frill into enormous pleats, and propped open the silk with sticks and made a fine bag that held about a wash-basketful of mushrooms without crushing them. It was a little difficult to carry, and it looked like an enormous striped bull's-eye and, of course, she met everybody she knew on the way home!

Another time I had to load the insides of two learned professors' open umbrellas with the mushrooms. They made fine trays – the owners carried them held aloft by their little stalk-ends. The little button mushrooms I poured into the dents of the crowns of their wideawake hats, and you have no idea how funny they looked walking steadily, talking gravely, carrying their umbrellas upside down. It caused quite a stir at the railway station.

I remember my father making remarks about long-legged nobodies turning meditative professors into 'mushroom brackets,' but man-like, he never said how else I could have got home enough mushrooms for four people, and the meditative professors mopped up those mushrooms for supper in a most manful manner.

That just shows you, that mushrooms are a law unto themselves, and with a little ingenuity can always be got home when found. But don't spread them on the roof of the car! They dry so rapidly they will blow off, and if you put them into a perambulator, put them on top of the baby. They are quite light, but go ever so squashy if sat upon. A newspaper coned up will hold a good few, and you can read the news in conic sections in the train.

The common mushroom is most eaten in England, but around Nottingham and Charnwood Forest district, they pay a higher price for blewstalls, an alabaster-looking fungus that to my mind tastes like mushrooms dipped in paraffin. In Oxford they eat inkheads, which are pretty good.

I believe the 'boletus' or rough top is good, but I hesitate to suggest it, because being difficult to describe, people could easily make mistakes, but the genuine field mushroom, with the pinky-brown gills and the plain white puff ball, are unmistakable and delicious. The puff ball is absolutely straightforward, and cannot possibly be mistaken, and when it is in the rich creamy stage is simply delicious. We used to slice it thinly, egg and bread-crumb it and serve exactly like sweetbreads, which it very much resembles, both in texture and flavour. It is as light and as easy to digest. Why mushrooms are considered indigestible, goodness knows! Probably some fault in cooking.

Beefsteak and mushrooms and 'a nicely-mushroomed chicken'

need no recommending, but some of these older simple country dishes may be useful to visitors.

This was how my old nurse cooked my mushroom supper: The smallest mushrooms were peeled and thrown at once into slightly salted water – when all were done, a pint of new milk was put into a double saucepan and the drained mushrooms added with a good dab of butter, and the least possible dash of pepper; the whole was left to simmer generally about one hour. The milk never actually boiled (and I think this slow cooking under boiling point was the value of the dish).

Before I had it, a little brown bread was crumbled in, to thicken the gravy, exactly like bread and milk, and it was eaten with another dab of butter, and a good stiff rusk. It was good! Bettws never gave me plain, dull, bread and milk while there was a mushroom to be found.

For grown-ups the same dish could be thickened with white roux and mace added, but the brown bread is really more wholesome for children.

Early morning finds are best – plain grilled – with the breakfast bacon (but do not do them both together unless you need) – fry the mushrooms first in butter till just done, then slip the pan under the griller and grill the slices of bacon on to the mushrooms, or, if you are camping, toast the bacon on sticks over the coals and lay it across the mushrooms as you serve. This way you get crisp-frilled bacon and tender buttery mushrooms, not a soft mash of both.

There was a country mushroom hot-pot we used to get in Wales. You peel the mushrooms and put them with two rashers of ham and a sprinkle of herbs and a small onion chopped up fine, and an apple, and pepper and salt and a blade of mace, into an iron saucepan with one pint of stock, and stewed slowly.

After three-quarters of an hour you turn it into a brown earthenware cooking pot, in which you have arranged your cold meat. You slice up cold potatoes, put them over the top and put the whole dish in the oven just long enough to heat through, but not to re-cook the meat. Broken and 'ugly' looking mushrooms will do for this dish, and the very ugliest of all make into ketchup.

If you have plenty, try drying a few for the winter – it is quite easy. Pick the young ones, wipe them carefully and leave in a hot, draughty room until they begin to 'curl.' Then lay them on paper in a cool oven each night for a week until they are perfectly dry and light, and slightly 'leathery' looking. (Do not salt them, or you will never get them properly dry.) When done let them cool and put them into paper bags and hang them up in the chimney for a time or in the warm kitchen – like ordinary herbs.

For the Store Cupboard

When they feel quite dry they can go into screw-top jars in the store cupboard. They should be soaked before use, and a few chopped up will enliven a pie very pleasantly, in the winter.

Country people make delicious sandwiches of brown bread and butter and thinly sliced-up mushroom, sprinkled with lemon juice. They are delicious. Similarly, thin slices laid on with beef sandwiches are much enjoyed by most folk in the fields. They keep the sandwiches nice and moist.

You see, I have not tampered with all the exciting, amusing other fungi that *can* be eaten! My father was an enthusiast, and we found beef steak fungus, red and white and juicy, exactly like beef steak, and there were others that grew in the beech woods; he would never let me experiment with the tiny scarlet frilly cups, a small poisonous mushroom that could be dried and smoked like opium, and was used long ago to give medieval dreams. But if visitors and new campers will stick to the pink and white field mushroom and the big, well known puff ball, they will be quite safe, and I hope they will appreciate the English mushrooms as much as they deserve.

Tuesday, 15 August 1933

There's more than one way of making butter

Butter of the richest quality and flavour and appearance can be made from sweet cream. Were such butter not super-excellent, would noblemen have it on their tables every morning? I consider butter out of the churn from sweet cream, and before it is handled, the most delicious.

For my own use I would never desire better butter all the year round than that churned every morning from sweet cream. Such butter on a new cool baked oatcake, sweetened with flower virgin honey, accompanied with a cup of hot strong coffee, modified with crystallised sugar and fresh cream, is a breakfast worth partaking of.

So says Stevens in 1870. And very pleasant too; and obtainable to-day anywhere in the mountains if you know where to look for it. The coffee pot could be shoved in among the soft hot ashes and settled with a dash of spring water, or a burning stick. (I have yet to find where the settling of coffee with eggshells came from – maybe from a district where they use them to settle the cider, or perhaps it's the general proximity of eggs and bacon.)

In all England I hardly know a farmhouse craft that varies more than the making of butter. I have found it still made in box churns, from milk cooled in round, flat milk pans, the cream taken off with a skimmer like a porcelain shell.

They are mostly block-tin milk pans now, but there are a few earthenware ones made, and glass ones may be found with luck; and there's many a bird-bath in a country garden or sink in some stone cottage that was once a square, built-in marble milk cooler and the pride of the dairy. Of the old tall plunge churns there is nothing left but their shape and name in the present-day iron milk 'churns' of railway and lorry and country carts.

One gets used to a churn, and one likes the churn that one has learnt as a child, and that's why there's a specimen of almost every churn that was ever invented to be found in use in England now. And as for labour-saving contrivances, I've known water wheels, donkeys and dogs all used to help out the monotonous labour of milk churning.

> *'That's reet, and they worked champion.'*
> *'Yess, yess, indeed, whyeffer not?'*
> *'And why for no?'*

Several of the old end-over-end churns retired to the smaller cheese factories; where they earn a modest competency as washing machines, and attend to the cheese cloths and overalls, and foaming up the soapsuds as willingly as they once foamed up the buttermilk.

Of course we tie charms to our churn, for certainly butter is a chancy thing and 'politeness costs nothing, and you never know' … and who would be wanting to offend the Little People, who know how to enjoy a delicate dish of cream, and know more about butter than any country judge at an Agricultural Hall ever dreamed of? No, you'd better not be stirring up the stardust with which we sand our dairies. I will tell you instead simple old dairy knowledge that you can appreciate.

Wool and cloth must not come into the dairy; old linen for the wood and scouring sack (hempen) for the floor. White sand from the brook to scour with, and lime 'set' with skim milk for the walls. Theoretically, soap ought not to be used at all, but if you must use it the best dairy-maids will make a fine jelly out of it, and use it with cold water only, so that it will not strike into the wood, and they rinse off very fine. The milk utensils must be scalded with boiling water, slightly salted, and they get a very clean rinse, and the tubs and jars must not be dried, but set to drip and drain in the wind until they are white as snow. The dairywoman's hands should be smooth as butter, white as milk, and cool as spring water.

Salt Butter Fashion

I've seen Janet rub them with salt and oatmeal, and she'd keep dipping them into cold salt water as she made up the butter.

The fashion for salt butter has changed and now you only get the fresh unsalted butter; but they used to pack down the butter, when it was plentiful and rich and creamy from the summer grass, into wooden kits with finely powdered salt. There was much controversy over the delicacy of this salt, our only real rivals being considered the Dutch, who 'made a very refined form of salt.' But there were those in England who considered the best products of Droitwich equally good. Certainly salt butter was put down at the best time of the year, and, far from being considered a second-rate article, was preferred for use on oatcake, or with cheese and meat dishes, and a few of us miss the cold fresh tang of the rather hard salt butter and wish more country people would continue to sell it.

The Dairy's Her Castle

A dairy is always a pleasant place, whether it's a modern up-to-date blue and white aluminium finish or the shady stone outhouse of a farm. The floor is usually tiled or brick or stone flats, and in some places where they can get it even the shelves are great slabs of black slate, cold as black stone ice. The fine slate becomes glossy black with polish and use, and how it catches the light and how the butter gleams and shines on it! Snow-white walls, black slate shelves and golden cream.

Give it a chequered floor of old black and red burnt tiles, and then a rosy-cheeked dairywoman, with her skirts kilted high and a big blue apron over a holland one over a pink frock, and you'll see the very cream of England swishing around.

And step back and wipe your feet, and speak respectfully, for the dairy is about the last stronghold of the Englishwoman on the farm, and she's queen in her own domain.

Tuesday, 29 August 1933

A day in the life of a scarecrow

'WHIRR-RR-GUP! Good morning miss. Nice day! Rather windy for my liking! But very seasonable indeed! On the whole, a very good season. Whirr-rr-gup!'

He grinned from ear to ear and his coat-tails flapped pleasantly. 'This is a fine field, *as* you say, miss. Very fine and full o' the ear. Standard Red it is, very popular in these parts, very close set, and don't shed like the white, but there, miss, I could tell you more about the different varieties of wheat than you'd be able to follow, no offence meant, but not having had my experience.'

'You been on this job long?'

'You may say so! It's been in our family down generations, miss. Why, my grandfathers on the trousers side have clung to the family stake for centuries! Whirr-rr-gup!

'As we were saying, heads of corn vary. Roughly, as a guide for you to understand, when all the grains are set so that you can see the main stalk down the middle between the rows, it's "open" ear. When the rows are so close set you can't see the join it's "close."

'Reasons for it? Well, it's a matter of judgement according to the climate. They say some stands the rain better, but there – as you say, miss, it's too deep for you, it's taken me years. Whirr-rr-gup!

Jack of All Corn

'Do I undertake all sorts of corn? Why, of course, miss. Barley, oats, wheat, I supervise it all in my time (never the same in two years running, of course not! It would not be suitable).

'I took over this field last autumn. Winter sown they call it. Ploughing by Caudwell for Wadkin, on X—'s two-horse plough. Sowing by Wadkin's Junior on X—'s duplex driller. (He spoke as a stable boy stringing out a pedigree.)

Mr. Boggart on his job in August.

'Very nice job they made of it; very nice. It covered the whole field in one day, very different from what my father's waistcoat used to tell me, of the old hand-sowing days.

'They'd walk forty miles a day sometimes, up and down the furrows, if it was a late season and likely to rain. A cloth they'd have slung about them, or a basket slung in front. 'Twas a lovely swinging movement. One swing of the arm between each footfall and the hand slowly opening as it swept round, so that the last grain left the palm at the end of the swing; and the corn spread in even waves over the rows.'

You occasionally see a broadcast field now on very small hill farms. You can tell them because they're all-overish, but, as Mr. Boggart agreed, the rows are much better.

I told him of an old fiddle I'd seen once used for spreading peas, a shallow box that the farmer bowed across, just like a fiddle; till it vibrated and the peas would hop abroad. He listened, leaning at an angle of 75 degrees. He could not remember seeing one in use. 'No!'

he shook his head vigorously, thereby arousing guilty consciences in two crows peering over the hedge.

'I expect, for peas, miss, they would have *imitation human* scarecrows.' This view of the boy with the sling or wooden clapper made me jump! I had not realised the pride of a boggart in being 'made' to the job, not born haphazard!

Truth in Verse

'They prefer to sow before rain, then?'

'As a rule, miss, as a rule. The ground should be light and moist; you must never sow when it's sodden with rain, or you'll have the grain enclosed in little hard clay bricks – nor, of course, during a hard frost.'

I quoted:

Leave little wheat, little clod, over his head
That after a time ye may go out and spread,
If clod or thy wheat will not break with the frost
If then that ye roll it it quitteth the cost,
But see when ye roll it the weather be dry
Or else unrolled 'twere better to lie,

from Tusser, and the Boggart nodded.

'He was quite right; you don't want too close a surface for wheat. At first it needs the shelter, and later, if you rolled after wet, it would either pull up the rows or cake the land so that the tender shoots could not break through. Rolling is nice work! I had a laugh out of my boots! They came from Selsey Bill, the chap there used to walk level with his horses when rolling, led them sideways with a stick. The boots said: "It upset their owner altogether walking in front of the team."

'I had great responsibilities in the spring, young stuff so *green* just coming up! Birds would pull up the green, peck off the seeds. Whirr-rr-gup! Pickling the seed is some protection, but doesn't last;

but there, a boggart's whole life is a year of responsibility! Birds can't do much after the seed's gone and the shoots and roots are set. Then I can close an eye for a month or two, but once the ears are formed – Whirr-rr-gup!

Degrees of Naughtiness

'What birds are worst? Well, that varies with the year and the place. Sparrows? No, miss. As far as corn goes, they are maligned, they hatch their families, four running in the spring, and the young ones spend their time feeding on insects and weed seeds in the field all day. I see them, whole families among the corn stalks. What they take in harvest is well earned, we think.

'Wood pigeons, now, fairly stuff themselves, they do! Rooks? Well, when there's one or two, it's nothing, but sometimes a whole rookery comes, from miles away, and makes a dead set, but if you notice, rooks always set a watching bird, and if I have a word or two with *him* – no rooks in my field!

'If he doesn't clear off *at once*, I tell the master to shoot the ringleaders!' and Boggart looked *fierce*.

'Magpies? Jays? Well, never both together. They each eat the same food, so there's not enough for both.

"Believe not in the pies chattering, it is no truth but false believing."

'Ha! ha! that's a very old saying. A magpie is a very noticeable bird. Tale went round that if you shot a magpie his mate would commit suicide by drowning. They found some drowned birds in water butts, but I expect the lonely bird balanced on the edge, saw the other bird reflected in the water, bent down to kiss beaks as they do, and toppled in.

'Yellow-hammers are terrors for oats. The laverock (skylark) eats corn, but the corn bunting earns its name, it's really knowing. In a hard winter they'll go to the stacks and pull out the straw till they get to a head. Real holes they'll dig in. The other birds are quick enough to see the corn when the buntings have shown them the way!'

The Scarecrow's afternoon nap.

I asked him if he believed in counting grains of wheat as bushels per acre.

'Well, it is a rough guide, but I'd not buy a field for it! The idea was thirty grains to the ear will give you thirty bushels to the acre. You see, a chap knows how much seed he's put in. Well, if each seed is multiplied thirty times – you get me? – but counting losses by weather or moles or insects' (we both politely ignored birds), 'there's bound to be less; but, still, you can take it as a slight guide if it amuses you. Excuse me, Whirr-rr-gup!

Inside Knowledge

'What's a strike? Why, miss, the old wooden bushel measures were filled full of corn, and the farmer ran a strike, i.e., a wooden rule, level with the top, so, so many bushels were so many "strikes."

'Why is that small piece left uncut in the middle of the field? That's left till Saturday afternoon, miss, till the boys come with the guns. There's always a good few rabbits and the master likes some good shots to keep them down.

'When is corn ripe? It needs experience to judge. I always consult the master. Better a little under-ripe than over-ripe. When *very* ripe wheat bends its head, barley opens till the beard bushes a little sideways, oats straighten out and the chaff loosens a little.'

I saw a blue cotton frock passing down the hedgerow at the side of the field. The boggart eyed it with approval. 'That's Nancy, miss,' he said. 'A very sensible, well-stepping girl. Dick thinks so, too.'

A Knowing Fellow

The idea of a boggart approving amused me; but he took it quite seriously. 'She's very punctual with the tea, miss, when she brings it to the field during harvest, *very* punctual, and Dick, he stops the teams for Sarah, but he gets down off the binder and walks half a row, quick, to meet Nancy; *besides, I've got on Dick's old trousers. That means he's been buying himself some new clothes!'* I bent quickly to hide my laughter and picked a patriotic buttonhole of white camomile, red poppies and blue cornflowers, and pinned it on to the scarecrow's bosom where his heart would be where he not entirely stuffed with straw. He looked pleased; and I went away down the hedge to join Nancy. The boggart waved to us as we passed…

I went back next week to find him, but the corn was carried. The hens were in hen-heaven among the stubble and my friend was gone.

Tuesday, 5 September 1933

Come where the bilberry grows

Up past the grazing grounds of the hill farms, up, up through the rocky foothills to the bilberry tops! Bilberry, blaeberry, whortleberry or whinberry on the hills. It's a regular Norseman's foot of a plant! Stand on any bilberry patch looking towards the blue, and see the foamy long serpents riding against the land!

With the Gipsies

Norway is the real home of the bilberries, but over all Europe and in England it grows in patches. The gipsies get panniers of them and bring them to the back door, purple bloomed and broken, dripping great drops of purple on to the stone floor, and their coral beads and gold ear-rings dangling, and their patter dripping and popping and spilling in flow; like the bilberries, and it's, 'Bless you, and cross me hand with silver now, and I'll tell you a fortune,' and isn't it bound to be an interesting fortune? For are not my palms stained purple patches – even before you begin?

Slow Work

The hurt pickers (in the south) use a rough comb and scratch the berries out. They get little bits and leaves among the berries, but there is such a swim of juice when cooked that the leaves float off, so it is little matter. The hand pickers slide brown fingers under, and pick with a scrabbling shake, and some pick delicately, each berry separately, but it is slow work, and you can't get more than a pint or so in an hour.

In the dales we had boiled puddings of the berries, crisp white crust, and then, when cut, a gush of luscious purple berries and juice and crushed brown sugar; or we made tarts, served with thick blobby cream, or in the south, stewed the berries in rough brown oven dishes, and served with a virginal white glass dish of junket.

They are difficult fruit to pack for travel, but they bottle well, and a set of purple bottles, heather packed into an osier crate are a real country present.

Picking Parties

You seldom get the berries in town. One firm sells bottles of the juice 'As Supplied to His Majesty the King of Norway.'

'Well, well,' as the gipsy said, 'now heaven help him! and would the gentleman be needing anything more?'

Besides gipsies, whole villages make parties and go off picking for the day. Such a party I found one noon. I'd passed a sun-warmed hollow full of the finest bilberries and filled my billy-can to eat as I went along, and then, scrambling over a low dyke, I knew I'd come across the bilberry pickers, for a plump brown baby lay asleep under the wall and a shaggy old sheep dog got up and stood defensively (wagging a friendly explanatory tail!) as I smiled and passed on, and then just beyond was the dearest little old Welsh body I have ever seen.

She can't have been much over five foot tall. Her skirts were tucked high over her neat little ankles and strong little black shoes. The decent black gown of her was green and purple with sun and rain of the hills. Her bleached hessian top-apron was over a linen apron, white as snow, and she wore the frilled white cap of the old people, close over black hair that would still try to crinkle a little above her brown neck. Her little plaid shawl was pinned down neatly. Her twinkly black eyes were set in a bird's nest of wrinkles, and she was picking for dear life.

Our Joke Lives On

'Hoo-ee-Bach,' I called softly; 'let me give you a leg over here, there are the best lot ever.' She nipped over the wall like a blackbird and I emptied my gathering into her little tin pail – it half filled it.

Quickly she looked at me and her eyes twinkled like wet berries through the rift of brown. 'Dyn Bach! child, do not tell the others! their legs are younger than mine – and – they thought I was ower old to come!'

'O, mamyn fach!' We looked into each other's eyes, and how we laughed and loved each other on that instant!

It's over fifteen or more years ago now, and you must long ago have curled up like a little brown leaf and be sleeping for ever, but still we share our joke; and still I hear you chuckling among the bilberries.

Tuesday, 12 September 1933

Country ways with blackberries

... the running blackberry would adorn the parlors of heaven.
(Whitman)

Once in our wild parts, the dealers gave the country people such poor pay for their blackberries that in self-defence they would not pick any next week, and there was a great outcry by the disappointed dealers, over the lazy country folk who would leave good fruit to rot on the hedges.

Don't you worry! The country people got all the blackberries they could use themselves, or give away, and made quantities of jam and jelly, and the wine casks were full, but there was something rotten afoot when pickers were getting less than a penny a pound and the berries were sixpence and eightpence in the shops in the towns.

They're a Special Case

As many of the country people have said over much of their produce – we wouldn't mind making so little if the poor folk in the cities were getting it cheap, or we'd give it to the unemployed, but the dealer bleeds us both, and there would come the centuries old cry: 'if our King were knowing to it, he would not let them deal so with his people.'

Blackberries are always a special case, for they are so plentiful.

Years ago they used to be bought for the dye works to make 'indigo dyes,' and for long were found useful by the country people to re-dip their black worsted stockings.

There's many a country housekeeper's crackling black silk has been 'refreshed' by a dip in the purple juice, and the delicate lavender ribbons in the housemaid's cap took their tint from the same simple laundry sleight.

The New Maid

I remember seeing an old trousseau chemise of old-fashioned fine strong country linen. The round neck and elaborate sleeve pieces were set with lace netted frills of lavender 'lace'. It was considered very advanced to have coloured lace underneath, and I remember the responsibility was laid to the 'new' maid-only-arrived-two-years-ago, at the neighbouring Hall, who was French, and said to have 'ideas' (she'd certainly a genius for curly dark haired violet-eyed Blodwen).

Some of the country folk would cook beetroot, or frost-sweetened parsnip, with their blackberries, to save sugar, and some (for economy, but we might consider the advantages medically), added honey sweetening; and it should be noted that the blackberry was written up in some of the very earliest herbals as 'good for them who would become lean!'

Bramble beer was made of the 'newe springes,' that is, the tips of the growing whips. They do 'cure the hote and evill ulcers of the mouth, and throat, and the swelling of the gums, uvula and almonds of the throat,' 'wash them out often with the juice thereof to fasten the teeth.'

Never Boil Them

The astringent juice of the unripe fruit is also used, and the ripe juice 'is good for all throat and mouth diseases,' and hot with honey for a cold. So now you know!

Now I will find you a few old country usages that may be old enough to be new to you.

Don't ever *boil* blackberries (unless you like tough brown berries floating in red ink!) Here's the country way.

Thinly butter a thick, deep, brown earthenware piedish, and pack it full of the berries, shaking down close with layers of crushed brown sugar. The correct country thing is to add a cupful of the clear juice as it runs fresh from the cider apple press, but an ordinary glass of sweet cider will serve instead, or failing that, enough extra juice must be squashed out of some more berries (a few elderberries added are liked by some).

There must be just enough juice to come level with the tightly-packed berries. Then cover your piedish closely, and bake it ten minutes in the oven!

You will have a dish full of rich, plump berries, floating in a thick, dark juice, and it's a delicious dish.

A Surprise

Jenny once achieved culinary unexpectedness by making the blackberries 'go all hot-house,' using some of the purple grape tumblings, a glass of Burgundy, and split almonds stuck all over!

An astonishingly good dish, of most 'party' appearance. But there's something very pleasant and homely about that thick brown oven dish of purple, spicy blackberries, and the slow-baked creamy rice pudding that goes with it.

A quicker method is to put the blackberries in a colander, or sieve, pour boiling water over them, and then toss them into a glass bowl, and break down lightly with crushed sugar. They are very nice and fresh served this way.

Blackberries are less successful in tarts, as they go 'down so,' and best in puddings. Make the suet crust as thin as possible, and lightly crush down the berries before packing them in. You get the right proportion of fruit to pastry then; and be sure you have a big jug of blobby thick cream with it! up from the farm.

Oldest Recipe of All

And please; if in your household you have any old people who 'can't manage' the seeds, do make for them this oldest recipe of all.

Take a folded square of coarse cheesecloth and pile it full of the ripest blackberries (so ripe that they almost squash). Knot the four corners over, exactly as if you were tying up a wayfarer's bundle, slip a stout stick under the knots and begin to twist over a china bowl.

Go on twisting, and as the fruit runs turn and press the bag with the back of a wooden spoon, till in the end you have a twisted purple string of cheesecloth, with only a dry knob of seeds and skin at the end and a bowl of thick rich 'blackberry.'

Don't add anything to it. It should set solid in about two hours, especially if you stand it in a sunshiny window. It will be the consistency of junket, and delicate and fresh and is delicious served in a china bowl with thin rolled brown bread and butter, or sponge fingers and a dab of Devonshire cream. I have never yet met an old lady who did not appreciate this dish; and she will appreciate the trouble you have taken to make it specially for her.

Blackberry Cider

Take new cider straight from the press and equal parts blackberry juice, strain both together and mix with as much honey as will float an egg. Boil gently fifteen minutes in an earthenware pot. When cool barrel it, but do not fill the barrel. In March bottle it. It will be fit for use six weeks after bottling.

Old Blackberry Wine Recipe – Date 1700

Take your berries full ripe, and fill a large wood or stone vessel with a spicket in it, and pour on as much boiling water as will just appear at the top of the vessel, and as soon as cool enough to bear your hand, reach in and bruise well (as if you were breaking curd) till all the berries be broke.

Then let it stand covered till the berries be well wrought to the top, usually three or four days. Then draw off the juice through the spicket into another vessel, wash out the cask and replace the spicket, and pour back the juice adding to every ten quarts, one pound of sugar.

Let it stand and work (with yeast floating on a slice of toast) for a week, then again draw off and clear it with four ounces of isinglass which has been steeped twelve hours in a pint of good white wine.

Next morning melt it over a slow fire and add to the blackberry juice, dissolving it in about a gallon of juice, and stirring till it mixes well. Strain into a barrel, bung it up and bottle late next spring.

Tuesday, 3 October 1933

It's the nice folk you meet on a country bus

I remember when the first bus started in our village. 'There was talk of a bus,' they prophesied, 'there'd be a bus,' then 'There *is* a bus! it's running.' And the first time through we all rushed down to the gate to see it. Round the corner it came swinging, dogs barked, pigs made a dive for cover, and hens exploded before it. Through the village it careered, Poot! Poot!! Poot!!! round the corner by 'The Ship,' and off —

My word! we all drew deep breaths, and crossed the road with a new trepidation to discuss the wonder. Old Scottie, the road man, sat down on his barrow and slowly lighted his pipe. 'This place' (puff), 'this here village' (puff, puff), 'it gets more like London every day.'

Would you believe it? For the first three or four days not a soul got into that bus. I don't know why; I think we were all a little scared of it. It was so *new*, we half disbelieved it was real. Then one or two people were 'seen in it,' seen through the windows as it went past, and we reported to each other. 'There was two people on it!' 'They say Mrs. So-and-so was *seen* on it.'

Then, 'Our policeman, he's been took on it.' (N.B. – *our* policeman: we shared his jurisdiction with the next village, but he lived with us, and only minded them, so he was *our* policeman.) Then, 'The Rector, he's been in it,' and the bus, having been duly sponsored by Church and State, we all went joy-riding shamelessly.

Here let me pay belated tribute to the conductors and drivers of those first country buses, their ingenuity, kindness and long-suffering patience. It was an entirely new technique they had to evolve – to persuade inquirers to get into the bus and continue the lengthy catechism while travelling, to answer innumerable questions *re* luggage.

We took baskets to shop, of course, then we put eggs in the baskets. Then if eggs? why not chickens? – then, venturesomely, fowls? ducks? Two geese survived, and the conductor even commended turkeys! But he had to draw the line at calves, though 'Mr. Wadkin took that great sheep-dog of his'n – that's bigger than any calf.'

Then we learnt the architecture of our bus. 'It's warmer top seat back of the driver.'

'Let me come here,' said fat Mrs. X, spreading voluminously over the front bench, 'I've got a box of day-old chicks that mustn't be chilled,' and 'set you your butter by the door, Mrs. Brown, or you'll be oiling the works.'

'And don't you sit by the radiator, Henry, or you'll get chilblains.'

And finally, after months, the verdict over the tea-tables – 'well, I reckon ours is a good bus, ours is, and if you're going by the lower road, Mr. Wadkin, will you just stop it and pass this box to the conductor?'

Running a country bus means more than punching tickets at the right holly-bush. The luxurious liners that sail on the A.A. arterial roads are a race apart. It's the cargo boats that do the work, the small country buses that plough their devious muddy ways through the network of English lanes, scratched by hawthorn, bedewed by wild roses, and pursued by pigs.

I remember once, in such a bus, we stopped at the bottom of a hill. We watched a cottage woman hurry out, signalling wildly. A child tottered up to her, its pinafore draggling. Automatically she tied it and, turning, stepped into a go-cart of apples. A frenzied collecting of the apples, and round the corner of the house came the Man, with the back of an old envelope and a stub of pencil, and we could see him producing that complicated masculine shopping instruction (every woman in the bus knew he said he hadn't wanted anything when he was asked).

Stop, Driver, Stop!

Then, just as she begins to run down the path, the clothes-line drops, and she picks up twelve socks and drops them into a gooseberry bush in her flurry. By that time the sympathy of the entire bus is with her and the men are laughing, and in she tumbles, panting and apologising. The driver lets in the clutch and we get to the top of the hill, and, 'Oh, stop, I left my purse on the dresser!'

Well, of course, a town bus would be restricted, but, being us, there was just laughter, and, 'Oh, stop! driver, stop! here. Let Henry run back for you, his legs are longer.'

'Well, well, we'll get started some time yet,' says the driver. Yet, curiously, one is seldom late to market.

Friendly Suburbia

One bus still takes us many muddy miles to a small railway station, wherefrom we catch a train to the country town. That bus sees some funny sights, for round the country station spread suburban season-ticket holders, and these, to give them full credit, are the friendliest allies on market days. When the bus disgorges fares, shoppers, families, market baskets, fowls, and livestock, simultaneously with their own neat-newspapered arrival for the 8.30, to see them grip attaché cases in one hand and expostulating ducks in the other, and charge down platforms, with beautifully creased trousers and baskets of eggs, is to realise the unanimity of English minds in a moment of stress!

'One gets to know a lot of nice folks on the bus,' said old Mr. Davis, thoughtfully wrapping a blanket round his beehive, because his neighbour looked nervous.

To appreciate the penetration of the bus, you need to go cycling along the country road between seven and eight in the morning when the market buses are going in. At each tiny lane-end, at each stile across the field, are people, waiting with bundles or even the bundles waiting by themselves, with just a label. One day I shall be a bold, bad buccaneer, and stop and make an enormous breakfast out of those bulging baskets. I can picture the new loaf crumbling under the golden butter, the honey dripping from my countenance, the cream frothing about my ears, but no – how could I break the honourable entente of the country bus? We trust them with our babies!

The 'School Bus' is an institution! and if the driver does not start with the mildness of the dove, the children soon teach him the wisdom of the serpent!

He Cured Them

One long-suffering friend bore with the racket and pounding of eighteen hobnailed boots to the final bump – and then exactly in the middle either way he stopped that bus, cleared them all out and made them trot a gentle half mile behind, up a level road, and 'they were glad enough to sit still when I let 'em in again.'

While another Man-and-Brother bearded a 'Head,' on behalf of six 'Lates,' with the plea that the children had asked him to do a 'Capacity' sum and it had fetched him so hard to figure it out that he'd forgot the time!

Our Special Buses

Then there are our 'special' buses. The stout-hearted Christmas bus that takes two hours to plough through the snow-drift and Mrs. Hallam produces the plum-cake 'that *was* going to me sister's,' and sustains us all with spicy slabs, while the old chap that we thought was so glum takes a hand with the driver with the shovels from under the back-seat.

The 'pictures' bus. There was a 'special sob-stuff number,' and the conductor could hardly get the return halves out of there 'because they were all crying so bad.'

The Saturday afternoon bus that takes us all to the football match; the Saturday night bus that (with difficulty) brings us all back, and deposits us (more or less) where we ought to be, afterwards.

It is times like these that develop the family feeling about our bus, and when the conductor, reversing the old seat with a split cover and wedging his ulster down the draughty, cracked window, says, 'We reckon to have a new bus come spring,' we look at the old familiar abrasions, peer comfortably through the rain-spattered windows, and say, 'Well, well, it has stood us proud, she's been a *good* bus, indeed I don't know what we did without her.'

Tuesday, 7 November 1933

Now the festive season's here, let us consider our drinks

Nowhere, not anywhere in England's country, have I ever had a good cup of coffee. It's not that they won't take the trouble. Watch the care with which they make tea: kettle rinsed, freshly drawn water, the pot warmed and polished.

Some little brown teapots even have special wool jackets crotcheted to fit neatly around their spouts, and pull up to their necks, and woolly mats to sit on. We aren't very *learned* about teas. 'Darjeeling' or 'Oolong' are names to us; we make plain 'Indian' or 'China'.

An Experiment

Once, for fun, I brought back a bag of the new Kenya tea and explained it was a new industry just started; the village warmed its pots and tried it, gravely experimenting; after dinner. They called it 'African' tea, and said, 'It wasn't bad for beginners.'

The first time I tried to buy coffee in a Midland village, I went to the little shop; the tallow dips hung from the ceiling, there were sweets, and clothes lines, and a flitch of bacon against the wall.

'Coffee?' said Mrs. Barks, 'now that's something I don't often get asked for; I know we *did* have some coffee. I remember getting it for the Rev. P—. Ah! there it is, in the back tin. May I trouble you to reach?' After we had sampled the coffee, we looked up the Rev. P—; he died *ten* years ago!

Herb Teas

Herb teas vary. Some old ladies make the English equivalent of the light French lime-blossom tea, but they are shy about it, and won't let you have it unless you beg for it, because it is thought rather mean and poor not to give a visitor real tea. (I wish they'd think the same about sage tea – the pints I've drunk of it!) But hoarhound-and-hyssop are made 'for a weak chest,' and raspberry-leaf tea if a baby's expected. The best 'coffee' drink I've had was some made by an old Leicestershire woman, out of dandelion roots, roasted and broken up, and dandelion coffee used to have a great sale in village shops; it was a stomachic, strong and men folk liked it.

Lots of medicinal herb teas would cure almost anything by contrast! But hot, strong black-currant tea, sweetened with honey, is delicious, and will loosen up a hoist (tight cold and cough) quicker than any linctus.

'Dour o' sweet o' scum?'

'I beg your pardon, only just milk please!'

'Weel, I ask you, dour *or* sweet *or* scum?'

'Oh! sweet, please!' and I got a brimming glass of rich fresh milk.

Buttermilk is called 'dour' in some parts of Lowland North Britain. 'Scum' is only sold in old places where they still skim by hand. The frothy remnants left after the separator has taken the cream contents are called 'separated milk,' which is much inferior. Buttermilk is a pleasant drink, often offered to you in the mountains: 'It's lighter on the stomach for a climb,' they say. In the Highlands they will lace your glass of cream with whisky, or if it's refused, you are 'sadly misguidit not to appreciate–' (and the lecture's as deep as the glass).

The egg flip and egg nogg of the Southern are not really milk drinks, but where else can I classify them? There is a recipe for an old milk punch and a Caudel that would have pleased our Mr Pickwick!

Beat 15 eggs VERY well and strain, put ¾ lb. of white sugar into 1 pint of Canary and mix it with your eggs in a basin. Set it over the coals and keep stirring until it is scalding hot. Meantime, grate some nutmegs into a quart of milk and boil it, and pour it into your eggs and wine (they being scalding hot). Hold your Hand very High as you pour it, and somebody stirring all the time you are pouring in the milk, then Set it before the fire for Half an Hour and serve it up.– (Mrs Glasse, 1742.)

And 'A Coudele' even older:

Nym eyren and sweng wel togedre chauf (warm) ale and do thereto. A porcion of sugar or a perty of hony and a perti of safron, boile hit and give it forth.

After these, chocolate is 'vastly modern.' The older makes of chocolate, you crushed the bean, stewed it patiently for hour, skimmed off the cocoa-butter and beat it up with milk and eggs to a froth. This form of chocolate crossed the Atlantic and remained almost unchanged for years.

Mead and Metheglyn

Meade is made of honney and water boyled both together, if it be fyned and pure it preserveth helth.

Mead was perhaps the earliest drink of all. Its basis is honey and water, though sometimes a thickening of barley water seems to have been used. The last mead in *use* on a country farm I found in Lowland Scotland, where they brew a sort of fermented barley water sweetened with honey, for the harvest folk. But well made 'home-brewed' mead can be a very heady and strong drink.

Of English wines I have recently written at length.

Bee Wine

'Metheglyn is made of honey and water and herbes boyled and sodon together.'

I've never found that in use to-day, but 'bee wine' they got a craze for in the village some years ago. We had a big glass jar of it seething in the kitchen window. Mater 'could not fancy anything in which these poor little creatures had been going up and down working so hard,' but the pater said it was 'purely vegetable matter.'

I'd sit for hours watching them, one going up and one coming down, and 'feeding' on the sugar at the bottom of the jar. They worked faster when the sun poured through the jar and the clouded wine turned yellow.

Ale and Beer
We will let Andrew Boorde speak:

Ale is made of malte and water, and they, the which do put any other things to ale, than is rehearsed, except just barme, or godsgood, doth sofystical theyr ale.

Ale for an Englysshe man is a naturall drynke. Ale must have these propertyes, it must be fresshe and cleare, and it must not be ropy or smoky. Cornish ale is starke naught! lokinge whyte and thyck as pygges had wrastled in it!

Beer us made of malte, or hoppes and water, and nowe of late dayes (1542–1547) it is meche used in Englande, to the delyment of many Englysshe men.

Cider practically replaces all other drinks in the West of England. They say the old Glastonbury monks, homesick for the wines of Italy, first undertook the regeneration of English cider. There is a fine cider-barrel carved in a very knowing way, at Glastonbury.

Verjuice
Curiously, the Hereford cider and 'Along-the-border' cider are made after the old recipes for making verjuice. Verjuice was the sharp crab-apple juice, used in medieval cookery as frequently as the lemon is to-day. It probably had considerable effect in mitigating the massive meat diet and salted-pork-and-beans of those days. Here is the recipe

for verjuice, because it is interesting in connection with the cider recipes:—

Gather your crabbes as soon as the kernels turne blacke, and having laid them awhile in a heap to sweat together take and pick from the stalkes, then in long troughs with beetles for the purpose, crush and break them all to mash, then take a bagge of coarse hairecloth, as square as the presse, and fill it with the crushed crabs, and press it while any moysture will drop forth. Turn it into sweet hogsheads and to every hogshead put half a dozen handfuls of damaske rose leaves, and tun it up and spend it as you should have occasion.

Ways with Brews

Now in parts of the West the best cider makers look out for crabs, and crab trees figure among the hundred odd sorts of apple trees that various makers of cider import, and plant, and transplant, and acclimatise to improve their brews. Hundreds of letters and MS. are about cider apple trees.

Down South they made the cider through straw and the variety of the brews show the antiquity of the procedure. Cornish miners used to put hot sheep's blood into it! Devon folks cream or milk! Kent writers mention the gum of cherry trees! Perry was never so popular, probably because the juicy eating pear, the Wardon, was prized for serving with cream and reverence, and the other pears were woody. Some recipes make a stew of them in cider.

Cider belongs to the apple-blossom South as surely as whisky belongs to the heather-land North.

Tuesday, 18 December 1933

Putting the turnips to bed

I was sitting on them and heard them talking together below me in the warm dark. Their low grumbling came to me through their straw-filled chimney. It was mostly low shuffling and grumbling – a grunt, and 'shift over a bit, can't ye?' and 'give ground yourself, ye fat lump.'

'Be quiet you,' I said, 'I'm writing about how you are put to bed.'

'What? What? What? Here, shut up, you others, what's that you say Miss? Are we going into print?'

'Haven't newspapers got mangels? Miss? Don't they know how to bed a turnip decent?'

'No' I replied. 'Now lie still, will you, till I get you written, and I'll read it out to you when it's finished.'

I took out my pencil and … chewed it thoughtfully … I was sitting on a clamp in the winter's sunlight. Theoretically I'd no right to be sitting *on* it at all, but the rest of the field was sodden with mud. Clamps are always built on the driest piece of the field and never another stick nor stone was there to rest on. The hedge was all newly plashed and dripping wet and the gate was being used by an elderly cow to massage her double chin.

We are so used to taking up and storing 'roots' for the winter, that it's part of autumn, as much as seeing leaves turn yellow, or expecting apples – but many people don't realise the amount of detailed care that goes into making the long low earthworks.

Medieval farmers used to kill off surplus cows at the end of the summer and the poor survivors had to eke out a thin time on straw and wisps of hay, and branches of trees, and broken whin bushes, and all manner of expedients.

Now, with cow cake, and cabbage, and 'roots,' cattle keep well and fat. Parsnips were one of the earliest cow 'roots' and are still liked on some North dairy farms, because they make the milk so rich; nowadays you wouldn't see any difference winter or summer, in cows themselves, but dairy workers know you get a very different cheese from winter milk and the finest Wensleydale workers won't consider the soapy 'hay' cheese, but wait for the fresh green 'grass' cheeses.

Milk varies so very much according to what the cows eat, that the winter feeding of milk cows is very important. You can't follow all the details and the infinite variety of 'roots,' and 'fodders,' and 'cakes,' that farmers study so carefully, but taken as an outline, white turnips come in first, so early that the sheep are 'put on turnips' in the fields, and they don't need storing at all.

Swedes come next, and are yellower and bigger, and last well till over Christmas, and mangels and cabbage carry right through till the spring grass is ready. In between and confusing these dates are the varieties of turnip – swedes, and earlys and lates, and halfs and halfs, that each farmer chooses to suit his own soil and climate and cattle. Some feeding suits milk cows better than others more suited to growing calves. On a large scale, carrots, and beets, and parsnips, and potatoes (specially potatoes!) are also 'clamped' in various ways. Roughly, all roots that would stay dormant in the earth all winter are clamped. Some of the roots that will be fed to the sheep in February are now out 'in a clamp.' Lots of the potatoes you have all winter don't come direct out of the earth, but 'out of a clamp.' ...

So – here sit I, upon a clamp in the sunlight, collecting its collaborators for you! The robin, who assisted at the building of the clamp, is tilting up and down in the hedge. He turned up as soon as he saw two men with spades, for he connects them with those delicious little yellow centipedes that he likes so much.

Robin and Co.

In fact, all the time the root lifters were working in the fields, plucking up and cleaning the roots, Robin and Co., had followed them down the lines, and if Bob Robin saw any small evil wrigglers he 'took them up' and 'ran them *in*' as a good Bobby should! Yes – anyone who has watched birds 'working over' a root field, considers them as collaborators, and Robin, having had his name duly registered, tilted off into the next field to join his friend the ploughman.

That near horse was responsible for carting the roots off the field to the clamp. He's rather heavy for the cart, but so clever at backing about, that he had a couple of days 'off' bringing the lumpy load along.

You can't really hurry loading roots, because they must be thrown by hands, or shovel, *not* spiked with a fork, as they can be when required for immediate use. Next, the blown straws, waving wildly in the wind, reminded me that they were 'refuse straws' left over from thatching the stacks. *Drawn* straw, i.e., the long straightly drawn-out straw, used for thatching ricks, or making rope, etc., would let the cold wind between the cracks. The more 'felted' the straw, the better, *and the straw must be bone dry*, and in many parts they use dry bracken for packing. It's almost better than straw. It's so warm and dense. For the rest, there were two men and a piece of measuring string needed to build this clamp.

They measure off along the top of a ridge; (about 5ft. wide, or so, according to the roots) and a matting of straw is laid down neat. If it's going to be a long clamp, stakes are driven in every few feet down the middle line (they will be 'chimneys' later).

Then the roots are piled down, in rows, tail in, head out, the big ones wedged in with small ones, – (or if it's potatoes, in layers of big and little). If there is fine dry soil on them, the better, but if damp, clear as clean as you can. If the clamp is large, and there's plenty of straw or bracken, they put layers of it along, like 'courses' built into the root mass, and where these layers reach the upright posts, they pull up the hollow straws towards the top, and leave it sticking up for a ventilator.

When all the roots are packed firm, a layer of 6 inches or more of straw is laid over, and lightly held down by cross strings of twisted

Lifting potatoes out of a clamp.

A heap of harvested bracken, useful for packing and bedding.

straw. Then the spades are taken, and very quickly they dig a trench around the clamp, piling each spadeful of earth upon the straw, layer upon layer, till the ridge is reached, and a neat triangular section clamp is finished.

Frost-proof Walls

The earth has to be 9 inches or 1 ft. thick, and is patted smooth and even. Then, within firm frost-proof walls, the roots sleep warm and secure through cold and snow (and look precious sleepy when the end of the dormitory is opened and they are pulled out).

They must not be too warm. They tend to 'heat' at first (or if they decay they heat badly) so the last thing the farmer sometimes does is to pull up the stakes he built in and stuff the holes left with straw – and it's these straw tufts, the ends of the ventilator shafts, you see sticking up at regular intervals along the top of the clamp; and if you go and *smell* the air that comes up out of one of them on a cold day you will smell the warm roots inside … and if it's swedes or mangels and they are heating! phew! it will knock you clean off the clamp.

N.B. – The Swedes in this clamp respectfully wish me to state that though originally destined for the farmyard, they are uncommonly good, well boiled, mashed with butter and pepper (two 'spares' came home with me to prove it).

Tuesday, 9 January 1934

Ever tasted laver?

Deos wyrt pe man sivn & oðrum naman Laber
nemnep byð cenned on woetum stowum

Anglo Saxon Chronicle

Which means 'that wort named Sion, or by another name laver is produced in wet places.' Wherefore – as it grew by sucking upon stones in the water, it was very reasonably used by our Anglo Saxon forefathers as a cure for the stone, 'Eaten sodden or raw, it draweth out the calculi' and anyhow, it was of good benefit against 'stirring of the inwards.'

There was a great deal of most plausible unreasonableness among medical men, even then. Their favour of laver seems justifiable. It is an edible sea weed, *Navel Laver*.

Soft as Silk

Purple Laver *Porphyra laciniata* and Green Laver *Ulva latissima* are common around the west coasts of Great Britain and Ireland. It is a smooth weed, soft and pliant as fine silk, almost translucent as it floats in the clear water, but clinging into a dark gelatinous mass when lifted in the hands. As the tide falls, it coats the smooth rocks to which it clings like a wrinkled brown varnish, drying off and spoiling under a hot sun or drying wind, but in water softening and floating free again with the returning sea. That's why laver gathering can only be carried on in the few hours of low tide, and the plant definitely goes out of season from April to September.

The Gathering

It used to be gathered entirely by women and children. The gatherer plucks it from the rocks, gives it a preliminary rinse in a clear sea pool, and finally washes it and boils it for two hours and packs it into a crock.

Old sea folk or the home tied wives of fishermen at sea had the gathering of laver for their own special industry and it supplemented their small earnings and they made possible many little extra comforts by preparing and selling it to the markets. But now it is one of the small trades that unemployed young men are gradually taking away from the old people. No blame, only the pity of it!

Strand Survivals

Laver is one of the oldest salads we have. A good example of our conservatism – for no attempt is made to introduce it to foreigners and visitors rarely find it. The tides of change sweep over England apparently submerging everything but when the tide subsides the old things are still safe stranded, rooted on the rocks ready to recover and re-spread.

'Stranded' is a good word, for laver belongs to Strands! Laver has survived down London's Strand. Here fine old restaurants serve it, piping hot from silver tureens, to true and hungry Englishmen – and down little wet 'Strands' of the West it's served piping hot from earthenware pots. It's equally good on either Strand.

A Cry in Bath

In fashionable Bath of the eighteenth century, where:

> *A Broker, A Statesman, a Gamester, or Peer,*
> *A Nat'rilized Jew, or a Bishop comes here,*
> *Or an eminent Trader in cheese, should retire*

and everybody specialised in noise and diet and banquets '*Fine potted Laver!*' was a street cry. Laver sauce was always considered a delicacy and health-giving but I'd judge its genuine medicinal properties more by the value set on it by old sailors, who classed it with watercress and limes for their hard life pent up for slow voyages in small boats taught them dietetic values. I believe it is a fact that our medieval English sailors were, for their times, singularly free from skin and blood illnesses.

Laver certainly tastes something like spinach but slightly iodinised and pungent. It is cooked best in a thick pot, with almost equal quantities of melted butter, pepper (it will not need salt), and a squeeze of tangerine juice, and served as sauce to roast mutton.

For Connoisseurs

Collins (1873) in 'The Squire of Silchester's Whim' writes 'A capital dinner – you don't get moor mutton with hot laver sauce every day' – but with all due deference to 'the Rector' (and his 'jaune doree with sauce of red mullets livers stewed in portwine'!) we think it best with *marsh* mutton. The 'salt grazings' for the hot laver or boiled onions and aromatic thyme, and hill-side mint, for our mountain jigots!

Probably for a first try you'll like laver best cold (almost iced) as a salad well sprinkled with oil and vinegar, and a *very* thin 'sanding' of coarse brown sugar, or, if you're west of the Severn, try cyder instead of the vinegar for your dressing.

Where to Get It

Anyhow, laver is in season now. It is never expensive. I've had it, fresh off the water, in West Scotland, Ireland (there are other seaweeds, better liked there), St. David's Head, Cornwall, and inland most of the old established shops in 'sea towns' will get it for you, ready prepared and cooked. It's really equally good wherever you find it, but I shall always imagine it most delicious from the West Countree, for remembrances of a blowing West Devon day, of frost cleared sea water, icy cold spray, and fresh wet sea wind – when I was the guest of the prettiest maid to Appledore.

Tuesday, 16 January 1934

Throwing the haver

I do love manchet breade, and great loves the whiche be well mowlded and thorowe baken … Mestlyng breade is made halfe of whete and halfe of Rye, there is also mestlyng made halfe of rye and halfe of barly.

Hauer cakes (of oats) in Scotland is many a good lordes dysshe.

A. Borde.

This form of oatcake has caused endless 'havers.' Haver is an old Northern name for oats. Its use is about as widespread as the oats, but the making of distinctive haver bread or clapper is confined to few localities. Haver is a variety of oatcake, very thin and of papery lightness, and the method of making is extremely individual. It consists of *flinging* the raw brose on to an almost red-hot stove and peeling it off again while still pliant, which is utterly different from the usual thick oatcake *baked* on an iron girdle.

Now certain recipes are traditional, and other recipes are the result of local commodities, and there are recipes caused by conditions (as the making of various sorts of cheese) that are almost geographical in their modifications, but there are recipes which cannot be accounted for by ordinary means, and these recipes usually follow certain trades or jobs.

Cookery Relations

The gipsy trick of baking in clay belongs to the potteries, and brick makers. The clay wrapped sucking pig or hedgehog in the potters' kiln, is the thick paste-wrapped ham baking in the farmhouse brick oven. Both have the root development of close encasing against slow strong heat in an enclosed fire.

Now here, in the oat cake, perhaps we have a trade tradition of some quarry workers or millstone makers? The strong tradition of some *stone* worker.

The First Baking

The occasional use of the word 'clapper' shows that it was probably first baked on the great clapper or hearth stones, over which most Northern cottages were raised. (Clapper-bridge is another use of the word.) The brose of oatmeal stirred into boiled water was set ready, the red embers were pushed aside, and the haver poured direct on to the almost red hot stone – a throwing action was used to make it spread, and a little brush of heather twigs to spread it out. When sufficiently 'set,' it was peeled up and hung to dry and crisp – while another piece was laid down, till the heat was out of the stone and the fire had to be moved back.

That was true clapper or haver – ordinary 'baked' oatcake is stiff and crisp from the moment it is cooked – but haver is almost as pliant as flannel when it is just made – and can be rolled up and carried in a poke!

Havercake Lads

This haver bread follows the Pennines and crops up again in Derbyshire, where they have similar stone, and other quarry men, and a form of it occurs in West Wales. The East Lancashire men were known as 'Havercake lads,' and it was equally common bread in the West Riding of Yorkshire. Some old stone cottages in the hills still have 'haver stones' built into the fireplaces, but with stoppage of the grain mills and the easier purchase of white flour and town bread, most of the stones have grown cold and the old haver is almost forgotten. The most Northerly place I found haver was Keswick, where the Lancashire wife of a tailor made it – 'to please the mon' and it was 'rare good hard brade,' and 'deal howsomer nor loaf for th' boawells.'

Historically, haver is connected with John of Hainault and the Scots wars, for the Borderers had a girdle under their saddle panel and a little sack of oatmeal behind, and they lay 'this *plate* on the fire and cast their paste thereon, and so make a little cake in the manner of a cracknell or biscuit.'

Now there was some controversy in translating that 'plate,' for some called it a stone, and the flat round stones of the riverbeds thereabouts looked very like girdle stones and may have made haver, but some stones 'fly' in the heat, or crack, like slates, so we can leave the Scots their iron girdles under the saddle flaps – but see how the question arose, among people who made true clapper.

One old clapper oven I've known since a child. The little bakehouse at the end of the stone-flagged yard in the grey Northern town is unchanged, the little shop is whitewashed skim-milk blue, wood benches and scoured bowls are yellow as cheese – and the baker has the same slow and friendly smile (like the polished oat scoop, it was his father's before him). The haver is slightly thinner than it used to be (fashions change), and the incredible skill is therefore even more wonderful. The thrower stands some way off and swish—! he flings the boardfull on to the hot stone, it spreads out about a yard long by six inches wide – there is a delicious oaty whiff, and it is coming up – brown smooth satin on one side and oatmeal rough on the other.

Up to London

Swish – another piece – and the little pile of oat dust grows smaller and the long lines of haver grow longer. Always the havercake baker has made for us. We took him for granted. And from that tiny old bakehouse haver goes all over England. Equally carefully he will fill a consignment for one of the largest clubs in London – or post a packet to a homesick wanderer like me.

At the club, or under the hedge, it's *our* own Northern haver; and the most delicious oatcake ever made in England or anywhere.

Tuesday, 6 February 1934

Foe to 'flu and chilblains

Curiously one always speaks of a field of oats, but not wheats or barleys. It's one of the many things that mark *the* oat as distinctive in origin and distribution from other cereals. The old Northern name for oat was haver, and haver[br]ead is a curious and delicious surviving form of our once staple oat bread which I recently described.

This cold weather, oatmeal should be used more. It's wonderfully warming and health-giving, and a foe to chilblains and influenza. The hardy Northerners of the 'cauld blast' swear by oats, and the more northerly grown the oats are the better they thrive and the finer the flavour, for oats have a very distinctive flavour and aroma.

Much Variety

Few people realise the variety of oatmeals and their many uses. Rough 'cut' or coarse ground oatmeal is hard and crisp and nutty in texture. This is best for solid food, and is put into meat dishes and broths, and is partly used for clapped bread, i.e., the thin flat oat cakes that are clapped or patted on to an iron girdle (and should not be confused with clapper or haver).

'Medium' oatmeal is most commonly used for bannocks, and for mixing with other flours. The 'fine' oatmeal is best used for dainty breads and bannocks, making scones with butter milk, or pancakes with eggs (and currants in them!) for flouring herrings, thickening soups and broths, or to boil with butter into a delicate warming gruel (like savoury milk,) for babies or invalids.

Janet's Recipe

We also use it to make a 'jelly' to serve with Northern soused herrings. In the days before there were so many 'easy' forms of oats on the market for making the morning porridge, Janet would take a 'fine' iron saucepan and have it one-third full of boiling salted water – bubbling 'fast as galloping.' Here's her way:

Have your coarse oatmeal dry and convenient by your left hand in a small wooden box. A tin box Janet will not use! She stores the meal in a jar, with a wooden lid, but I can never tempt her from the lidded wooden box she considers 'fit.'

With the left hand she sprinkles the oatmeal very lightly, 'dancing it' down on to the bubbling boiling water. So that (this is the crux) every grain falls separately into the boiling water, and is sealed up instantly, and stays crisp, and the porridge grains never soften to slime.

Never does Janet scatter fast enough to stop the water bubbling, never does she stop sprinkling and stirring till the last handful of meal is sprinkled in – when she seizes her spurtle and drives all vigorously round and round till the porridge suddenly thickens; – then she claps on the lid with a triumphant thump, replaces the ancestral spurtle in the kitchen draw and twenty minutes later it's 'Awheel, you have it the noo.'

Quantities vary with the age of the meal and individual taste. We use roughly a small cup of oatmeal to two large cups of water and a teaspoon of salt to a cup of oats we think not too much, if you eat it Scots fashion.

This is how Janet serves it. The porridge is poured smoking hot direct into the bowl, and by it set a mug of cold, creamy milk. Then with a spoon you take up a helping of porridge, dip up the cold milk into the spoon, and so get a good tasty mouthful, solid and grainy enough to chew and fresh and cool with the milk. This is the test of good oatmeal porridge – that each grain is distinct and clean tasting and nutty and *does* have to be chewed – though soft enough to lie level in the bowl, porridge should 'cut' cleanly, and never cling to dish or spoon.

When as a child you had eaten all the porridge, you drank up the remainder of the cold milk, wiped your face, and got down feeling very warm and full! – (there was no idea of anything else afterwards: – porridge served this way *was* a meal in itself, and lasted well). That the oat is sustaining is proved by the old 'brose' of the mountain shepherds, which was a handful of raw oatmeal put into a hoggin and filled up with burn water from the hillside, about two hours before use. The soft peaty water and continuous shaking of the mountain walk churned up the sort of cold broth or porridge that was 'brose.'

Supper Porridge

Hot, freshly-made porridge with cold milk is best, but most children, on a cold night enjoy porridge with hot milk and brown Barbadoes sugar, or 'lacey' with treacle, and it's a healthy supper in winter. For variety, we sometimes had little one-inch balls made like porridge, but stiffer, and rolled in fine oatmeal and fried in the fat after the breakfast bacon – they were very good and warming – with a dust of pepper over each. Haver and oat cake were served at dinner with cheese, and for breakfast fresh new baked oatcakes with creamy butter and honey.

Oatmeal pudding was delicious. I had it the first time made by a sailor cook in a Northern lighthouse! It was made with buttermilk like a bannock but had raisins in it, and chopped peel, and a kernel of butter in its warm brown middle, and it was tied in a cloth and boiled and boiled.

Then There's Haggis

We had it rolled out smoking hot on to a dish of rhum sauce, and ate it with lumps of butter and brown sugar for six o'clock tea! It *was* good! The maker explained that as it could *not* be over-boiled he put it on for the nights the 'boys' would be out late with the boats, (and I've thought it would be fine for those football evenings when no mother knows when the muddy, hungry players will come back!)

Oatmeal is the basis of many meat dishes. The renowned haggis is largely oatmeal. The black-puddings of Lancashire, (that mark the disappearance of the farmhouse pig) are of oatmeal. For grilled herrings the fine oatmeal is a better dusting than any other flour, and gives them a savoury crisp crust.

Tuesday, 13 February 1934

Learn your bread and be a man

The louelyest corne that men ete.

(Robert of Brienne, 1303)

Has it occurred to you that cereals suit the climates and peoples where they grow – perfectly?

In our pride in transport, and having the treasures of every land brought to our kitchens, we neglect our primary English cereals. The rice of the Indian is delicious with his curry, and takes kindly to our pie-dishes; sago, tapioca, cassava, and many other cereals are excellent – *for a change* – but they are tropical cereals, and we do not live in the tropics, and the good simple food grown at our doors is probably a lot healthier fare as staple diet.

We cheerfully accept the fact that the adapted healthy food of a foreign country is usually the safest diet *in* that country. So on the same principle these three standard English cereals should be appreciated by Englishmen, on the reasonable basis of 'know England first!'

Every Boy Should Know

Now wheat is specially for you younger ones (younger in mind, whether you are in years or not!), because wheat is essentially the standard flour of our native *bread*.

Any boy scout will tell you a man does not need to do a lot of fancy cooking. But every real boy ought to be able to skin, or pluck, and dress his own meat, and be able to make some sort of bread that's wholesome and satisfying to eat with it. You are not all going to be city dwellers for life, dependent on cooks and caterers and valets to look after you. Some of you (thanks be!) will go to the colonies, and some will be great explorers, and adventurers, and the least travelling of you all will spend holidays in camp and learn to do things with both your hands, as well as your heads and heart as well.

I was only as high as the table top when I had my first bread lesson, in a tiny cottage in a little village called Appletreewick right up among the Yorkshire moors, but since then I've had to produce edible bread out of the assorted strange flours of many countries and using varied fuels. So – will you take my experienced word first, that the boy who's got the working knowledge and can make good bread – and teach others how to make it, is likely to be a popular person, and prove a reliable English chap in other ways too, the sort of boy who gets a working knowledge and then uses his gumption how to apply it, as required.

Exiles' Food Dreams

It's queer the number of home-sick Englishmen who (like myself) have sometimes been living on outlandish interesting indigestibles and filling up with whatever queer thing falls into the foreign cook-pot for months on end. When they plan an English meal, in home-sick moments, they picture a big glass of beer and a good plate of cold beef and farm butter, and a good cheese to cut at and a large white country English *loaf.*

They dally with the picture, adding a head of fresh lettuce from the garden, new mustard, or an apple pie to follow, but from the detailed description of the exact shape of that English crusty *loaf* I've often been able to place their exact home county! It's the fine nutty English bread that completes the picture. Other countries have good fancy bread, yards of it, but for a good English *loaf* we praise wheat.

So let every English child learn the simple wisdom of bread-making; it's not much trouble, in coal, gas or electric ovens, and you can be as 'modern' as you like in your old-fashioned accomplishment.

The basic facts are flour, 'raising,' salt and water; an 'oven to your hand, and a loaf to your ear!' for the oven's heat is traditionally tested by the smooth, capable palm of the housewife's hand, and the baking of the loaf by the sound of a firm 'rap' on the bottom of the loaf.

I can see now the scrubbed white table-top in front of the deep-set little cottage window where I first 'learnt bread'; outside the early winter tea-time dusk, and inside the yellow firelight, flickering on the yellow-lined bread bowl, and Old Nurse, her blue apron over her white one, and her grey hair drawn smoothly over her brown forehead and into the black chenille net bag of the old people.

Her neat white neck tucker is loosened, and the hooks of her black bodice undone at the throat; her lips are compressed and tucked in, like she tucks in the folding dough, and she pummels briskly up and down, dump and pummel, at the elastic spongy white dough. ... Then the maternal pat as she puts the shaped loaves down to rise before the fire, and tucks the old white table cloth over them.

I do not think her recipe was ever written, for she could neither read nor write it – bless her clever old head! – but there is the simplest old recipe that I could find for you. If you follow the directions you can't go wrong – but there's a knack in it, as in butter, to make it 'come well' – and that knack is best learnt in childhood. So go ahead!

To make two loaves about 2lb. each

Flour 3½ lb. (called a quartern) or half a gallon and salt (1 tablespoon). Put it in a deep bowl, make a hole (round like a bird's nest) in the middle that will just hold a tablespoonful of yeast, broken up into a cupful of warm water. (This should be mixed overnight and next morning thinned down with ¾ pint of warm milk or water.) Some yeast takes up more water than others, but about 1½ cupfuls of thick creamy yeast mixture should just fill the hole.

Cover a little layer of flour over the yeast, and place the bowl in a warm place for an hour, or more, till the yeast has risen through the covering flour and is spongy.

Then pour in about a pint more of warm water and, as you stir, mix in the flour till the whole panful is spongy dough and ready for kneading. Knead well (pummelling the dough in a friendly fashion) till smooth and elastic. Then leave to rise in a warm place till it's swelled to twice its bulk (about 2 hours), shape into 2 loaves, and after giving them another short rest in a warm place bake about 1½ hours. Tap the underside to see if the loaves sound light and evenly baked through – cool slowly in a dry, warm place, and wrap up till used.

Don't put hot loaves into a cold bread-pan, and don't cut your new loaf till next day, no matter how good it smells.

N.B. – Cut a cross (+) on top of your rising dough to 'let the devil out' if you think he's got in. Our Jennie always did this. She said 'it was as well to be on the safe side!'

Tuesday, 20 March 1934

Round Britain with the spring cleaners

Cleaning of chambers and houses ought not to be done while any honest man is within the house.

(Andrew Birde, 1490)

In England *Now* everybody is beginning to do it! It takes us all in different ways. I only know one clue in common, between the Northumberland lady and the Kentish lady – up North, down South, East and West, the only thing we do alike – we all begin with the sweep!

The town people coolly telephone to the sweep, country houses send for him, lesser folk arrange with him to come.

In country places where there are not enough chimneys to keep a real sweep in countenance, there's always someone who obliges in the spring.

In really remote places we do it ourselves – oh! yes; tack an old wet blanket over the fireplace and poke up a bunch of holly twigs tied to a mop.

Hen-terprise

In crofts it's simplest to drop a hen down from the top. No, it doesn't hurt the hen. It takes a lot to unsettle a hen, and a crofter's animals are always wanting to get into the kitchen, anyway. Afterwards you take the soot out and put it on the young cabbage plants against slugs.

Mining towns and quarries, where the men folk are used to blasting, the women get them to 'fire' their chimneys: of course, it's strictly illegal, but nobody minds.

Washing goes forward as fast as the warm weather discards blankets, coverlets and winter clothing. Users of laundries are spared a lot of trouble, but miss a lot of interest.

Laundry Tricks

The older washing processes were divided into steeping, bucking, boiling and scouring (before you got to pressing, ironing and finishing), and they all had complicated sub-divisions. There's nothing 'catches on' in a country place like a new trick in the laundry.

Some French nuns came to a Northern town – and one of the things that most impressed the house-proud Northern women was their skill with the clear starching of their straw goiffered ruffs and stiffly-pleated linen! In a week there wasn't a curtain or tablecloth in the district that didn't fairly crackle on the line *and not a man could sit down in comfort in his shirt for months!*

Scotland has most elaborate clothes-prop erections that shove out from the upper stories over the wynds. They have them in the Lakes, too, and Northumberland; it's likely you can't walk up a wynd on a Monday or Tuesday, the whole air is flapping solidly with washing!

The gypsies make most of the clothes pegs.

In country villages, specially in the Midlands, there is usually a woman who undertakes your washing 'by the week' as a job; this being new to me when I moved South it was puzzling to be told 'Mrs. Abraham has had Monday and Tuesday for years, the Rectory's taken Wednesdays and Thursdays but if Saturday delivered is any use to you, you're welcome to it on Friday by the milk float.' It took me as long to sort this information as to sort the washing!

Fountains of whitewash are loosed by the melting snow. The West of England, perhaps, whitewashes most; the South puts it on thickest, the burst of apple blossom along the West borders brings a burst of pink wash and yellow wash on to the houses. Anglesey uses a round rush besom for its whitewash, and puts it on solid! and, as they have learnt the sensible trick of cementing over their wind-shifted roof tiles, they sometimes (like a bald-headed man that doesn't know when to leave off washing his face) white-wash up over the roofs, too, so the neat little low houses nestle among the green fields white as mushrooms in grass.

'We all like to get that honest man well out of the way before we begin!'

Some of the old Scotch and Devon crofts have had such layers of whitewash, that the rough granite below has softened till the angles are rounded as the Pisé building of Devon, and you can watch the firelight trip out faces and forms in a century-deep gesso.

Pink and yellow is the West, blue the North, where the clogs clatter over the holystoning. Going into Yorkshire or Lancashire, over Glossop Hill, into the Black Country, in the early morning, you will see all the women holystoning doorsteps, window steps, ledges of walls and hearthstones. Time was when we holystoned and sanded fine patterns all over our stone floors, now we have fallen for linoleum, but if we cannot burst into bloom so early as the South, we can burst into holystoning – and we do. Nowhere but the North do you get such snowy gleaming white hearthstones.

Lancashire shines in blacklead, because the elaborate iron kitchen fireplaces are in the sitting-dining-rooms, with convenient red tile floors, where the chaps in their pit and workshop clothes can sit in comfort.

Fireplaces 'Go Spring'

Give an ex-mill lass a pennyworth of blacklead in a gallypot with mysterious vinegar and beeswax and she'll produce a gleaming miracle of black satin.

Fireplaces 'get the spring' as variously as they are built. The big, open fireplaces get washed over with soot-water, and the outsides are tarred till they are as black as black cats.

A funny style I found in Central Ireland. They blacked or red-raddled the entire fireplace and then imitation bricks were pains-takingly drawn over the black with whitewash. 'Shure, it was so neat you might be living in a brick house entirely.'

Nottinghamshire has a passion for red raddle (the red earth you mark sheep with) and in spring around Nottingham the lace curtains spread like hoar-frost upon the fields (if you dry a lace curtain on a hedge you will never get it off again if it blows).

Another Quilt

In South Wales, and some Northern markets, patchwork squares made from the patterns and cuttings of the cotton mills machined together have a sudden sale, for old worn blankets (yes, and flannels and shawls and woollies) get sandwiched between two brightly-coloured pieces of patchwork and sewn together, with a fancy border, and another 'quilt' has come to flap on the family line.

Feather beds and pillows get re-made. The hams swinging against the walls get new paper mats to sit on, hen-houses are upheaved, the dairy is whitewashed and spare dairy-pans and cheese tubs come out and are put to soak 'against the new milk.'

Perhaps the bonfire of the rubbish is something of a beltane fire, but who am I to admit it?

No Place for Man

Chintz covers come out and are glazed and fresh white muslin frosts at the windows; womenfolk get new hats, children get brimstone and camomile; outside the menfolk are whitening the cow byres and liming the fruit trees; carts, after the toil and mud of winter, are getting new spokes and fresh paint. In the garden, cucumber frames have sudden white squares of new glass, thatching starts up and 'sets' appear in the markets, lemon puddings, spring chickens, duck and green peas.

Oh! I cannot tell you one-thousandth part of the odds and ends of domestic spring tokens in England, or the joys of spring cleaning, but on the one thing we are all agreed, North, South, East or West, *we all like to get that honest man well out of the way before we begin!*

Tuesday, 27 March 1934

By a woodman's fire

I was freezing on the Pilgrims' Way. I had been frozen for three or four miles. My fingers were claw curled with cold, inside my gauntlets. The east side of my face was stiffly frozen and my mind was numb. Suddenly … a faint blue scent? … more a wraith of a blue purple colour than a smell? … an intangible magic, in the air? … Wood Smoke!

I turned and crashed into the undergrowth. Uphill the wraith led me over the ridge. The first faint mist drew visibly through the trees. And I followed, winding between them, and stumbled to my knees, over the burning wood ashes of a white encircled fire …

The air melted around me and I uncurled slowly, numb to everything but returning life. I was sitting leaning against a tree ruddy and tingling and rested, before my eyes cleared to take in the surroundings.

It was a three days' clearing, for three burnt-out fires lay spaced in regular circles, white-ringed black up the spinney. It was a one-man camp, and he could not have been gone long. Warmed by the fire, I rose, and stood looking round me. There was his axe, laid sideways, not covered, as he would have covered it against frost in the metal, had he been leaving for the day … No dinner-bag … No billy-hook, then he must be living close and had gone back home to dinner. Then I found a bicycle leaning against a standing hazel.

I back-tracked the bicycle to a path, well worn, so my solitary worker had evidently gone down the woods on foot, probably to join another camp for company. I returned to my fire and sat still. The charred sticks lay radiating outwards, burnt into a perfect circle like the spokes of a spinning-wheel.

When I stirred the fire, a fluttering show of white ash drifted off down in the blue smoke. The haze of heat hung quivering over all, so that the far trees and eaves beyond the fire swam like a forest seen under water. Idly I slipped my empty billy out of my rucksack to dry it in the warm ash. I'd have liked a hot drink, but the frost wind had dried every pool or stream for miles. I sat still, watching the fire in the quiet wood.

A red squirrel, disturbed from sleep by the cutting, moved slowly down a distant log and went into a low hole. He looked as paralysed with cold as I had felt myself an hour before. I moved across and dropped in a crust of bread, and lightly plugged up the back door with moss for him. Poor little cold chap! That will keep the wind out for a bit, I hope you will find the crust when you wake. I wish I had a fine bushy red tail to wrap my nose in.

I was half dozing by the fire when the woodman returned … 'Yes,' laughingly, he'd been down to the other camp for dinner hour and they'd got talking, so he hadn't hurried back. It was his own time. 'He'd brought a drop of tea over, would I like it?'

I showed him the empty billy. 'Would I not!' (Lovely and hot it was!) it set me on my feet wide awake and inquisitive again.

The woodman was getting on with his job, and talked as he worked carefully and swiftly. He'd been abroad in his time, West Indies and China; there was not so cold as this!

I'd find several other workers down in the main shed. They had just about finished that spinney, and he was clearing on ahead before they came to this one next week. It was pretty good wood, grown straight and clean, most of it hazel.

I told him of the squirrel, and he repeated what you hear almost everywhere in England, that the larger grey squirrel is turning the red squirrel out. Like most wood workers, he'd a poor opinion of the grey squirrel compared with the red.

The spinney was rapidly coming down and sorting itself out into orderly piles as he talked, and I went down to find the shed in the lower wood where the finishing work was going on. It's always a marvel to me how they 'split' shafts of timber so level and true. Try

it yourself and the wood runs out into short wedges. Yet a woodman will split a twenty-foot lath even to a hair, from end to end, with only an old fixed axe that looks like a Chaldean remainder.

They were making split palings for fence work, the neatly split and pointed palings were bundled and piled in stacks. They'd got the most ingenious bundler that I ever saw! Just two zinc pail handles set downwards, swung from four stakes. It was a perfect device. He piled them full of stakes and ran a wire round as I watched, forcing the stakes tight with a bend of the knee on the woodman's vice (which is a mechanic's strip-vice designed by Pan).

The great pile of peeled bark was softly brown and grey green, the palings of creamy white, streaked silver, the birds tilted and shivered along the base of the hedges ... We were back in the primitive ages ... transported by the magic of wood smoke ... unto the age of the axe, and skill.

A prehistoric monster came crashing through the wood ... a lorry! ploughing along over the lower pastures and negotiating ditches in an off-wheeled sort of way. (I think English lorries graduated during the war as much as their drivers; they take anything in their stride these days!)

Then the procession of workers started, taking the new white bundles down to the lorry and loading them up. Work was nearly over for the afternoon ... and a thicker flurry of snow in the wind set me hunting for my road again, so I turned regretfully back up the wood.

The lorry wheels showed black tracks broken through the ice over the pools, in the clearings, and beyond the golden catkins swung gaily above their tiny scarlet blossoms, fearless of the coming axe. I scrambled back on to the Pilgrims' Way. I was warmer now and friendly. Almost I could hear the thawed-out ghosts of Chaucer's riders, their horse bells tinkling down the path like melting ice.

Tuesday, 3 April 1934

Toffee apples, or what's the use of history?

I'm stuck! 'Toffee apple' has got me up a gum tree, glued to the spot am I by a toffee apple!

You see, all things in England come to greet me through an introduction of historical tradition. I've become so used to asking a Thing 'How's its father?' and 'Where's its grandfather?' and 'How's its great-grandfather keeping?' that it is part of my eyesight. I can't see a Thing without speculating on its interesting past (and possibly involved future), and now, here is a Thing obviously simply stuck full of Traditions; and mute as an oyster.

Can you remember a time when 'Toffee apple' was not? *No*, you can't! Nobody can. There have been references to toffee apples for centuries, and the toffee apple tree probably branches back to the flood. Julius Cæsar may have eaten a toffee apple, William the Conqueror probably did, but do we know who invented toffee apples? No. Now, what's the use of history when it leaves you stuck on a little thing like that?

Recently I've conscientiously taken down much evidence (about fourteen pounds of them) and got no further mentally. Toffee apples have reached the state when they are getting on my nerves (at least, it must be nerves or indigestion, I never had either, so can't be sure which), but just as I am getting it out of my mind I meet a new toffee apple, and it will wink its shining, varnished eye at me and waggle its little stick to diddle me – till I'll be bound to eat it in self-defence!

Only last week I went on a pilgrimage to Canterbury, and there, in that very stronghold of English tradition, just as I was dreaming happily and pottering about watching the pilgrims ambling in, there was a toffee-apple cart right plunk on the bridge by the 'Weaver's window,' and I had to sneak off and eat six in exasperated research and the Monk's Refectory.

> ## Toffee Apples
>
> There are inspired parents who sometimes provide toffee apples for 'seconds' at nursery dinner-time. This is a simple, good recipe – boil it sharply:
>
> *¼lb.* butter. *Melt.* • *½lb.* treacle, *add to it.*
> *1lb.* brown sugar, *add.* • *Tablespoonful* vinegar.
> *Boil twenty minutes.*

Toffee apples can't have begun much before the general importation of sugar, about 1500. Before sugar became cheap they would be quite expensive, unless they used a boiled honey toffee mixture.

The probability of this early honey coating is not to be overlooked; it probably struck somebody quite early, and probably 'caught on,' in the stickiest sense of the term, with the very young.

Presumably small windfall apples dipped in toffee bedabbled the fairs of St. Bartholomew even before sugar (as we know it) came into general use. Probably as early as the wind shook the little apple trees the toffee apples of England burgeoned upon their little sticks. Anyhow, it's one of the most thoroughly old-fashioned English sweetmeats you will find, and thoroughly wholesome and pleasant and to be commended in every way.

Don't think there's anything haphazard about the output; not lightly is this epic produced. Anyone can jab a chip of firewood into an apple and dip it in toffee – you can do it twice with two hands – but what are you going to do next? You can't wave them about indefinitely!

Suppose they never harden? There you are stuck up for life! No, the making is serious and varied as the locality of the sale, for (mark you!) toffee apples defy transport. They must be made and sold on the spot, Creator to Consumer direct (many a more important commodity has achieved less).

In old times they would only be had in the early autumn and winter (the little summer apples would be too sweet). Nowadays, thanks to Empire products, they bristle on the barrows twelve months to the year.

Angels' Ice

Only the smallest apples must be used, *or you don't get enough toffee*, and the apples should be tart and on the sharp side rather than sweet, soft enough to bite well and yet hard enough to stand up to the toffee. Then, too, the apples must be clean and smooth and the sticks white and sharp, and the toffee must be just of the right consistency to coat deeply, with that iridescent luscious gold varnish that crackles so crisply, like angels' ice!

The problem of how to 'dry out' the toffee apples in sufficiently commercial numbers is the real difficulty of production, and has been solved as variously as we solve all our national problems.

Cambrian toffee apples (like Welsh spoons) hang up by their tails, just a split in the stick over a long string (so easy), but the sticks must be driven in deep, strong as a sturdy Welsh pikeman would drive. This method is good, for it keeps the sticks clean, and the apples shapely. And, oh! what a lemon-nosed transparent drop accumulates at the 'drip'! a very amber dew-pond of a most seductive shape!

There is one great fault with this overhead treatment, there is a tendency to scant the depth of the dip. (This is regrettably noticeable in the commercialised border towns.) This leaves a bare green patch unlicked by toffee around the upper side. This leaves the stick un-cemented in. I have had repeated juvenile complaints of toffee apples thus nakedly exposed above their tails losing their sticks. This should be checked!

The English Usage

The standard of English usage is to up-end the stick, prodding them into a lump of clay, or I've seen a half-potato used. (N.B. – I don't know what happens to the potatoes.) This gives a clear unvarnished field and no flavour, but the 'runs' drip down the handles and you get ever so sticky.

The oil slab of the urban district is quite a convenient compromise. The apples, after dipping, are laid down upon an oil slab in rows, their tails all pointing one way, as though some sweet-laden wind from the Barbadoes had swept the toffee apple orchard. The 'drip' spreads out, and each apple sits on a little pool of toffee, which accounts for all toffee apples made this way wearing neat little amber haloes at precarious angles.

From Inverness to Bermondsey

Excellent toffee apples are made north, south, east, west, all up and down England. You may buy them in Inverness or Bermondsey, on barrows in markets, at root shows or garden parties, at night clubs or church bazaars! It's astonishing the individuality that you get into an English toffee apple!

Only last week I found the most enterprising new variety. In Canterbury I met an apple-cheeked old lady, whose eyes were bright and shining as her own toffee apples. She had on a spotless white apron and smiled the sweetest smile, and she flung a big, soft flurry of white desiccated coconut all over my toffee apple. It was 'toffee apples in a snow storm'!

Tuesday, 10 April 1934

Where to go in blossom time

Now, of my three score years and ten,
Twenty will not come again.
And take from seventy springs a score,
It only leaves me fifty more.

And since to look at things in bloom,
Fifty sprigs are little room.
About the woodland I will go,
To see the Cherry hung with snow.

A.E. Housman, 1896

I am only just back in time to catch the cherry blossom – I have missed weeks of an English spring. And don't believe I'll ever catch up with all that's been happening.

When I left the ground was hard and knobby with frost, and about the last thing I did was to put brown curled bracken fronds over the bulbs' noses. (It's always a risk whether they shelter the bulbs or the slugs, but slugs don't like bracken much: it's too scratchy for their tummies to walk on.)

Cowslips Already

Before I left a few cold primroses untucked themselves gingerly out of the hedge, and the snowdrops, cold and green, were trembling in an east wind. (All our early flowers are white, or pale gold, like winter honeysuckle.) Now the daffodils belong to be over, but the primroses are creaming over the ditches, and the aubretia and arabis are plump, pink and blue and lavender cushions under the handsome dusty millers in the cottage gardens.

And, the chiefest of spring, the cowslips are just beginning. I found the first thin little three-flowered cowslip shivering in a hailstorm a month ago, but now – oh, the fine sturdy fellows. A foot high some of them, and tasseled thick and smelling so sweetly. I think the baby that hasn't held cowslip balls, soft, dewy fresh cowslip balls, in its two hands can't know how to fall in love properly, even when it's grown up. Daisy-chains are all right to please little girl babies, but the country Boy-baby whose clumsy fingers have held sturdy cowslip balls; he'll know just how sweet his young love is going to be later on when he meets her!

It's really serious to miss the tree blossom in England. The wild cherry comes first. The soft, loose blossoms sway in sudden laughter among the grey-brown trees in the spinneys. North Wales has perhaps more wild cherry trees than anywhere else, or perhaps it is that they show more exquisitely among the rough hills and have the very colour of the Dee water splashed over their boughs.

Up in the slate quarries they lean over, white against the black wet slates, and, as the wind blows, the loose blossoms float off, and drift against the rough black rock, and cling there, the wet turning their whiteness translucent, like clouded ice, and the next gust of wind brings down a whiter drift, so that the black slate comes clouded with the drifting blossom, and in one small quarry I know an old worker, in an old grey-green coat, smiles and brushes the delicate blossoms from his head and shoulders as he works.

In the Severn Valley

The pear blossom is chill white and frail, after the soft loose, brown-dusted cherry, and the apple blossom sturdy and pink and thick, comes just a little after the pear.

If I had only a holiday at Easter, I'd go down to Devon for the daffodils, to Dunsfold, or later up the Doone Valley, or further in Cornwall, down Truro way, because in some sheltered Western cove I could be sure to feel the spring earlier than anywhere else, but by Whitsuntide I'd go along the Severn Valley, up past Evesham and Tewkesbury, and see the orchards, right up as far as Worcester.

There is a hill, above Cheltenham, where you can stand and see the Severn shining silver, winding down to the sea, and acres and acres of soft pink and white blossom, and by Uley Hill, too, across to South Wales, and right down to the estuary as far as Weston-super-Mare.

I think I would start across the flat green marshes of North Somerset, where the cowslips shake gold over the fields, and white ducks splatter in silver dykes, and the osiers are cut, and the willows dusty gold with the sun behind them – and go upwards along the hills, seeing the valley below like fallen clouds of blossom all up to Malvern, and at Malvern (on a May morning) I'd climb St. Anne's Well Hill, and look out across England, West and South, and see the loveliest view in spring.

There is a good chain of youth hostels for walkers, from Dursley upwards to Malvern, or if I were a walker starting from Birmingham, I'd probably train to Droitwich and start with a prosaic salt tub, because the hot baths there are great fun, and make you tingle all over (for our English spring can have a nip in the air of a morning, enough to crisp the blossom, and stiffen the lambs' legs with a black frost, as the country folk say).

For One Day Only

If I couldn't go so far I'd go to the Cotswolds, beyond Malmesbury and Tetbury, and wander down those foot tracks and gated roads that go by Nymps Field and Owlpen way. Or, if I couldn't get so far and had only a day, I'd spend it at Tiptree in Essex, or go to Harwich, and ferry across the water and walk to Pinmill, to have lunch while I waited for the tide, and scrambled a happy muddy way along the Estuary to Ipswich.

Or I'd go to Kent – there are walking hostels thick all along to Canterbury, and though the best of the blossom is farther South you could reach the cream of it in a week-end – but – 'since to look at things in bloom'—? Well, they are in bloom now! and waiting for you. Go and see —   *Tuesday, 1 May 1934*

Women down on the farm

Get up in the morning as soon as thou wilt;
With overlong sleeping a good day is spilt.
See all well served, without and within,
And all things required before supper begin.
Provide for thy husband to make him good cheer;
Make merry together what time you be here.

(Old verses – 1557)

The largest change in English country-side life, is the women going off the land. The whole economic and political situation is involved and complex. But the big resultant change, is that 'the farm' has altered from being a family life, to a possible (or impossible!) commercial proposition.

In old days, you went on to the land to live, and if you were lucky you made money. Nowadays, you go on to the land to make money – and if you are lucky you live. In olden times farming without a wife was considered a hopeless proposition, a thing that no man, single-handed, could afford to do. Nowaday, it's – can he afford a wife?

Sharing the Work

This looks better for the woman, than it is in reality, and I am not sure we have not lost more than we gained when we left the soil. For definitely we have left it.

The arrangement that the man should do the field work and the woman the house work, was equal and fair, but labour-saving appliances in the fields and changes in farm structure have overlapped this primitive division. Nowadays, most of the field work that used to be done by many hands, is done by one machine, and what was 'house' work is now 'field' work.

The specialising of farm work, the running of huge dairy and poultry farms (I nearly called them egg factories!) are modern, urban necessities, but they have very queer unbalancing effects in the country.

No Dull Moments

Indisputably, womankind has an easier time of it. In the old days, they'd not only to undertake the cooking, washing, feeding and entire clothing of the household (and a household that consisted of perhaps 20 or 30 residents) and making the clothing for their own family, but they saw to the grinding of the flour, sold the meal in return for its milling (and a medieval note tells the hussife to keep an eye on that miller!), made the candles, the cheese, salted the winter meat, etc., and brewed and baked also.

A sensible farmer's wife had to note how the weather and carting was going on, and try to get her grain to and from the mill, or her wood and coal brought in at times when her men folk did not need the horses and carts in the field. Also the few weeks' slack time after harvest, was a good time to undo the household purse strings, and replenish the house, and if you could get away for a short change and a holiday and see how the rest of the world was faring it would do you good, and you would bring back fresh ideas. The woman was not so tied at home as one supposes.

The winter storehouse, far more difficult in those days, the farm suppers and harvest homes feasts were her affair, and it was often a hundred or so that you had to provide for. And those feasts needed a considerable amount of cooking and planning.

Manlike, the farmer himself usually lent a hand with the brewing, or in the West undertook the making of the cider himself.

(Somehow, one can't believe mankind ever trusted a woman entirely alone with his drink.) But the actual planning and the work of catering was much heavier than it is on any farm now and the whole of it was her job.

For the daughters, and the farm and field servants, the difference has been even greater. Statements describing the sordid, miserable lot of the 'woman farm labourer' are nearly as inaccurate as the pictures of the bareheaded 'harvest girl' dancing down the hayfield.

Farm Fashions

A reliable decent Scots body of a century ago, when quoting prices and conditions, states firmly that 'women workers should kilt their skirts high and have a change of dry clothing in the barn and a hot supper after the heavy muddy work of potato planting,' and 'workers in the hayfield should wear sunbonnets to protect the nape of the neck and drink plenty of barley water.'

And you can tell me either of these jobs isn't a more jolly and healthy occupation for a sturdy growing young woman than bending over a machine in a stuffy room from 9 till 6?

The work *was* strenuous, but it's interesting to note that the provision of two large barns, one for the men and one for the women, with 'plenty of clean straw bedding and two clean blankets apiece,' and a 'place where they could wash.' *These provisions are exactly the same as the accommodation provided and enjoyed in a modern Youth Hostel to-day!*

Plenty of Fun

Now, as always, the conditions of the woman on the land depend upon the individual manager than upon anything else, but those big work meetings, the supper all together every night in the farmhouse kitchen, or the big harvestings (rather like our hop pickings now) meant a great deal of fun and social life, as well as work. And as old farm pay sheets show, when Sarah X and William Y have arrived on the same day with suspicious regularity for three or four years, usually they leave the pay-roll simultaneously and settle under one name.

As nowadays, in actual stock breeding, mankind dealt with all the heavy work, the shepherding and calving and horses, but the woman of the house took, naturally, the care of all the young stock. As one old farm book puts it 'it is the natural work of a woman and they be loving to it.' Or, as another farmer writes (and you hear the exasperated man putting it tactfully) 'they have a *natural* patience.'

That womankind was expected to assist at the killing of pigs, and the slaughtery of poultry is less pleasant; but there were one or two firm-minded wenches about in those days. Of course, the real value of the woman having worked on the farm nowadays is that she knows what farm work feels like, and what mankind needs to eat when he is in the fields, and how rest on his return, and the blessing of peace and amusement in the evenings. And her workgirls can be supervised with the insight and knowledge of her own experience.

Please don't think this is advocating a back to the land movement and general exodus from the farm parlours. But going up and down the land, always I found the happiest places where womankind understands the farm's jobs and enjoys to lend a hand, and the trouble is where she despises country things, and neglects the fun and work that belong to the land.

The ease with which country folk can now run into town and often share town pleasures and conveniences, ought to add to the joys of the country, but sometimes, they make us forget the near country pleasures that rightly belong to us. You must really love the country and take a pride in your country work if you are going to enjoy it, and the hundreds and hundreds of happy farmers' wives in country places will tell you the same thing.

Tuesday, 15 May 1934

Seaweed for dinner

One good thing they use in Ireland, that I have not seen for ages, is Carrageen. It used to be gathered in Dorset, and I have heard tell of it in Devon, and around St. David's Head (but that is Ireland's other landing stage, anyhow).

Some French nuns used to make it as a rather special dish for high days and holidays. They used to set it in elaborate tinned copper moulds, with a lion couchant and a bunch of fruit and an architectural stand. The lion got poured in first and was frequently coloured bright pink, which made him look very fierce. He would tremble on the dish, high above the maidenhair garnishing, with ominous gelatinous resilience, as if he quivered among the jungle growth of his native land. He had citron and almonds and rose water in his inside in those days (those French nuns were marvellous cooks!).

Try the Chemist

We loved him less when we had mumps, and he became softer and lemonish, but perhaps that was association and not the lion. It certainly was not the good carrageen, and his native strand was Dorset, for he was just plain seaweed and milk, really.

All old recipe books quote Irish moss, and note you, it is always considered a delicacy and figures among the creams and pastry dishes. One could always buy it from the chemist, but there were few who knew its use in the kitchen save trained cooks and chefs, who continued to use it.

Last summer I spent some time in Dorset trying to trace our English carrageen seaweed. Two or three people knew of it, but it had acquired a medicinal use. The old man who produced a dried handful out of a jar, used it hot with whisky for a cold. He remembered when a great lot of it was sent to London market. But its ordinary cottage use is all gone, and the delicious creams the country people would make you for supper did not seem to be made any more from the weed.

On Its Dignity

There are a good many edible seaweeds; laver, like wet brown silk, remains in Devon and along the Bristol Channel up to Bath, but my 'Irish moss' was forgotten from the English cookery book. Now imagine my astonishment when I find it neatly packed and offered for sale in the best shops in Dublin as a 'special product!' Joyfully I brought some home, and if any of you like to try it for yourselves – this is what it looks like:

I have seen it around our coasts, chiefly in the rocky West. What you buy loose from the chemist is crisply white, faintly streaked with pinkish brown, and crisp, like curled shredded gelatine. In the water it is soft white and very pliant.

The pinky brown streaks seem to vary locally. Some that I found off the stony beach of Dungeness was quite darkly streaked; at St. David's it was almost white, but the quality seems to be the same.

It needs no preparation, except picking over and washing and soaking in several fresh waters to rid of the salt. It is clear and fresh as salad while you wash it, and springy around your fingers, like white fern. When you can bite a piece and not taste the salt, toss it out and dry it, and keep it in a box ready for use. (My old Dorset man told me that his mother kept it in a white cotton bag, hung up in the dry kitchen.)

This Way, Please

Use it exactly like gelatine, soaking it a little first to soften it, and then steeping it in a very hot milk with flavouring. About a handful to a quart is plenty; don't get it too stiff. After about 15 minutes' simmering, strain it out.

It is very little more trouble to make than the starch blancmanges, but whereas they are solid and chewy and stick to the spoon, carrageen is lighter consistency, very creamy and cuts with a 'brittle' clean cut, like jelly or junket. You can make it as stiff as you like. Given time, it almost dissolves away in cooking; when you strain it, you need only use a coarse sieve.

In Ireland, in the cafés, they were using it chiefly as a sweet: ginger creams, chocolate mould, coffee and raspberry creams; but I liked it best with the old-fashioned flavourings of honey and cinnamon, bay leaves or almonds (with whole almonds and whipped cream on top).

Rattaphilla

If any of you treasure old recipe books, it is fun to try some of their suggestions, including what my own treasured copper plate MS. book calls 'Rattaphilla*!' It has many other uses also.

The soused herring sits more solid if his jelly has a little moss dissolved in it; the clear soup clears as if white of egg were used. The stuff is full of iodine and protein and is really, under analysis, a very health giving food.

One reassuring word if you go to gather it for yourself, as I hope you will; don't be nervous, you can't go wrong as is possible with mushrooms. There is hardly anything that you could find by mistake nor anything poisonous like it. Carrageen is the only nearly white weed we have and is perfectly harmless and very delicious.

Tuesday, 22 May 1934

---

* Ratafia.

Across the apples and round the fruit

It's good to have fruit all the year round, but the effects on the market are very, very far-reaching. They reach down to a tiny shed in Kent, where one man is working alone, making slats – pliant split bark covered saplings that nail across the apple boxes and around the fruit barrels.

'There used to be ten of us in this shed,' he said, 'and more, and plenty more about the woods. No, they still use barrels,' he explained, 'but the grapes and the foreign fruit they comes over in barrels and boxes and it wouldn't pay to send back the crates and barrels, so they have to be sold off cheap.

'Some firms undertake that their packings must be destroyed.'

'Why?'

'Oh, they won't risk other folk's goods passed off as theirs. One can't blame.' (The patience of the country people sounded in his voice.)

'One can't blame anyone for picking up what's not wanted and using it, if it's what they want, or they can get it cheaper, but it means there's few want new-made barrels and fruit boxes now – compared with what there was.

'We have some orders. These have got to go off now, and some more, longer ones like that' (he showed me a long strip) 'for going round spring onions. The watercress growers use willow and pack in flat baskets. These slats are best for a nailing job, wrap round as pliant as a bit of tape they do and never split in nailing.'

I remembered seeing the dark brown pliant strips nailed across English dessert apple cases, and told him so.

'That's right. Better-class stuff uses them, and a few firms that cater for some special London houses they'll pay a bit extra for specially made crates, but not much now – not much – ten there used to be here.'

The slat-maker.

He peered across the empty shed. The sunlight coming through the chinks pointed to empty work benches with blue soft shafts of light that made gold pools over the bark-littered floor, and moved slowly as if looking for somebody.

The slat maker was using the simple wooden foot grip of the wood-worker that held the thickness of the sapling easily, and released it with one movement of the knee. As I watched, he slid the long knife down and down the strips, adding the finished strip to the pile with the same hand that brought back the next sapling on to his bench. Not a moment was wasted, not a movement careless. His fingers were automatically feeling the strip under the tool, his mind automatically judging its thickness, avoiding weak places, thinning coarse ones.

His mind was free, he could talk to me, yet, so well the unconscious knowledge of years served him, that a thickened sapling, a knot in the wood, was reflected through his words, the grain of the wood as an inflection in the voice (just as the rock patches of a hill pasture can be seen through the thin grass).

The roof of the shed was thatched with the bark shavings. It gave it a shaggy look. The fire bucket outside the door was smouldering quietly under the big kettle. A coat was hung on a pin driven between the slats. The pin was worn smooth and polished with use.

His father had been in the same trade – 'woodmen all – we were' – (the past tense hurt). He went on talking, and working, telling me a hundred things, giving me at random gleanings of woodlore, the experience of a score of winters, a wisdom that had grown with the wood itself, experience as to what would grow well, shape well and 'last out.'

Knowledge worth gold – Nay! there's the rub. Not worth gold these days, but worth the very heart's blood of England…

A woman came down the field to the shed with a bundle wrapped in cloth, and a basket, and the slatworker came out and made up the fire. It was dinner time. 'Going? Have you bothered me talking? Not a bit, not a bit! T'other way round, one gets to remembering… Ten there used to be in this shed…'

'Wait a minute until I get my dinner off the missus. She'll put you on the road to that wood. Ask for Joe Gates and tell him I sent you. Here, mother! here's company for you on the way back. She'll show you the turning into the wood – it's just past our place – well! I wouldn't be surprised if you *did* find the kettle on, as you went past!'

Tuesday, 29 May 1934

Inishbofin

INISHBOFIN originated as a 'Phantastic' – a heap of cloud rising from the water – and some sailors, thinking it a whale spouting, went out to capture it. They chased it two days, as they would a shark or whale, and then hurled a red hot harpoon into it.

That fixed it. Iron being, of course, the end of all magic. But actually, if the harpoon was one of the heavy iron contraptions still in use by the islanders of that wild coast, it would settle anything.

Anyhow, there *is* Inishbofin – about eight square miles of solid island, and the queer thing is, that all the other islands, that used to be marked on the map, queer 'Brazils' and 'Fortunate Isles,' are gone, while the island of Bofin, which was the most legendary of all, has become solid.

Islands That Go

It makes one curious about the others. To be sure, that coast changes a lot (and 'islands that are found to be not there, go' as Irish islands do) but there are stone walls on islands that were built when those islands joined the mainland, and rocks at sea that are all that's left of islands which have been broken away or crushed and pounded down by great seas. There are causeways and reefs out at sea where a man might have gone dry footed on turf. So maybe many a fable island really existed, and was fastened to the map by an iron pen of a scribe as securely as Bofin was fixed by the iron harpoon.

Brasie is the only mystic isle left now, and that to be seen only once in seven years, by any one man. And within living memory died a man who saw it twice, and if he had seen it a third time he would have got it; but he died with excitement the night before it was due (and this is a fact well testified by learned antiquarians from Dublin), but there are those less book-learned and more knowing who say those Ones on the island had no mind to be fixed, and had him taken at the back end.

A Little Mistake

'You have to be taking care about Them,' they warned me. Giraldus nodded in agreement, and quoted the popular error, that the sailors landed on the island while it was actually floating, and lit a fire there, which, as he finally remarked, was a legend stolen from St. Brandan, who made the same mistake over a whale.

'But this island of Bofin,' they told me (we were sitting on a wooden lobster raft, while the clear blue water lapped and sucked below us). 'Whitecow Island is the name that does be on it, on account of them that did be in it, for the morning after the sailors had caught it, they sleeping on it, lying by the fire of turf which they had covered over, one of the sailors, getting out to blow up the lighting of his pipe from the fire, saw a girl driving off a white cow.

'"Arra!" he said, "there's Them that do be on this island would be leaving it!" and he up and ran and laid hold of that cow by the tail – and it was seaweed in his hand... So *Those* were the like of the Ones that be on Bofin before us.... And I would not say they were all gone yet.... There be holes on the Island that no man knows of, and the sounds that do come out of them – Whist! as if They'd no mind to be heard....'

A trail of kelpie weed, long as a cow's tail flapped lazily across the tide drift at our feet.... Behind us, Diamond Mountain shone green in the sun, lit with a sparkle of fine quartz. Out across Cleggan Bay, the mail-boat was beating her way in slowly, losing the wind as she passed within the shelter of the headland.... We watched her come up into the lee of the harbour.

An American Scientist

'There's one man that does be knowing all the rocks on Bofin and putting the names to reefs, the like of which you'd never believe....'

'What does he do with them?' I asked. 'Sorra a thing he has done, but he has put a pass on himself to have all the rocks on the coast named, and faith! 'tis a life time he'll need, and he but young!' He had come across from America, they explained, with his family, 'a Scientist, he was!'

My old Giraldus pricked up his ears;

'Before my day' (i.e. 1186!) 'learned men came from Italy, Spain, and all over Europe, to study in Ireland. I would have speech with this man of unknown race. We heard, in our time' (Giraldus spoke of the 12th Century as if it were yesterday) 'tales of strange doings of dark-skinned natives from across the Western Seas.'

I got up hurriedly! Giraldus, old historian, was my friend, but I had no wish to hear him talk medieval Latin to an American geologist under a hot sun!

I wandered off alone around the island. The small sheep were cropping the short grass; on the west, three long interarched caves threaded far inland, in the great rift where the soft rock had washed out in a winding passage, exactly like a huge harpoon jab.

High Island, to the south beyond the Stags of Bofin, has a hermits' settlement of small stone cells, to the west, Inishark lay watching us. The rocks of the islands were folded and bent in weird shapes – and showed a hundred volcanic colours. The old fort, built at the harbour entrance, had lost all its corner stones; they had been limestones, brought over from the mainland, and the islanders had burnt them for lime for their tiny fields and houses.

I returned to the quay. The American geologist and two fishermen had just landed, and were hauling cameras and fish nets out of his curragh. (I noted that he handled the fish nets very scientifically!)

I prepared to collect old Giraldus, but the smallest American in Ireland, astride a donkey, laughing and talking alternately in island Irish and American, blue-eyed, freckled, curly headed, and 'almost five' had taken possession of him.

Saturday, 2 June 1934

Our toys in England now

The toy industry of England has, in the main, passed into the jurisdiction of the mechanic. There are several good wooden toy workshops and well-run toy industries, but it is perhaps suitable that in this new mechanical age, the very babes should begin on clockwork.

Still, the unmechanical toys of England stand firm. Stuffed animals hold their own, rabbits leading slightly, dogs and cats going strong. Doll-houses are in request, paints and chalks all smell as heavenly on a wet day, and the large pull-off sheets of drawing papers *are* an improvement on the blackboard, because you can keep your best efforts to show, and not have to rub out one inspiration before you have corrected it on the next.

Rocking horses continue active. The old carved wood rocking horse has lost much paint, but there are still good craftsmen, with a nice eye for good points in wood, and the old-fashioned skin-covered horse (with real tail) is beautifully made and finished with real bridle and stirrups that let up and down.

One of the most exciting things I ever saw in an interesting life was a travelling caravan-show spring cleaning; and forty-eight new painted roundabout horses were brightly shining in a green meadow, all among the varnished buttercups.

In Rhodesia, one English family, unable to get a horse, had sensibly substituted a leopard (shot from the veranda); and six healthy youngsters had kicked the fur off its side and galloped on the '*rocking leopard*' as happy as any ancestral equivalent.

Knucklebones

It was farther up country I met two little English girls with their dollies strapped on behind! Because in that country they had never seen babies carried in any other way.

Spinwheels still spin in the English wind as they have done since the 12th century.

Up North, on pavements, the children still play knucklebones with special bright pottery knobs, and complicated hopscotch with strange chalkings and a piece of tile. In the London parks it's various forms of cricket and footer, kites, boats on the ponds, and for the younger, hoop and stick, down the walks.

Skipping ropes, 'proper,' long ones, that will take three or four skipping in them at a time, are the Lancashire toy. On summer evenings, if you incautiously hop the first rope, you will be let in for an enthusiastic hurdle race to the end of the street. In London it is the lamp-post swing (why do these incredibly frayed and knotted ropes never seem to break?).

Marbles

Among small boys marbles appear as spasmodic as measles, usually ending equally suddenly. Those striped glass marbles one can still buy in little country shops, and 'Hims,' if you are lucky, though I am told on good authority that 'Hims' have gone out and the best people play with marbles all of one size nowadays.

Tops are lighter than they used to be, and more agile. Soap bubbles are leaving the pure realms of skill and infringing on the scientific via glycerine and special mixtures.

The grown-ups have appropriated our battledore and shuttlecock to play badminton with, but left us their old tennis rackets. They have also pinched our ninepins to revive skittles. Sport games involving real rackets and hockey sticks and so forth are quite different (like books!), and the sort of 'table games' that they 'give-you-to-be-quiet-with' aren't toys. (N.B. – Musical instruments of all sorts are ruled out by this provision.)

Again, I am assured that scooters, single roller skates, etc., are a 'means of transport' and more a means of getting about than a toy. (The upkeep of a commercial scooter is almost prohibitive these days.)

The gramophone, the typewriter and the wireless are so contemporary that I hesitate to include them among toys for fear of offending some of my youngest and most elderly friends.

Tuesday, 5 June 1934

Here's a pretty kettle of fish

Do you know where little boys go to who go fishing on Sundays?
Yes, sir; they mostly goes down Johnson's Creek.

The shops are full of fishing tackle, and I've never warned you about freshwater fish. Of course, if your family boasts a slayer of salmon and a master of trout, then you, in honour bound, will know how to deal with them respectfully.

But, remember, time was (and not so very long ago) when the apprentice boys of London supplicated that they should not be made to eat salmon more than once a week, and many a smaller fish was considered a greater delicacy when they were better known and better cooked.

Cooking the Catch

A lot of new adventurers will be beginning on the Broads this summer, and let me warn you straight away that the technique of cooking *flat* water (i.e., usually muddy-bottomed water) fish is absolutely different from river or sea fish; and if your men folk are going to land you with 'fish,' they'll expect you to know by a kind of instinct how to cook it correctly, and be unnecessarily disappointed if you spoil the catch. There is never a man or boy that doesn't expect his fish to expand in the kitchen. (N.B. – Fish seem to grow larger the minute they take their eyes off them.) So hie you to your fish-kettles!

Now I speak for amateurs. Of course, if you've got a natural-born float fisherman in the family, then you're happily blest. I don't know a pleasanter sight on a sultry summer afternoon than a fishing club along a flowery, peaceful canal bank – each man on his little stool, with his little lunch box, and his little flask, beside him so careful … and knowing that there they are happy and out of mischief and being properly good all day.

Carefree Wives

When you see a sight like that, you run round behind and you'll find a party of carefree wives in some café in the little town having a lovely time. Of course, the wife of a big-game hunter can be sure of a fur coat – but I do think a fisherman's wife makes up for it in peace of mind.

However, it really is important that you know how to cook the boy's fish properly. Don't you remember happy Huck Finn's catfish that they caught on the island? 'We haggled him open with a saw, his meat as white as snow, and he makes a good fry.'

When the sportsman has ideas about cooking fish, then you just obey orders (after all it's *his* fish), but whiles they hand you the most dubious-looking catch, and hopefully expect you to make the best of it – well, that puts you on your mettle.

Now for Bream (that's very common on the Broads) or any muddy-bottomed water fish. Do not wash them, do not wipe, nor on any account scale! Cut and trim off the fins with scissors, but handle them as little as possible because the scales of them are different from fresh-water fish, and the least movement after the fish has gone limp lets the mud in under the big loose scales. Especially washing under water lets the thin mud rise and work up between the overlapping scales and the skin, and once this is done no matter how you cook the fish it will taste muddy.

The best treatment for any sort of flat water fish is to flour heavily. (I've seen a gipsy trail the fish over soft mud *by its head* so that it was smooth-coated like a crust.) Then lay the fish on a gridiron, and grill, roast or bake before a very hot fire. If the fish is fresh and the fire really hot the scales ought to loosen and crisp up into a protective crust almost at once. If it doesn't, try sprinkling with oil or melted dripping to start with. Cook *extra* well, till the meat is white and soft, and slides easily off the bone. (Test this at the back of the head, not near the tail, which is thin and apt to be cooked too much before the thick part of the fish is done through.)

Serve straight from the grill on to hot plates. Slices of lemon and a hot tureen of melted butter are good with almost any of these fish. You will find you can lift off the loosened skin whole, and the fish will eat clean as fresh water, no taste of mud at all.

An old way of cooking pike was called 'Pike under Ashes.' The way was to clean it, stuff the long slit with chopped onions, put pointed head into tail like a whiting, wrap in white oiled paper and then several thicknesses of wet brown paper (or bracken), and bury deep in hot ashes for two or three hours.

This original recipe was done in the deep ash of an open peat or wood fire, but it is very suitable for camp-fire work if you have got a good depth of ash. Before serving remove the wrapping, skin, and give the hot fish a good basting with dripping, and sprinkle with breadcrumbs or flour and brown till crisp. Good beef gravy is best with pike.

Stones As Frying Pans

Incidentally, in camp the best way to roast flat fish is to hang them by their tails over a well-greased hot stone. Find a flattish stone and prop it slightly slanting close to the fire. This brings the head and thick part closest to the fire. Make the stone hot thoroughly through before you put the fish against it, and turn it twice at least. They cook nice and evenly this way.

Long-shaped fish can be lain across or hung up, according to which is most convenient (put a piece of butter inside or baste them well with butter if the fire is rather drying). Well-washed watercress is the ideal garnish for fish out of doors, and a squeeze of lemon juice is a great improvement.

I do not include eels, because I have the countrywoman's firm conviction that they must be dead through two sunsets before they are cooked, and any reliable cookery book will give you good recipes for cooking eels. By the Lancashire and Yorkshire pits they like them stewed with onions and white sauce. Jellied eels are popular in

London and Liverpool, and in East Anglia I've had good eel pie with anchovy sauce, slices of egg and onion and a buttery potato crust – very savoury.

Crayfish are delicate as lobsters. They will only live in very fresh water, so are quite safe. The monks used to breed them in streams as a great delicacy Many of the North-country becks around Malham and Gordale were stocked originally from the running water fish ponds of Bolton Abbey. Only use the very large crayfish (the rest should be thrown back, as they are not worth eating unless full grown).

The Method

When the fisherman has 'settled them' thoroughly, plunge one at a time in absolutely boiling water, and keep it boiling until they are cooked.

Take them out and throw them at once into clean, slightly salted water (or, if you are going to eat them at once, milk and water). Otherwise the shells will be part empty and the fish dried up in cooling. If you leave them to cool in the slightly muddy water in which they have been boiled, that will soak back through interstices of the shell and spoil the fish.

When cold, clear out of the shell and use like lobster, with mayonnaise and salad.

Now all this wood lore and countryside fish tales are the result of experience and firm tuition at the hands of fishermen, and it's worth taking trouble, because when your fisherman feels that you have done justice to his prowess he'll go and catch you another.

Tuesday, 19 June 1934

Just a Gloucestershire cot

There were roses round the door, but not exclusively. There were also virginia creeper and a sprouting of jasmine, and either side of the doorstep neat little knots of daffodil leaves, so the doorway would have had a welcome all four seasons.

The test of an English cottage garden is a nine out of twelve month test – in the fields we are either 'nice and forward with the work' or 'terrible behind.' In gardens we are 'very early' or lucky to be 'very late.' If you notice, it's only towns-folk or English foreigners who talk about English 'weather'; in the real country, where they've lived through it, man and boy all their lives, it's seldom mentioned. We say '*It's* terrible dry,' '*It's* terrible wet,' '*It's* gae saft,' '*It's* wunerful!' 'Yes, yes, *it* is.'

I believe half our lethargy in dealing with the present water shortage comes from our interior conviction that *It* will only wait till we get a scheme started, and then drown us.

Anyhow the predominating characteristic of English country homes, whether cottages or castles, is the comfortable all-the-year-round look about them.

Always Busy

This little country cottage, though nestling among flowers in warm sunshine, had nothing of the summer-house look, but defied all the gods of bad weather with thick stone and a well-tilted slate roof. It was a busy little cottage, polished and spotless and yet full of the signs of work continuously going on in it. It gave you the impression of having just settled down for forty winks between a very busy morning and a very busy evening. The sun was pouring in through the window and through the open door the sound of the hay-making machines whirred and whirred steadily, cutting the hay of the rich Gloucester meadows. There was a little garden with a red brick path down the middle, a white painted gate, leading on to a white road, and beyond that the hayfields.

Inside the cottage it was very warm. A cricket chirped steadily, gaining about four over six with the grandfather's clock, who tick-tocked solidly in the far corner. The kettle was on, and singing.

A Very Fat Cat

A cat was asleep on the thick pieced-rag rug before the fire; he was a very fat cat, with fine wide whiskers – his fat paws folded under his tummy – his eyes closed. He purred a little louder in his sleep when a cinder fell from the fire, but didn't trouble to wake.

There were white lace curtains, crinkly stiff at the white painted window, on the ledge of which was a barricade of potted geraniums – their handsome scarlet set off against the red raddle of their flower pots, and the scarlet picked up again in the red pattern of the hearthrug. It was a very thick hearthrug. Those bits of red cloth had been a hunting coat – they always get a good price for hunting coats at rummage sales because they put the pattern in the rag rug so good. The rest of the pieces were mostly black and grey and dark blue, skirt and coat pieces, diamond squared and close set.

The polished open range shone like black satin, and the brass knobs on the fender gleamed. On the mantelpiece, in the middle, was an ornamental clock that had stopped bothering to go, because the grandfather clock did the work anyhow, so it said five always, which was a very convenient time, because it meant you could always put the kettle on. On either side the clock were two tin boxes with pictures on them that had had tea in them, but now held bits of things. There were four brass candle-sticks – two on each side – a brass boot on one side matched a china cat, with a slit on its back (for pennies) on the other.

There were two china dogs, one at each end. There was a fat stock and farm calendar on one side the fireplace, and a treadle sewing machine, with a white crochet top put over it, on the other. Above the sewing machine was a wireless speaker, and on a shelf by it an old knife-box full of tools and some man's oddments where he had been fidgeting with the wireless.

On the other side of the fireplace was a boy's desk with some books and a newspaper rack, very full.

Something About Hay Time

The men's coats were hanging on the scullery door that just led out of the kitchen. The owner of one coat was at that moment riding round and round the hayfield on a mowing machine. His father had gone, too, to-day. In the winter father complains 'he is getting stiff,' but there's something about hay time that warms the blood, and few can stay in a cottage when the scent of new hay comes in through the door; besides these Gloucester meadows have a way of tilting themselves up on to surprising hills and then there is plenty of need for an extra man or two with the old pitchfork to work up the corners and spare the tedding machine…

Phew! It's warm in here, though there's only enough fire just to boil the kettle.

The woman of the house is away in the scullery, where it's cooler. Through the open door I can watch her cut even slices of close, white bread and creamy butter – slice after slice gets piled up steadily, for the men are to have tea in the fields.

On the table by me stand two large green glass bottles (the large brown teapot is warming on the hob), a bass basket, a clean white tea cloth, and two thick china cups wrapped in newspaper lie by the glass bottles.

'Yes, he had a tin tea-can one time, but my boy, he fancies it better in the bottle. Keeps hotter, too. Cold tea? No. Hot tea's best for cooling – there's nothing like it.'

She reaches down a bowl of rich yellow double Gloucester cheese from the shelf by her hand (the shelf is covered with paper, cut into fanciful edges with little holes cut in it like paper lace), and the cheese is yellow as egg yolks. She cuts smooth, thin slices and lays them overlapping like tiles in a thick layer on the last slice of bread and butter which is just cut, covers them with the thin bottom crust of the bread to stop them breaking, picks up a crisp, creamy custard tart that's been baked in a flat tin and comes back laden, to the kitchen table.

The kettle has stopped singing and the lid is hopping round, so she picks the kettle holder off its nail, in the mantelpiece, and, pursing her lips, lifts the heavy kettle on to the side of the hob and wets the tea. Then she puts the tea-pot in the oven to draw, while she wraps some lumps of loaf sugar in a scrap of white paper and pops them in one of the teacups, with a teaspoon reminder; she also hunts up a special knife, and four tomatoes are brought in from the window ledge in the little porch.

The tea has drawn now, and a cupful of milk is measured into each bottle and then the tea poured in in a long gold stream gug-gug-gug, and the corks rammed home. She looks down the road enquiringly. 'There now! It's ready and he ought to be – Ah, here's Sam now.'

The bottles are packed, one at each end of the bass with their necks sticking out over the top. The big pile of bread and butter and cheese is wrapped in a white cloth and wedged between them, and the cups fitted in on top between the handles.

'I did put that sugar? – Yes, I did.'

The teapot is refilled from the kettle; the cat gets the remainder of the milk from the empty jug, and, with a rose in my buttonhole, I go off with Sam down to the hayfield, carrying the custard tart in its tin.

Tuesday, 10 July 1934

[197]

Sheep are not so silly

It has got to rain plenty before it refills the hollows in the hills. Casual holiday makers crossing the mountains don't see much amiss, but shepherds and workers on hill farms who know the shape of the grazings see the change that the long dry spell has wrought. The shrinkage of the bogs and slow draining of many of the wet places has lowered whole stretches and there are queer white sandy drifts, with black rims, where there used to be still brown peat pools.

In our houses on the hills we have not much shortage of water, and can still run taps, and water the gardens, but the air seems dryer and our skins feel tight and dry, and the fine dust troubles our eyes and throats more because we are less accustomed to dryness than the Lowland folk. Specially so troubled are our animals. It isn't that they don't get enough to drink when watered, but the fodder has changed its character. Usually they eat about as much wet grass as they do dry, for though the hill grazings are short, they are good, and hill sheep are very cunning and clever at finding tasty pieces.

Sheep Are Scientific

The young sheep are very fond of the thick bottoms of the rush tufts (look close and see where the little sharp mountain teeth have bitten down in the juicy damp grass at the roots of the rush tufts); I've watched them picking off the little brown tassels from the rushes as neatly as we'd pick peas, and chewing away busily. Well, all that fodder is dryer. Luckily we have heavy dews on the hills, the grass is soaking wet in the early morning, and sometimes where the slope of the hill lies turned from the morning sun, the dew will lie till nine or ten o'clock, and the sheep get busy enough cropping the rainbow grass.

People not knowing the hills seem to imagine sheep wander loosely and chance upon fodder anywhere, haphazard. Don't you believe it! There's a lot of science to sheep feeding, and the creatures themselves need to 'learn' a mountain as much as a shepherd. They have regular feeding spots and walking places. You have found those little foot-wide tracks that lead to the heather? How many strangers think they are human paths. 'Oh, here's a little foot track,' they say, and feel surprised when it peters out into several branches, or leaves off at a shallow pool.

Afternoon Nap

The sheep have made those paths for themselves, and if you think of the hundreds and hundreds of tiny footprints that have trodden out those little tracks, you will realise how methodical sheep are.

About dawn, or earlier, they start feeding – and crop till the dew has gone, and after. About noon they find a shady spot; if there's a favourite tree or rock they will gather there from miles around. If there's no cover, they will find a deep heather clump to shade them; there in the shadow, they will doze and sleep all noonday – till long shadows and cool air start them off cropping for the evening.

On moonlight nights they will be awake cropping half the night. That is one reason why the moon is so important in planning the breeding times for sheep, or killing them for food. They are in very different conditions at the end of a bright moonlight spell, or dark nights. On some steep hills sheep will go as regularly up and down the mountain sides as the mist rises and falls over its top.

Once, for interest, an old shepherd and myself mapped out a small mountain, as the sheep themselves had mapped it out for the year's grazing. It was only a rough map, but there were regular highways and by-ways leading to and from the drinking pools, and shallow places in the streams, and regular 'dormitories' and tracks to and from the old salting stone, and one or two queer worn places which were evidently favourites at regular seasons, but why (not

being sheep!), we could not be certain. Probably some small thyme plant that the sheep were fond of, sprouted specially thereabouts, or perhaps (the shepherd gave it as quite a serious reason) they liked the sound of the water, and knew they could get a drink handy when they were ready for it.

What We Miss Most

That 'Sound of the Water' is what we miss most. Unconsciously we mountainy folk are tuned to hear always running and trickling water. In the evening going back to the farms we hear streams, gently talking over the pebbles, and on the hillsides, between the stills of the wind, comes the silver splashing of small waters falling on stone. The bogs sing to us, and the mist-wet hedgerows drip as we pass by. Down the longest, hottest, driest country road in summer, we stop, and the horse edges in where a pipe juts out over a stone trough, and slops away below the road. After a quick rain the little surface drains chuckle and gurgle down our sloping fields. Always and always, we are surrounded by the little soft voices of running water. Now that they are still, it feels unnatural – and without knowing quite what it is – we listen for it; *and the sound of water isn't there.*

Last week, where I have gone for years often knee deep through pools, and bogs, and spongy furry wet bog-moss, there was but dry dusty powder, and little beaches of white bleached stone, and the sheep were walking round and round the edges, puzzled, and dry and hot. They were in fair condition and were not wanting water desperately, for there are few hills where there is not some stream still slowly running, but animals hate change and the fourfold tracks crowding around that little dried up patch voiced enormous indignation.

A few of the old hardy sheep came close and stamped at me reproachfully. Most farm animals know the look of a bucket and all consider we ought to carry them about with us this weather.

Of course, the high hills are in some cases better off than the lower pastures, and anyway it would be impossible to clear the top grazings, but on many of the lower hills the shepherds are bringing down the sheep at intervals to 'help out' this season.

The dryness is having dreadful effect on the little wild things also. The great hawks swing steadily over the water courses much more often, whereas they used to quarter on the open bare hillsides. Curiously, the moorland fruits are not much affected. The wild raspberries on the way up the slopes are fine, a little small, but plentiful; and surely the bilberries have never been so purple blue and luscious. (The bilberry pickers are out on the hillsides now, with their purple-stained baskets and tin pannikins, and the piles of the fruit are for sale in the country market – the nicest fruit in England, and so slow to gather!)

The lizards flickering over the hot stones are flourishing, and I saw a long brown adder drawing himself through the heather stems (that one will have a long track to his bath!). In the low places masses of frog spawn have perished this spring, and surely we shall have a crop of athletic frogs! for they, like sheep, are very 'set in their ways' and choice of pools.

The long-beaked moorland birds, who feed in the soft bogs and muddy places, ran and cried and peeved heartbreakingly, and a few curlews have been seen in undignified domesticity down by the muddy edge of the river hayfield down in the valley, where all the dry corncrakes will croak endlessly: 'Rain' – 'rain,' 'rain,' 'rain … rain,' because what time the wild moorland creatures start coming down to the valleys to get a drink, we hill folks know the drought *is* being serious.

Tuesday, 17 July 1934

The intricacies of hay

Hay-making is a good example of the variety of methods one finds in use in this one small island. Years ago the only real hay made was off the flooded water meadows down by the rivers. Many old dykes from rivers mark out places where of old the spring floods were deliberately led across to deposit their silt, and the juicy lush grass of summer was the old English hay.

The importation of foreign seeding grasses marks one of the innovations of modern husbandry. In the North a seeded mixture of rye grass and clover is 'hay,' though, roughly speaking, a sown grass crop, including vetches, is not properly called hay.

Anthoxanthum Odoratum

Hay is the natural meadow grass, but so many varieties come under the same name of hay. They used to say that sown grass crops (including clover) were best for young things, and the natural meadow grass was fed to general stock and horses, and that may be a slight guide for beginners in country lore to the intricacies of 'hay.'

Anthoxanthum odoratum is the official name of the particular grass that gives the delicious smell to a hayfield, and that is English. Now, apart from the variety of hay (and its specialising locally according to the climate and the necessities of the district), there is a tremendous difference in the *way hay is made* all over England.

Mr. Jones Speaks

This month I have travelled across England, west to east. In Cardiganshire were small hilly hayfields set about with rocks, where the sturdy Welsh ponies pulled about the low, two-wheeled carts, and Mr. Jones plunged about on the sweet-scented load guiding the pony

about the fields with no more communication between them than his own persuasive Welsh voice.

Discussing the modern improvements, says Mr. Jones, 'Indeed they are very remarkable, but I would have no room for them whatever.' And far away, along the wide west road, drives a slim, intelligent, Modern, wearing horn-rimmed glasses, and guiding a swift scientific contraption behind an up-to-date agricultural motor; and he would have no room for Mr. Jones's old methods!

One bond between them. They both grinned and said 'it was fine weather for haymaking.' Though in the east the lack of rain was sadly felt in the weight of the crop and in the west they chuckle at the lovely weather, and still 'much water in the ground.'

Between these two extremes, the old and the new, lies the study of haymaking. At the old beginning, the scythe, still in use in the small inaccessible meadows, and also in the large up-to-date ones to 'open out for the cutter,' i.e., a man with a scythe goes in first and cuts away clear around the gate and a path into the field, so that the great cutting machines can drive in.

The rakes for hay in the old days were one of the jobs that filled the winter evenings by the fireside, for cutting and fitting the strong wooden teeth (usually oak) and setting on to the strong ash handle was a long job. Many of the rakes in remote country districts are still entirely hand-made. In the more up-to-date agricultural districts they have now sometimes metal finishings, and the teeth are turned in a lathe, not split out of the grain as in the old rakes.

The pitchfork with its various lengths is extraordinarily little changed by centuries of use; (pictures in old manuscripts show pitchforks hundreds of years ago that might belong to the most up-to-date experimental farm to-morrow morning!)

The tedding machine for tossing the hay has dozens of forms, and is in use in all except the smallest fields. So is the horse-rake.

It's impossible to lay down hard and fast rules for the time for cutting and leading hay ('leading,' or 'carrying,' or 'lifting,' all districts have different names). In good weather it has to be down about two days, but that's a very loose measurement.

'Wiping It Up'

In the flat, open fields the modern machinery turns the hay so smoothly and efficiently and gathers it up so quickly that, as an admiring farmer said, 'they just seem to wipe it up.' Sometimes when the weather is bad you only save the hay by turning it and keeping it aired and in condition till you can get it in.

Generally speaking, in the north and west where there's more rain there's less spread and bigger cocks. In the Midlands and East, where there are flat fields and good weather there's sometimes no cocking done at all. It's just gathered up straight from the swaythe. In Scotland, where it's unsafe to leave the hay uncovered overnight, they make huge handcocks, six foot high (there's a lot of skill in making a handcock so that it doesn't topple over), and it's a funny sight to a Southerner to see the horses going round the field with a low trolley, for the world like a tea tray on wheels, on to which they dish up the fat handcocks and slither them off to one corner where they make four or five round Scottish field-stacks.

The Irish Way

On small farms sometimes they don't have this gathering board, but hitch a rope round the base of the handcock and a man walks behind steadying it into the corner. In Ireland (where it's going to rain anyhow!) they make up lap cocks, which is a handcock covered with a dexterous swish of hay, like a little thatch or hat on its head, under which it shelters, till the hay can be got in.

A haystack is loosepacked when it's first piled up, and drops and packs down closer 'of itself' as the hay heats and matures. Roughly a 12ft. wide stack drops about a foot, almost at once and if it isn't evenly piled may topple over.

The heating of a stack is something very scientific. It's what turns the gathered-up meadow grass into real hay. The process has got to be very slight, and very right, and is very subtle, but any woman who's ever made a spiced cake, she'd understand it easily.

A Very Sweet Year

You know, when you mix all the dry ingredients together, if you cover them up and put them away in a warm place overnight, next day the whole mixture is more permeated and when you make up the cake it's evenly spiced and savoury? Well, *that's what happens to the hay*, and is what makes it so good, but, like our cake ingredients, the hay has got to be just dry enough to mature itself savourily.

Damp hay and an over-heated stack is waste. The animals can't eat it. Sometimes it will even set fire to itself. But this year there oughtn't to be any trouble with damp hay anywhere, and I don't know when I remember the hay smelling so sweet.

Tuesday, 24 July 1934

When the cherries come to town

'No man can gather cherries in Kent at the season of Christmas.'
(The Courtship of Miles Standish)

Cherries are so particularly English that it comes as a surprise to find botanists declaring them not native to Western Europe, but brought by Lucullus to Rome from Cerasus. The wild cherry trees are spread pretty well all over England. Whole plantations of them grow on the sloping lands between the mountains and the rivers.

Wedding Presents

Cherrywood was much used for light furniture making. In the beechwoods in the North of London are men who made 'sets' of cherrywood chairs. A set of cherrywood chairs, (hand turned on a pole lathe in the woods and sweetly seasoned) was a rural wedding present worth having.

Somehow they are specially a children's fruit. A schoolboy in the fourteenth century is 'Readier cherry stones to tell Than goe to school or hear the sacred bell'! One of the prettiest, oldest carols we have, is the 'cherry tree carol,' and all down the centuries the cherry blossom floats through our English poetry.

Lovable Time

The song of Piers the Ploughman tells of the pretty novice who 'had a child in cherry time and all the Chapter knew it – knew it'; the doubling thrush song music, breaking through the line; as is the joy of English language. (Another version says 'The caponcote,' (i.e., the fowl house) but – that scribe had never seen the cherry blossom from St. Ann's Well on Malvern Hill, as Langland saw it – Cherry-time is so much more lovable!

In old times Worcestershire and the Western Vales of Evesham grew as many cherries as Kent. (Worcester had a big cherry fair.) Nearly all the cider-making districts grew cherries, because in many localities they added cherries to the apple 'must' for colour and flavour, and there are bills and shipping invoices for cherry trees sent from one district to another.

In the 17th and 18th centuries, those times of possets and cordials, they favoured the Morello cherry, sour, dark and spicy. Sweet edible cherries were a favourite conserve through the 18th century, but English recipes for cooking cherries are as old as the cherry trees.

He Loves Me...

In 1425 a cook begins: 'Take Chyryis and pike out the stonys'; we all know how that recipe goes on! Cherry stones made a love charm, and the gipsies trading them up to London sold them by the sprig or branch, and you counted – your witchcraft of the cherries – he loves me, he loves me not – and it – it always came right!

Kent cherry time means a whole county at work. Two months ago I saw queer splay-foot cherry ladders, lurching and swinging down the lanes on lorries, to be re-runged and mended against the cherry harvest. Later, round baskets piled up by the gateposts and bulged out of sheds; all the paraphernalia of Kent cherry harvest.

Sign of the Picker

A very special shape are cherry ladders. They are about 3ft. across the foot and taper like a Comice pear. 'Why? Oh, they reckon there's not so much weight on the tree.'

Far away on a citron estate in the Tropics I heard two Englishmen discussing the ladders for their crop. 'We can't afford steps yet,' they said, 'and the trees won't bear ladders, but that young timber would split into fine *cherry ladders*.' So I knew him for a man from Kent! They don't have those special ladders in many parts.

The cherry basket. Iron hook and splay cherry ladder.

The sign of a cherry picker is a hook and a ladder. The hook is to sling the basket into the tree, and leave his hands free – a good strong iron hook about a foot long.

They start picking as early as the dew is off the fruit and it's properly dry, and they go at it all day. The bird man is there practically all night. He has to be there before it is light. For weeks before the crop begins, all through Kent, are the bird men popping away; one man, one gun, one orchard, and mostly one little shed in case it rains and one neat little fire with a kettle on it. There's a lot of fun in a cherry orchard, as the baskets are filled, emptied into the big bushel baskets, numbered up and carried to the shed.

In the evening come the lorries, and then if you are lucky and have good friends, you put an enormous supper inside you, a sack of cherries behind you, and clamber up and drive back through the warm summer night, slow and steady.

Up to Covent Garden

'You don't want to bruise fruit, but you've got to make good time all the same...'

The wet misty Queen Anne's lace in the hedgerows brushes the lorry as you pass down the lanes, and the white lamps show the

The bird man in a Kent cherry orchard.

hares, their coats matted together into little points with the dew crossing the white road. And sometimes along the road you pass a house that's opened and awake, and meet other lorries, and stop (and have a quick one) and say how the other orchards are going, and what's the fruit like this year? and how it ought to be better, or it couldn't be better. And so, in the early morning's cold and quiet, you reach Covent Garden, and – the Cherries have come to town.

Cherry Wine

'Pull cherries full ripe, and beat fine, removing stones. Into every gallon put two pounds of sugar and beat again, and stir and put into a vessel (earthenware) which must be full' (a very little spice is added by some old cooks, but others say if you have delicately flavoured cherries, 'let nothing come near,' for Morello cherries they favour mace as a flavouring, a little nutmeg, and a stir with a branch of rosemary). 'When it is done working and making a noise stop it close for three months in an old brandy cask and then bottle it off.'

Cherry Brandy

(This old favourite is more popular than ever to-day, and there's no reason why the most modern of you should not make it by this old recipe.)

'Pack an earthenware jar with dark Morello cherries and shake in some brown sugar candy, crushed, so that it will goe into the cracks between the cherries, and fill up with brandy and tie down very tightly and wax over and keep for several months before use.' (And I'm sure if the old cook had had a screw top jar she'd have used it!) After the brandy has been poured off the cherries they are 'good with melted red currant jelly poured over them and a nice whipt cream syllabub.'

Marmalade of Cherries

'Five pounds of cherries, and then stone them (and it depends on the size of the stone,) but probably rather more than 2lbs. of sugar. Cut your cherries and wet your sugar with the juice that runs from the cut cherries, and when melted boil all pretty fast till it be stiff. When cold put up in glasses.' (Again if you are using the dark, sour Morello cherries, a little spice is an improvement.)

The last recipe sounds like a picture of the 18th century wainscotted room – 'To preserve cherries with the leaves and sticks green.' 'First dip the stalks and leaves in best vinegar boiling hot and stick them upright in a sieve till dry. Meanwhile boil some sugar to syrup and dip the cherries, stalks, leaves and all in the syrup and just let scald, then hang them up to drain while you boil the sugar to candy height. Quickly dip the cherries in, stalks, leaves and all, and then stick the branches in sieves to dry carefully, as any candied fruit. They look very pretty at candlelight in a dessert.'

These old recipes are chiefly taken from an 18th century cookery book.

Tuesday, 31 July 1934

Put me on a haystack

B y the form of a haystack know the county. Haystacks are extraordinarily interesting. The number of people who take haystacks for granted, without even noticing the difference in their form, and the comparative few who *know* the details of their making is really remarkable.

Most people (not agriculturists) consider a hayfield as a picturesque place in which to have tea, and the hiker's idea of 'sleeping in new mown hay' is idealistic but inaccurate. Actually you would probably *die* if you slept in *really new* mown hay while it was still heating! even after new hay has been in a barn, thrown down loose for several days, the air is heavy as a drug.

Bad Hay

In all good hay a certain amount of heating takes place as soon as it is gathered off the field and piled up. The temperature varies with the comparative dryness of the grass, and a little with the kind of grass. As everyone knows hay gathered too wet may heat to such an extent that it bursts into fire, and an immoderate amount of heating will make the hay uneatable and useless. There is practically nothing for which you can use spoilt hay, except as manure, if it's worth carting to the farmyard first. In some cases the farmer won't use it for that, if he thinks there are too many weed seeds in it. So much for a bad hay harvest. This year there ought to be very few troubles from damp hay.

Now consider the makes of the stacks. In the South they run somewhat oblong. Some of the Sussex thatchers finish off the best haystacks in England – 'thatch them down like a house, they do!' – finishing them neatly with straw rope and peggings of split willow. In Kent sometimes the square stacks are thatched with reed; south-

The hay slice.

west way the stacks will be square rather than oblong, and the tilt and form will be more 'bulgy.' There is no more descriptive word for it, for whereas many of the square and oblong haystacks in the Southern and Midland counties are almost architectural in their straightness of line and trimness of surface – away to the West they 'bulge.'

Up in the mountains in Wales they build round stacks in many places, and often they're later building them; and in some parts, specially in the West and South, they thatch them with rushes – green rushes off the mountains – and very interesting work they put into the patterns. Some of them have top-knots, and finished edges of most intricate design. (I showed one of these to a world traveller once and he took it for a Zulu Boma!)

In the mountains in Yorkshire mostly the haystacks are built square, and they are called 'ricks' up there. An old-time farmer demanding education for his son required that he should be able to 'Read, wRite and measure Ricks.'

Irish haystacks are built round, but they are like mushrooms almost at once, because the animals eat away at the bottoms, and there the haystacks stand in the fields, not knowing which way to lean next, and half of them having a stick to prop on.

In Scotland

Scottish haystacks are of several kinds – that's not counting the little Highland stacks, which aren't so much stacks at all as little cachets of hay tucked down behind a stone wall to prevent their blowing away. In the Lowlands there are the fine big haystacks, and the small round field haystacks, and the haystacks, round and fat and sturdy, which cluster together in the Scottish farmyards. The small haystacks on the islands and in little places round the coast usually cower down under a rick cloth, or if they are thatched, are criss-cross strapped-down with a perfect hammock of ropes, and each rope-end with a rock the size of your head tied to it (and even then there are places where the wind would shift an elephant, let alone a wee haystack).

So between the opulent architectural haystacks of the middle of England and the little carefully-gathered dumps tucked away in the odd corners there is a whole field – a hayfield of investigation.

The construction of the haystack varies equally. Most of the Northern ones have spikes in their middles. In the picture you can see the preliminary building of just such a ventilator. They are usually made of larchpoles, three or four, set apart with cross bars of split larch. Roughly as high as a man, because, mark you, the height and width of a stack depends on the height to which a man can raise comfortably a prongful of stacked hay; or the width to which two of them working together can conveniently spread with a stack fork. Where they have proper hay lifts you can have larger stacks.

Carts and Stacks

For the small round stacks the height of the hay cart is usually set for the height of the stack, and in Scotland they're a pretty regular

A centre spike for ventilating a stack being put together in the North.

size, and it used to be customary for dealers to buy from the field stack and cart it away themselves. The wooden ventilators are less common in the square Southern stacks. And with hay lifts (and hay wagons that can be piled higher on the flat Midland roads than they can on the rough mountain ones), the stacks can be made almost any height.

The hay lift is sometimes the mast of an old ship, well strutted down, and the pulley that draws up the hay may be worked from a small oil engine in the steading, or more commonly an old steady farm horse, good at backing, is given the job of walking forward and pulling the hay up; and walking back and letting the grip down again. And a testy job it is, and the horse that's on that job looks enviously enough at the fellows who have got the job of leading their empty wagons down to the field, and bringing them back full, and able to get a decent forty winks while they're standing against the rick.

In the East, a machine attached to the back of a haycart is seen lifting hay straight from the swaythe.

Platforms for Hay

Again, the modern hay lift that lifts the hay from the swaythe on to the wagon in the field can be used to lift it direct on to the stack with great advantage all round.

In the dry level fields the squared stacks may stand direct on the ground, provided it's well drained and there is no fear of flooding in the district. Elsewhere regular platforms are built to receive the stacks (both hay and corn). In some districts these are made of stone, several feet high. Particularly on sloping land around hill farms these platforms of stone levelled out for the stacks need to be strongly built. Over the stone is laid a layer of brush wood or bracken, and then the hay (or corn). In some districts they make wood platforms, and where these are high enough, isn't it a nice cool comfortable place for the pigs to find, and go to sleep under!

Thatching

In an old MS. it is noted that 'Seldom is time found to thatch hay stacks while the corn is yet uncut,' and often the straw from threshing, though broken, is still good enough to thatch a haystack (and much better than the hay itself). But the ornamental finishes of twisted 'birds' with plumy barley tails and plaited straw 'vanes' are ornaments reserved for the corn ricks. A haystack is usually plain – but not uninteresting.

Tuesday, 7 August 1934

The gentleman gipsy

I t was on the level plains around Glastonbury; I was pegging along peaceably watching the round white clouds moving up in the blue, and the small soft shadows dappling the fields … The white dusty by-road lay between dykes of willow, squaring the green marsh fields.

The little raised islands of King Arthur's land stood up suddenly here and there, each with its little crown atop … like ornaments. It is a good peaceable piece of England around there.

I saw a whiff of smoke under the green hedge but should have passed with no more than the civil 'good-day' that the sunlight called for between us; but some random recollection, or was it the uptilting of the phrase of his 'good-day' brought me up all standing. (There is a tilt up to the end of a Welsh phrase as if a laugh had caught its foot on the Border doorstep that runs from Caerwys to Ludlow.)

'Aberystwyth Tom'
'Are you "Aberystwyth Tom"? ' 'I yam.' 'That's all right then, because I've got a message for you from So-and-so.'

He checked up and approved his whereabouts and identity satisfactorily and I delivered the message that had been given to me on the top of Pen-y-craig a month before, and we plunged straight away into a business indaba about a mistaken right of way and certain closed quarries.

It was a simple explanation, and the difficulty was cleared up on both sides in five minutes. Tom would take word along, and they'd be meeting the van within a few weeks, so that was O.K., and with good wishes both sides I got along on my way South while Aberystwyth Tom turned up into the hills.

A gentleman by the wayside. Jones in Wells. The milk my contribution.

The Gipsy Language

Herewith let me interject that Romany, the Gipsy language, does strongly exist and is in common everyday use. Dictionaries and histories of it are compiled, and any gipsy will laugh and teach you words and phrases, for they are proud of their language, but it is wrong to believe all wayside conversation plentifully besprinkled with 'Chals' and 'Lavengro leaves,' for your genuine gipsy is a courteous person, who would not willingly speak an incomprehensible foreign language to a guest.

I have heard the merry brown-eyed children, racing around and chattering, rebuked for just such a small incivility. The majority of gipsy children are very well brought up and are quick-witted, friendly little folk.

The years since the war have made things difficult for gipsies. Many old landowners who for centuries have let the same tribe of gipsies pass through year after year have been obliged to sell out, close or let their lands, and strangers from the towns, knowing less of country traditions, or owning smaller territories, have closed their new possessions to all vagrants, seeing only the illegal trespass of the caravan.

Many a gipsy encampment drawing in and settling down for the night where they have settled all their lives have been hustled off by a new gamekeeper, and in some cases had great difficulty so late in finding other ground. Sometimes the reluctant local policeman is forced into breaking the unwritten truce because an old caravan and a new landlord were unknown to each other.

Some, perhaps, the luckiest gipsies, were those who found a corner where they could dig themselves in permanently throughout the unexpectedly long years of the war, and in some cases that has meant the break of the wandering tradition, and now they are living in small houses in the neighbourhood – with a caravan in the back-yard.

The Potteries Settlements

Around the Potteries settlements of this description are very distinct. And a compromise that has helped is the old gipsy trade of collecting 'misfirings' and the 'spares' from the kilns and trading them in the markets around (far up into the Welsh hills penetrate the gipsy pottery carts). Something of the same sort of settlement has happened by many of the derelict canals.

Curiously the new hiking movement has not helped the gipsies much, for the interest of hikers is chiefly in keeping open footpaths and old bridle paths and *small* rights of way, not wide enough for a caravan. At many open camping places (especially round beauty spots!) the owners now find they can make more by charging tent and camping fees than by the small payment or service they had from the gipsies. (Oh, yes, gipsies often pay fees for the right to draw in off the road and the outside fees connected with some fairs are quite heavy.)

Another erroneous idea is that gipsies wander about haphazard. Their route is often marked out a year ahead. The route maps of the regular gipsies track out an older England than ours of to-day.

The gipsy family that taught me clay cookery.

Pack-horse Routes

Some of them follow the old pack-horse and trade routes very closely. In time and date they lead from Fair to Fair, the large old country Fairs whose Rights and Charters date from the first century onwards. (Did you know that the old Court of Law, held during the Fairs, was called 'The Court of Dusty Feet'?)

Don't confuse gipsies with show people. Lots of show people are gipsies, and many gipsies attend shows and fairs, but there are all sorts of distinctions and levels in the life of the road just as there are in settled societies.

The raggle-taggle gipsies, dirty and picturesque, are one level, but you can be sure that the aristocratic gipsies are clean as the most fastidious house dwellers. I have slept in a gipsy caravan and know it!

I am a house-proud Yorkshire woman myself, but I would have been proud any day to have turned out Lizzy Smith's batch of washing. She had plenty of linen, and it could wait slung in a waterproof bag behind till she satisfied herself with just the right windy day, just the right drying place, running soft water and plenty of time, and then – gleaming white it was, fresh smelling and beautifully pressed.

Built-in Box-beds

The box beds were built in, the blankets embroidered with the mark in the middle (like a steamer cabin). The sheets had fine crochet lace a foot deep to the hems and pillow cases matching. One small dodge interested me, the sheets buttoned down on to the blankets. They had little button-holes right through, so the linen held steady and the blankets never tickled your chin! Now that is a Russian dodge!

The cooking stove was built in, boxes for clothes slid under the bunks, the brass winked and shone (it was from a gipsy girl I learned that fine wood ash dusted over polished brass takes up the last film of grease and leaves it simply sparkling). The entire small caravan simply shone with cleanliness, and a tiny kitten on the step was polishing away for dear life, pink tongue out, to do a credit to the family!

Gipsy caravans vary as much as their owners, and you could find the family ancestry, Italian, Spanish, German, etc., very distinctly marked. By now it is pretty well decided that the 'Egyptians' are all spindrift of the great nomadic tribes who swung to and fro across Asia; some maybe (it is a long way down the dusty road) are relics of the people whose tents hung purple and gold thread, when carved ivory buck and lion with jewelled eyes sprung across the folding tent poles by the water-courses under the willows of Babylon.

But – hey day! the gipsies are only part of the people of the roads. There are the pedlars, relics of a great trading community, and the drovers, the 'regulars' and the 'small traders' who frequent common lodging-houses. Then there are the tramps royal, with their codes and signs and the earmarked casual wards. The real trouble about a casual ward is that you have got to be destitute before you can use it, which, as a reasonable tramp pointed out, makes it difficult for a chap to save up enough to buy new shirts and boots or outfit, because if you have got 10s. in your pocket they'd say: 'What are you come in here for?' so you have to spend near 1s. a night while you *are* saving up.

Curiously the water shortage caused more indignation in some casual wards than anywhere, because many regulars come to consider Saturday and Sunday as bath night, and a sympathetic tramp master (it is the personality of the man rather than the letter of the law which counts) can make it easy for a decent chap to get a clean-up and do a bit of laundry.

But the vaunted laughter of the road dies out in the twilight and old age, and there is left only a numbness, and a longer sleep in the cold, and then there is another 'Unknown; aged apparently 80, clothes worn, etc.,' on the police notices.

Tuesday, 28 August 1934

Mysteries of clotted cream

Rawe cream undecocted eaten with strawberyes or hurtes is a rurall manne's banket. ... I have known such bankettes hath put men in jeopardy of theyr lives!

(A. Borde)

Clotted, clouted, clowted, clawted, cream – cream thin and silky, cream smooth and bland; thick creams, falling in great soft dollops from a brown jug – cream rising in the pans, wrinkling up in thick leathery folds before the skimmer; beaten butter-cream, smooth and yellow; whipped cream, swept around like warm snow and frosted with ice sugar. ... Warm sweet cream, white as ivory and fragrant as meadow sweet. ...

Let the howl of the separator be heard in the land, there is still cream in England! – and it's thickest in the West!

How It's Done

Separated, or plain skimmed cream is the 'pure cream undecocted' of the old MS. The clowted or clotted cream of the West is come to by a different process.

All cream originally was skimmed from open pans in the dairy. They do it still at our old hill farm. It's one of the prettiest sights I know in the cool, shady dairy to see the milk pans spread out; wide, shallow, round bowls, standing in the dimness like a brood of newly-hatched young moons, shining on a black, night-dark slate floor ... and Jean with her big white apron skimming them into the big cream pots.

It's a careful job. She purses up her lips, and makes satisfied little talkings to herself under her breath, and there's a clink of china against the pot, and the soft 'blop! blop!' of cream falling into the big jar, broken by the hard, sudden clatter of wooden clogs on the black slate floor, as she steps from one pan to the next.

Creamy Controversy

All large dairies used to have fixed marble pans for raising cream. Round wooden hooped milk pans were of Scotch use, yellow Wedgwood ware was common and clean; glass (green glass – treasure now of the antique dealer) was a favourite near Chester, but Devon used its panshons of Devon red clay; and Cornwall – rarely, had china pans, whiter than the yellow cream.

In those days there was a great controversy among agricultural experts as to which material made the milk 'throw up' best, for indisputably it did vary (probably according to whether some materials were better conductors of heat).

About four inches deep was considered the best depth to skim cream off, but the rich Western milk had panshons four to eight inches deep.

The Present Way

This is the method in use at present. Realise that it varies locally. You can't ever make a definite law about anything in England, without finding the next farm upsets it completely by a traditional variation, but *this* is the method of one of the best-thought-of farms that I could find near Exeter.

First the milking is put to cool, then when it's just cool it is poured into the pans as they stand in rows on the cold larder floor. The pans must have been washed in very cold water and left to drip dry, and are given a quick polish just before the milk is poured in.

The milk must stand eighteen hours – if the weather's good. Then the pans are lifted gently, one by one, on to the hot stove (it used to be on to the warm wood ashes of the old open fireplaces) and left to warm through slowly. When the milk is quite scalding hot, then the pans are withdrawn, and the cream lifted as it clots and cools.

The making does vary, so that it's impossible to make hard and fast rules, but in general the reason the Cornish cream comes smoother and more all-overish is that in skimming they fold and 'tuck over' the cream glouts, and put it into a jar – so that all the cream is mixed. The best Devonshire cream-makers try to lift the clots separately and unbroken, and pack it lightly into wide basins, so that the layers are unbroken and the slight 'crust' on the top can be seen.

Many Colours

The Devon cream in its big red brown panshons is vari-coloured, white, ivory, primrose, almost daffodil crusted. ...

The name is still controversial. Clotted seems to be the generally accepted derivation, but clout, old name for a mending or thickening, or a thick wrapping of cloth, is good enough cause for naming the folded wrapping of soft 'clouted' cream. Compared with the raw cream it *is* thick and clumsy.

If you have to keep clotted cream, put a lump of sugar into the middle of the bowl and that will help to preserve it.

It is very good eaten with junket. In the West Country a junket is just about an excuse for cream. Supposing (only supposing!) you have any cream left over to go sour on you, it's still good with fruit, or if you don't like it so, beat it with pepper and salt and a very little powdered parmesan cheese, and pile it on dry biscuits and dust with coralline pepper, and you will have the most delicious savoury cream cheese (garnish it with watercress when you can).

Warning

Never let your cream get warm, or it will oil. (In the thirteenth century, Chrism or holy oil was referred to as 'noytede wyp creme.') As for the idea of mixing raw cream with a thickened cooked cream, it is a highly immoral procedure!

In the North and East eat raw cream, in the South and West, eat it clotted, but (as they said so firmly of old) 'Cloutyd crayme and rawe crayme *put togyther* is eaten more for a sensuall appetyte than for any good nowrysshement'!

Tuesday, 11 September 1934

Come down to the orchard

It is autumn and we cannot stop summer leaving us: No: and not all the brave coloured dahlias nor the cheery chrysanthemums in the world can make us pretend that we do not care. The big round-faced sunflowers hang heavy heads with crumpled yellow leaves. The drying straw in the rickyard whispers and sobs as the stacks settle and the leaves drift down.... The blackened walnuts rattle down pretty lively, and it does make a pleasant half hour in the sunshine, picking the little bone-white walnuts out of their split blackened cases that strew the ground (and doesn't it give you a time afterwards getting the stain off your fingers!).

The foals in the field don't mind. The youngsters don't know what is happening, the new nip in the air excites them. It's just right to crisp their new grown-up coats, so their baby fur stands up fluffy and loose – they stamp little enterprising hooves at the new frost stiffness in the grass hummocks, and the brown hedgehogs that are out slugging, in the fields, make tracks for home!

The lambs don't mind. They are fat and muttony now, and thick-wooled, against the cold. The crows are holding their winter parliaments, and the visitor birds have nearly all gone home.

Only Thing to Do

It is no good being depressed about autumn, because you cannot help it. It is no good crying over spilt milk, and if ever there was a month soaked full of spilt milk it is September. The spilt milk is all over the hedges, the cobwebs are white with it, and so is the Old Man's Beard.

By October one is sort of resigned to autumn; and set to wondering if the jam is going to keep. But now – oh! let us go down the orchard and eat plums. (It is really the only thing to do in September.)

Let us go down then, where the rank green grass is wet around our ankles, and where the yellow leaves drift down over our shoulders, and pluck…

There are some fine plums still left, a few black diamond plums on the big standard (purple-black, skinned, with golden greenish pulp, free stone, and as big as goose eggs)…

Then a few greengages, warm, off the sunny wall of the barn, and, in passing, a handful of those little round, dark Maid of Orleans (the most delicious little eating plums of the lot)…

Those pink, speckly oval Victorias are really rather dull eaters (but 'stew nice').

The yellow egg plums look beautiful with a bloom on them, but you might as well chew soft turnip … ('they bottle well').

Now screw up your eyes and wrinkle your nose over a Johnny Raw. My! They are a pretty plum, round as a peach, purple red with a bloom like grape, and clear amber pulp ('splendid cookers').

The old tree gets so heavy sometimes that we prop up its branches with broomsticks and old ladders and spars. Even so, one old bough has cracked … (How queer the plums look on the dead bough, wrinkled and greenish.)

The damson trees are one of the compensations of autumn … There is something so reliable about the sturdy dark little damson. Bulaces are rounder, 'plummier' damsons. The older damson is more sloe-shaped, and the country people use that sort for their wine, they say it makes a richer colour…

Damsons Always 'Do'

Which reminds me; (and I tie a knot in a very juicy handkerchief) to take a basket along the lanes for sloes, for sloe gin.

Damsons are the cottager's great stand-by. Plum trees 'may or may not,' but damson 'do' nearly always. Country people wisely set great store by a good crop of damsons. They reckon they are wholesome. They say they are cheap. They boast they are plentiful – but the fact is that there is something about a damson pie, baked in a *deep* dish, with cream, plenty of thick blobby cream in a brown jug, and a yellow short crust...

And a bowl of extra sugar ... brown sugar is best with damsons. ... *Some* folks put just a suspicion of cinnamon in the pie crust, not more than to be a faint echo of the spicy flavour of the damsons in the pie ... but, *all* the best people insist on a *deep* earthenware pie-dish ... swims of juice. ...

(That is the worst of September, you can't feel properly sentimental and love-lorn, because it has got such a lot of good things to eat in it.)

Damson Cheese

This is an old-fashioned dish, that all country folk like very much, this is a very special recipe.

Put one gallon of damsons into an earthenware pot, and stand in the oven, close covered, till the damsons are tender, then stir and mash, and rub them through a sieve to get out the stones and skin; it won't take long if you use a coarse sieve and a big flattish wooden spoon. If there are two of you at it, and you have something nice to chat about you'd better do two gallons of damsons between you.

Weigh the pulp and add equal sugar, boiling rapidly and stirring fast about one hour, or until it jellies quickly on a cold plate. Pot it up in *wide-mouthed jars*, because after a month or so, it should 'turn out solid' and cut like cheese.

You can eat it as jam, but it makes a very special sweet dish, turned out, stuck over with split almonds and whipped cream and eaten with wine biscuits.

Damson Wine (Thick)

Four quarts damsons to each gallon of boiling water. Pick the damsons into the boiling water gradually, till all be in, then scoop all out into an open wooden tub and stir twice daily for six days. Crack any stones that rise so that the kernels flavour the wine.

Let it settle till it looks clear (probably four or five days). Strain the liquor into another tub and set floating on top a slice of brown toast, spread with ale yeast. If the weather is cold (or you work in a cold back kitchen) heat a little of the juice and pour it back into the tub, just enough to warm the whole a little.

When the yeast has done working, strain into a cask. Leave open till the wine has done singing. Stop close and in two or three months draw it off clear.

It is the cunning of the various farms to add a handful of raisins, a bag of spice, or stir with a branch of sweet brier, to give a subtle special flavour to your own wine, so that no two brews are quite the same. The best is thick and dark, and smells spicy when opened. A glass of damson and hot ginger-bread are favourite on a winter's day before setting out on the cold drive to town shopping.

Monday, 17 September 1934

A real shrimp tea

The traveller dines on potted meats,
On potted meats and princely wines,
Not wisely, but too well he dines,
And breathing forth a pious wish
He fills his belly full of fish.

Robert Louis Stevenson

There was a little house that said SHRIMP TEAS, at the turn of a stony highway. You went through a little wicket gate down a flagged yard (for it was in the Grey North). There was a holly bush growing over a stone wall at the end of the yard, and a wooden bench went along the wall. There were three strong round wooden tables, and against the three tables leant twelve strong square wooden chairs – (straight backs, well down, square back legs flung out behind).

The Order

On the tables were white cloths, coarse, but snowy white. You told Betsy 'You'd come!' Then you went into a shed and washed your hands (dipping rain-water from a cistern into a yellow-lined basin, and wiping on a rough brown roller towel), then you went back into the yard and 'drew in.'

There was a pot of tea, with a woollen tea cosy on it (knitted and drawn up round its neck into a frill, and the handle and spouts sticking out through holes). There was sugar and cream, and a cup and saucer each, and a plate each, and two big plates of thin bread and butter – brown *and* white – and a big green plate of watercress, and a big pink plate of shrimps. And that was all, except an armoured salt-cellar, and a robin. Then you 'reached too' —

Conversation Tea

And presently Betsy Tatterstall came out with a big white apron over her decent black gown, and took the teapot in to replenish it, and see if you wanted any more bread and butter, and you always *did* (and it always came out at once, because she cut it before she asked you!). And you ate, and talked ... desultory fashion (there is something very conversational about a shrimp tea), and the robin hopped about on the table.

Presently, you began to feel comfortable and full, and said: 'No more, thank you,' and wiped up, and sat back, and Betsy carried the bowl of pink-bewhiskered debris to the hens, and you bought some fresh eggs, and a jar of potted shrimps to take away with you...

Betsy sold fish paste, too, pink, in white jars, with whole shrimps embedded in it, and smooth white melted butter on top ... it was the best fish paste I have ever eaten and I don't reckon it's because of memory's flavouring, either. It *was* the best in the district, and that, mark you! in a district that was notable for fish paste.

Just Appetisers

There was a white jar of potted fish, or potted meat, on the table for the big Yorkshire high teas. Sometimes (if it was a new jar) they would thoughtfully cut 30 degrees out, and lay it neatly across the top just to *show* you; and to take off any diffidence you might feel about breaking that smooth expanse of melted butter top. Of course, there would be the usual chops, or steaks, and game pie, and cold round of beef, and apple tart, and pie, and pikelets, and boiled eggs, and hot tea cakes, and jam, and plum cake, and cheese, and all the *usual* things one had to one's tea in Yorkshire; but you always left space for the potted meat, and butter and home-made loaves, because they were *good*.

Where Shrimps Are Unpopular

I am not telling you this to make your mouths water or in depreciation of southern tea tables. I have had some very refreshing jams south of the Trent, but just to show you what Betsy Tatterstall's shrimp paste had to stand up to in the way of competition.

There are parts of Scotland where shrimps are not eaten, but there is hardly a small seaside town in England where they can't boil you a serving of shrimps if they are encouraged to do so. (They boil plenty for themselves!)

The Market

Roughly, where sandy estuaries (like the Humber or Morecambe Bay) give access to towns inland, there is a good market for shrimps. London gets quantities off the south coast, and besides the local sales, many go to the regular fish market, and to large firms who tin them up to sell again, and to the restaurants.

Shrimps are caught by women fishers in the north. In North Wales and up in the lakes the shrimp women kilt up their skirts and wade along behind the wide fish nets. The men and boys do it in the south.

With the Nets

The beam of the shrimp net is anything up to six foot long, and the handle slopes up, through a cross piece which rests across the hip. You shoved it along in front of you, and when the net was full brought it to land, sorted it, put the shrimps in the basket, went back and dredged some more; till the basket was full, *then* you went home and boiled them. A shrimp net is one of the most expensive nets you can have, for it is very fine and close and very brittle.

Prawns are caught in round nets, that you bait for them, or in prawn pots like a sort of lobster pot in which you put a piece of meat or other bait.

Home with the shrimps.

A Different Family

But the largest shrimp can't ever be a prawn; because they are a different family.

The long tailed decapod marine crustacean *Palæmon senatus* (*or prawn*) is of the palæmonidal family; and his first two pairs of legs are chelate. A shrimp is crangonidæ family, *Crangon vulgaris* (*or shrimp*) and his first legs are subchelate and the carpus of the second pair not subdivided...

But Betsy Tatterstall didn't bother about *that*, she boiled them all!

Monday, 24 September 1934

When the cider sings

The old pony in the orchard stops crunching – a moment – slowly swings round a wise, aged, grey head, and pokes forward an ear. Then he shifts his weight on to another leg and goes on chewing peacefully ... He's located that sound. Years of steady experience supplement memory. 'It's that cider beam begun creaking! Derned monotonous job – but well fed – Hup!' And he stumps off through the hummocky autumn grass to lean his head over the farm fence and watch his humans getting on with it...

Getting Ready

Way up on a green hill top where Hereford tilts down off the Welsh hills to the Gloucestershire valleys, there is my special favourite cider mill. For years now I have managed to get up there when they're cider-making . It is one of the oldest orchards around, old but prolific. The small mill is just a convenient size to be loaned friendly to neighbours around, who come up the steep cart track with their own creaking apple loads and do a couple of days pressing for themselves. The brew he makes for himself is to my taste just right.

The apple mill is an old stone trough with wide splayed wooden rim, slanting well out to catch runaways. The stone crusher revolves, pivoted on a worn oak beam. The trough is wetted out, the press set, the grinding circle is cleared, and bump comes down the old harness and collar from off its pin and up comes the pony from the orchard.

Fifty Varieties

The apples are waiting in a pile on the floor, and tumbling in the trough, browned just a little, a well-chosen lot, not very large, but juicy, yellow, bronze and green, with splashes of scarlet. Those, the scarlet, are an old apple, red skin and green pulp, and good eaters. (So agrees the pig snuffling in hopefully 'Hoy! hoy! out with you! you'll be coming close enough to the apple sauce presently.' With which ominous warning Mr. Porkus is hustled resentfully out!)

Once researching into the culture of cider apples I located about fifty varieties all mentioned before 1850, and there were many more; the names, echoing their localities, sing sweetly enough: Deux Anns, Jerseys, French Longtails, Culverings, Rusticoats, Holland Pippings, Cowley Crabs, Kentish Pippins, Burlington Crabs, Cackagee, Kendrik Wilding, Herefordshire Styne, the Foxwhelp, the Woodcock, the White Swan, the Warrenden (can't you hear them trundling along?), the Redstreak, Rubystreak, and Longstreak Redstreak (they sound like a cidermill creaking!), and a dozen others.

They say the monks of Glastonbury helped develop our English cider (there is a huge cider cask among the stone carvings). Certainly after the sweet, sun-warmed wines of the South, our raw English cider must have wrinkled their mouths.

The carriage of appletrees from one part of England to another is an endless tale of patience and loving enterprise. Wharf lists and cargo records, shipping logs, private letters from shipowners to orchard planters, all pile up information on the care given to English cider orchards.

In Kent, cherries were used with cider. A late red cherry juice was kept and used to darken and flavour the early pressing. In the West sometimes blackberries were added. In Devon, milk and cream, and the hardy Cornish miners put a whole sheep's blood, warm into the cask. Real strong drink they demanded.

Perhaps it was the Spanish influence that taught the scenting of casks with aromatic spices and herbs. One of the ways was to soak linen in strips in aromatic gums, or sprinkle with crushed spice and set to burn slowly within the cask, pouring in the cider while the 'smoake' was still in the cask. Metal was never allowed to touch the

Cider-makers.

pumice [pomace] or pulp. Staves and shovels had to be of wood.
The gum from the trees was used sometimes when bunging up the
barrels, and sometimes like isinglass for clearing.

Points and Pints

The old notes about 'racking' become as lyrical as the singing of the
casks. You are not to rack when the cask is singing too loudly, but
best in frosty weather, when the cider 'is singing low and sweetly.'
Then, there was a controversy as to whether the crushed pips did, or
did not, improve the brew with their slightly almond flavour. (And
this discussion still continues in all parts of England.)

In Hereford they use great horsehair blankets, or (nowadays) coir
mats, to wrap up the pulp before putting it in the press. In Devon
and West they use straw (oatstraw for preference) for packing the
pumice. The blanket-users maintain their juice is clearer and purer.
The straw-users contend that 'there's a power of minerals raised up

out of the soil into all grass, and the apple is searching acid and will track it out,' so proving that the straw is of genuine flavouring importance and adds value to the cider. (Certainly the variety of the straw does make a difference.)

In England now, all along the Border, the little horse presses are at work, stones rolling and juice running free, and men are piling up the presses and tightening them down. (In one inn you must give a turn to their press before you fill your flagon.) Serious-faced men are everywhere straining off cider into vats; and hurriedly bringing up other barrels. Here and there a small engine is chugg-chugging away and a tiny factory is working.

Some of the huge cider estates are now being earnestly scientific, while even in the smallest village there's plenty of grave discussion goes on! And the argument's fresh every season, because – if you start arguing about what's the best cider, it's another pint all round to prove your point, and that's why arguments about cider will never end.

Tuesday, 9 October 1934

Quick work in a Welsh kitchen

Mrs. Jones is to show me how to make Bara Ceirch. Mrs. Jones lives half way up a Welsh mountain. Below her the wide road sweeps down the valley to the busy town by the sea. In the early dawn when Mr. Jones goes to fetch up his cows the lorries are thundering past with goods and crates and oils and animals. At eight, when Mrs. Jones takes down the clean scalded milk pails the cycles are passing, young folk going to work. By eleven the morning's work is done and everything pushed ahead, the fire crackling, the world shining. Mrs Jones is going to show me how to make Bara Ceirch!

It is cosy in the kitchen, the fire crackles. I sit quietly.... Mrs. Jones has gone to the barn to fetch the oatmeal.... I sit and look round. Over the open stone fireplace is a high mantelpiece where thick china figures of mountain-shepherds and dogs, and poets with trees, live combined pottery lives. Two fine china dogs sit either end.

If you have never lived with immobile china dogs on the mantelpiece you don't know what a comfort they can be. When the skies fall and disaster trembles at your feet you look at the dogs – they sit firm, placidity personified, nose to eternity, one leg out – it is very sustaining.

Getting Ready

Below the mantelpiece are hooks with bellows, and kettle-hangers, and pot-hooks. On the fire itself is the big round iron girdle plate, nearly a yard across and about an inch thick – getting hot. At the other end of the room opposite the fire is the big harmonium, with piles of music, and books (you would know it is a Welsh cottage by that), and in the corner a grandfather clock tick-tocks steadily and clears his throat and says 'Tut-Tut' in a friendly way every so often as being indeed one of the family for years.

Back comes Mrs. Jones with the bag of oatmeal, dumps it on the table, rattles in the fender busily and settles some extra large logs under the girdle and 'we iss ready.' Mrs. Jones has to translate as she works, for she thinks in Welsh, but she is a natural born teacher and here and now will you realise the difficulty of her to translate from a language which has over 40 words in it for the exact describing of our one word Bread? This is Bara Ceirch – Oat bread Bara Ceirch (it is also Bara LLech or Greibell).

There are only three things on the table. The oatmeal, a cup of warm water, a bowl of butter.

'Or lard? Yess it will do very well, but I make this special for you – good.' A double handful of oatmeal goes into the big brown basin, a piece 'see you it iss only a little piece' of butter into the warm water, and there is a scurry of Welsh, a beat of a wooden spoon and 'Now it iss you divide.'

A row of lumps sitting in a semi-circle (like a hut circle on the moors above!)... 'Now we must be quick – while still warm,' and pressing with one hand and rounding with the other vigorously dump No.1 [which] flattens out meekly into a brown round oatmeal moon about as big as a dinner plate.

'It iss quick now.' And a small Welsh rolling pin fairly hops into play rolling this way, that way actively. It is an old-fashioned pin, barrel shaped like a Babylonian seal. Mrs. Jones imperils the chilling Bara Ceirch while I measure it. Eight inches round the middle, three inches round the ends.

Making It Smooth

As the round, flat oatcake spreads out under the roller, the edge splits and quickly she beats it in with the side of her little brown hand.... 'It iss so that you get it smooth, no breaks – Now – I will show you how we make it very nice, specially good for your picture.'

And a blue plate off the dresser flaps down and the moon is trimmed 'very round because I make it very good for you, to *show*, but not always; when we make much it takes too long – there!' – and the first Bara Ceirch lies before us, thin as a penny, round as a dinner plate.

It is skilfully slipped on to the hot grid-iron (and an indignant cat disputes the settle with me while I watch it brown). Now Mrs. Jones fairly flies around. 'It iss a quick time now.'

Browning one cake, beating down the next one – few more sticks on the fire – drop more hot water... . As soon as one cake is brown it is lifted up off the grid (stiff now!) and laid on the table flat one moment to steam. It is then popped on the iron fender to dry, and here it will – our Welsh-English completely fails us and I supply the word 'warp'!

One a Minute

The flat, round cakes bend themselves up in the middle so that, when they rest in piles, one on top of the other, they look like flat, shallow saucers. When they are made for harvest time on the big farms, one woman mixes, one rolls flat, and one sits always by the girdle turning the browning oatcakes and mending the fire, and all are kept busy, and the round brown moons slide off the girdle at the rate of almost one a minute (four minutes is the average time on the girdle).

As Mrs. Jones says, 'All men they do like the Bara Ceirch, and it is good to work on, yess – indeed they will have it for a harvest, it iss good indeed, yes you may eat it now, but to-morrow it is better....'

But I do not wait till to-morrow, I have a dish of Bara Ceirch, sweet cream butter and a glass of chilled butter milk... and I come away with a whole morning of the kindest teaching and the present of a big old blue platter 'to measure by' – *Thank you very much, Mrs. Jones!*

Tuesday, 16 October 1934

All about tea

All well regulated families set apart an hour every morning for tea and bread and butter.

(1711. Addison)

'I've left your tea all ready for you, dear,' says the wife of his bosom tying her bonnet strings, 'so you've only got to wet the tea,' And when the abandoned man comes to do it, there's even a tea caddy scoop inside to show him how much to use.

It's not only woman's prerogative. Take your navvy, with his billy-can of yellow, hot tea, and the lumps of sugar (so neat in a screw of newspaper). First thing he does, on a job, is to fix the bucket of coke fire and settle the blackened iron kettle to boil. And it's 'Keep your eye on the tea kettle, Bill.' In the factory the apprentice boys come and fetch the cans, at 'mashing time,' regular to the tick.

A Varied Performance

They carry them threaded on a stick sometimes, two boys to ten cans, and the married men have real milk in glass bottles and the bachelors use 'condensed' out of a tin in their locker.

The procedure of tea making is most varied. In some localities they 'wet,' in others they 'brew'; in others they 'mash,' in very few places do they 'make' tea. Barge men on canals, they 'boil' it. 'A well-boiled cup of tea' only means real boiling water and well *stood*. On the road one makes shift to 'set-to' a cup of tea, because that means kindling a handful of fire, and '*set down to it*' and light a pipe.

Discourteous past becoming would be the back door that would refuse boiling water to a proffered tea can, and offer the drop of milk and sugar that a chap can't carry. 'Save your screw (of tea) and have a filling out of our pot,' is the courtesy of the road any time after four o'clock.

Little teapot, how I love thee.

When It Was Chaa

Tea came to England in about the seventeenth century. They say it was imported to Europe first by the Dutch, at the very end of the sixteenth century. It didn't sound any too good at first.

'*The aforesaid warme water is made with the powder of a certain hearbe called chaa*' – later 'tay,' later tea. One traveller from the East explained carefully that the water should remain on the tea leaves 'for as long as it takes to say the Miserere Psalm slowly.' There was a tremendous lot of controversy about the new drink. The first tea cups did not have handles. They were little round bowls, and you went to take tea with tremendous ceremony and palaver.

In 1660 Pepys sends 'for a cup of tea (a China drink) of which I never have drunk before.' (It's nice to think the date is in September, with the evenings closing in when Pepys first fell for a nice hot cup of tea!)

Fifty Shillings a Pound

By the 1700's tea was well away as an English drink, pervading the coffee houses and washing in an amber sea of complacency over the strongholds of the rich. It was ruinously expensive, anything between 16s. to 50s. a pound, and the used tea leaves would be dried, rolled and resold again by the servants of the rich.

In the 1800's they tried to make wine of it (because about that date they made wine, good, bad or indifferent, of everything), and tea was fermented probably flavoured with briar, and casked and bottled, same as any other wine.

There were two main types of tea known, *Thea bohea* and *Thea viridis*, that is to say, black tea and green tea, and the names of Gunpowder, Pekoe, Formosa, etc., were all mixed, locality and variety, for ages.

Tea Was Not Tea

Probably we fell for tea because so well previously trained on our own English infusion drinks. Instantly foreign tea arrives, the old infusions and waters become called 'teas' also. This is a very interesting point, as it probably means that many country drinks called 'tea' were for many years not tea at all, but the old well-known plant infusions which continue in use in country places even till to-day.

The medicinal teas crossed the Atlantic, and still flourish in America (sage tea vying with sarsaparilla as universal and all-pervading).

All the old cordials and water brews become 'teas' – even the strengthening soup becomes 'beef-tea.' Sweet balm, camomile, hartshorn made tea. Cowslip tea is delicious and lime-tree tea I have bought in shops in London. It is made of the blossoms of the lime trees and is very fragrant and supposed to be soporific.

Raspberry leaf tea is known to village mothers, and black currant tea is sovereign cure for hoarseness of throat and cold in the chest – especially when it's sweetened with honey. Wild thyme, bugloss, willow, and mint are other country teas; so is the stinking valerian used somewhat dangerously.

Lime-stone Tea

The medicinal waters of Bath, so popular at the period of tea and coffee houses, were referred to as lime-stone tea!

Sallop, that transparent starchy brew that preceded tea, is still occasionally made; it used to be sold about the streets of London and though once very common it has practically died out of use. To my astonishment I had it served to me in a cabin in Ireland.

Luckily for our nerves, and the medical lecturers, the old black-strong long brewed tea of country folk is paling – they still tend to buy readily put up in 'packet' blends.

Tuesday, 30 October 1934

Our village wedding cakes

In our parts we make our own wedding cakes, and there's usually something very individual about them, too. Most families stick to the same recipe. It gets diversified a bit, and trimmed up differently according to the generation, but it's pretty spicy with reminiscence anyhow.

You see, in a small community that gets used to entertaining itself, we each begin automatically to specialise in the thing we do best, and in cakes it's really remarkable how hall-marked we become.

Quite simple reasons. One person has got a light hand with the eggs, or another a slow oven, or another a good firm knack with the beating pin, or maybe it's just some kink, but one gets to rely on it, and when one's reputation is made *in* it, one has to live *up* to it, and one can't live it *down*.

One gets to know one's own particular cake so well that it becomes a sort of vintage. Certain it is, that in all our parties and 'doings', when we get together, we come to rely on 'Mrs. Jones to make a nice sponge' and 'Mrs. Roberts will do the scones,' and 'there'll be Miss Nora's tarts.' I mean, we know where we are when our village sets to baking.

Years and years ago I compiled a local cookery book of the special recipes we all had all round, and it was awfully funny to index, because it read *by the names of the things that had been asked for* and it went something like this: 'Whist Drive Scones,' 'Cricket Match Biscuits,' 'Wesleyan Tea-cakes' (two sorts), 'Rectory Cake,' and so on.

But to come back to our ovens, there are all sorts of cakes that we consider rather specially our own, and they have special times.

Seasonal Cakes
Plentiful eggs in spring bring up the golden sponges, cold frost and hot wine bring out the gingerbread; summer tea parties bring out

[247]

the little cakes (so that they pop about all over the village tea tables
– and very tasty, too!). In winter we like 'a large cake to cut at,' good
and solid; where there's men folk or children we think well to keep a
wholesome 'loaf cake' on hand.

Importations from foreign parts can be traced by name. 'Mrs.
X … s' Welsh Yorkshire parkin,' Mrs. Gillespie's real Scotch shortbread.' (This is a mystery to us, because *we've* had the recipe but it
doesn't come out the same; it's whispered that she uses 'laird' with
the cream; we'd none of us dare. Anyhow, we feel it needs a Scottish
constitution to achieve shortbread!)

'Bridle' Cakes

Funny how the least trace of North-British blood gives a traditional
standing among the dry cookies. We Southerners don't envy them
exactly. We accept the ascendancy but we bridle a little and say our
'cream flans *are also*,' 'etc.,' 'etc.,' implying that they may have *their*
specialities, but so have we! In the same way a French strain subtly
accounts for a skill with the syrups. We don't analyse this exactly,
but if it's a question of cowslip wine? or hot cordial? or 'you'd expect
Mrs. Stubbs's to be the best because she was a Miss Delacey before
she was married.'

There's the personal touch, too. There's 'Mary's cake,' and 'Annie's
Madeira,' and 'Mrs. Parker's seed-cake-that-her-mother-makes,'
which is *quite* different from 'Mrs. Parker's *own* seed cake.' And the
'Roman Pie, like-they-have-at-the-Hall' is not ordinary Roman Pie
(any more than a 'Good Hot Pot' is plain 'end-of-the-week-hot-
pot').

So when there's a wedding cake in the village, it's a matter of
traditional interest. Actually, you know, they say the wedding cake
had Roman origin, because the bride held ears of wheat in her hand
for a symbol of plenty. Afterwards, they threw wheat and corn over
the bride for the same reason.

The Real Thing at Last

And in Scotland it was the custom to crumble an oatcake or bannock over the bride, so they should always have 'plenty.'

By Elizabeth's reign small biscuit bride cakes were thrown. It wasn't until Charles II's time that the corn had settled down into a real cake, which has been getting more elaborate ever since.

In the real country it's not so important to send away a lot of little pieces of bride cake (so small they're no bigger than a card and about as dry!), but to have a good big cake so that you can send a nice large friendly slice to people who can't come to the wedding, or friendly old folks who live too far away.

Under Your Pillow

The bride and her bridesmaids must cut and pack this cake themselves; and a really nice sympathetic bride will cut up plenty of cake with her own hands, and see her special girl friends get a chance of a piece quick.

Because – you know – if you are a maid and get hold of a tiny scrap that a bride has really and truly cut specially for you and slip off quietly and put it under your pillow – that very night you will dream about the man you are going to marry yourself! Which, my dear, is a most circumstantial superstition, considering he's most likely been at the wedding too.

Tuesday, 27 November 1934

Our weather is changing

The snow was nearly a foot deep as I came down over the tops of the mountain, but the small active sheep were scuttling about through, and feeding over it. Grey brown their wool looked against the white snow. Here and there, they were scraping away the snow with their hard little front feet, but mostly they were snatching a knowing bite from sheltered places under the tussocks.

The sky was leaden and dull. I thought there was going to be more snow, but, by the sheep being left still loose, I reckoned it wouldn't be heavy before morning.

At the Cottage

I came down to the valley, where a narrow rocky watercourse pencils a winding black path down the hillside. The snow made going perilous, and when I had sat down ungracefully several times, I was altogether very wet, and turned in to 'dry out' at my usual cottage.

In the shepherd's house they were sitting either side of the round three-legged table, the dish of lobscouse was just emptied, and puss was licking the savoury scraps of cold white mutton fat from the edge of her dish, with great satisfaction. A sheepdog pup disputed with my wet boots for the middle of the fireplace, and the boots won, for 'indeed he iss no right to be there, it is bad for him, he must learn to be a strong dog.'

Talking of Weather

And the soft bundle that will presently be a fine white tipped tail sheepdog was hustled unceremoniously out of the door. He finished off the cat's dish in passing.

It was warm by the fire. The teapot was warming on the hob, and some sticks were shoved under the kettle to hurry it up.

The talk turned on the weather. The shepherd said if it had been in his father's time those sheep would have been brought down, and he told the young shepherd so yesterday! If the snow held off it wouldn't matter. A little snow would do the sheep no harm, and this year's lambs (that had not seen snow before) might as well learn first, as last. As long as snow did not *lie*, they could get a good bite among it.

Light dry snow did not hurt anything. He told me much about the cleverness of the old sheepdogs in the winters of deep snow. 'That one's grandmother' (the black puppy had insinuated himself back into the circle). 'That one's grandmother knew every inch of the mountain, and had been a wonderful dog for snow work.'

The working dog a shepherd wants on the mountain is, 'bless you,' a dog able to 'use his judgement,' but now dogs were trained more especially for close work.

It was quite true that in the old times of snow, a wise dog would go far on his own to hunt up any snow-caught sheep, and if he couldn't get them out himself, would come back and fetch the shepherd. Nowadays it is seldom that sheep get caught out in heavy snow. There are fewer sheep, for one thing, and more roads up the mountain perhaps make them easier got at. The shepherd doubted if some of the present dogs would ever have the 'snow sense' acquired by some of the old dogs.

'Is the weather really changing?' I queried. The old shepherd of fifty years experience thought it a fact that the winters on the mountain were not so severe as they used to be. 'The snow doesn't lie like it used to,' otherwise, we must be having exceptionally good winters.

Everywhere this puzzle of changing climate is talked over among the older country folk. The great sheep stells on the moors, and notes in the old farming journals, testify that they speak truth, and it is not only that the easier winter feeding leaves less sheep on the moor through the bad months.

Deadly Snowstorms

Almost exactly a hundred years ago, 1836–1837–1838, hundreds of sheep perished on the Scots moors in long, continuous snowstorms, and that, mind you, in a country well used to making winter provision.

The great round stells on the moors used to be filled with sheep hurriedly gathered together in emergency. The snow blowing level across the moor, swept aside around the stell, or over it, and dropped a long trail of white snow on the leeside. (You can see this to-day in light snow). A provident farmer would take up a small stack of hay on a sledge early in the autumn and batten it well down in the middle of the stell, and the sheep could shelter there, protected and fed, for a month.

In 1823 snow lay solid from February to May! The old shepherds were wise in their generation. It was not that they didn't foretell the snow and bring the sheep down in good time. It was simply, as the shepherd said, 'More sheep and worse weather.'

Of course, the lowland sheep can be fattened up on turnips in the valley. And in the mountains they do definitely clear the higher pastures about October.

Mountain Mutton

The clearing of Snowdon, or the sheep drives on the Berwyn are wonderful sights. But one thing all shepherds of mountain flocks agree on is the unsuitability of root food for mountain sheep. They say it 'spoils them for the mountain'; they do feed them hay, but even in the winter, for the health of the flock and the economy of the farm, they like to get them up on the hills as much as possible.

Your mountain mutton is characteristically small. Some of the true, best Welsh mutton will only be about 4lb. weight to a leg, and the mutton is very lean.

Youth is Respectful

That is why the lobscouse on the table had been so savoury and good. You cannot make mutton stew with fat, large, greasy mutton. And the old shepherds say, 'It's the grazing and the weather has made the stamina and the quality.'

The old shepherds of the mountain are very valued friends to the younger shepherds. They are exceptions to the rule of antagonism between the old worker 'set in his traditional way' and the young one who is 'all out for something new.' Dear knows! we need youth and enterprise and fresh ideas for our mountain sheep industry. It is in a terribly bad way; but the youngest and the most hopeful shepherds wisely treasure the wisdom of the old shepherds who have already learnt so much.

Tuesday, 22 January 1935

The goodness that only bad weather supplies

The ward is very quiet; dimly lit for the night. ... The white painted walls reflect streaks of light from the street lamp, shining through the uncurtained windows. Long dim streaks of light shine along the polished floor – the white screens around some of the beds seem luminous in the dusk, and the electric light bulbs overhead pick out small spots of opal white.

At the far end of the long, long ward, a pool of shaded white light lies over the big table, where the night nurse sits, padding splints. Among the white piles of gauze the little blunt ends of her scissors shine bright... the first is shaded, too, but the ghost flowers of the red flames play over her white apron, and throw soft little goldy pink lights over the white stuff piled up on the trolley beside her. The ward is cool and fresh, with a faint smell of antiseptic, and an elusive iodine odour fills the air...

I open my eyes – Snowdon is high above me, white as gauze clings the mist – the faint scent of iodine still hangs in the air – *they are taking down the sphagnum moss for the hospitals.*

Years ago during the great war it was a London chemist who introduced the old new use of sphagnum moss for dressings. In those days, Boy Scouts were sent out to gather in the sphagnum in Companies, and the hillsides rendered up bales, and bags of moss to help over the shortage of dressing in the hospital.

Far up on the clear windswept hillside the moss grows clean and cold. Frozen, even ice held, perhaps a month at the time, so that the pure green moss only needed drying to be safe bedding – safe padding – safe to use fresh for each case, and then to burn and replace. Screwed up in a scrap of gauze it was safe to wipe and swab with, in the emergency surgeries, where cotton towels and swabs got so dreadfully scarce.

The worth that sphagnum showed in those strenuous times, fixed it again securely among the few genuine English materials which have not yet been superseded by importations. We are used to importing many medicinal plants and drugs, which could not ripen in our climate, and many that need more sun that our island air can give, to bring them to perfection.

Age of Substitutes

A great deal of medical material that used to be gathered in England has passed out of use, with the discovery of better substitutes.

Broom, and the sulphur-strong gorse flowers, are no longer gathered in great basket loads to make skin ointment, and few now harvest the foxglove (digitalis). The saffron which once yellowed all the eastern counties, now only yellows a few fields, and the Cornish and Devon saffron cakes.

Our climate is *not* the best for products which want sun, but here is a product that wants a wet climate, which requires our island rain and damp air to bring it to perfection. A product where the very goodness of the plant depends upon the very badness of the weather. Sphagnum moss will grow only at certain altitudes, and with very certain rainfall. It is more a loose filling of moss (that rises and falls with the rise and fall of the damp in the water-logged hill) than any solid vegetable growth. It branches and branches. To try and tease out one piece would take you hours.

It lies feather soft and light in the wet places of the moors, and its very capacity for living depends upon its ability to use up water – *and stay resilient*. So its absorbent properties are natural to it. Of course it is not used wet. When nurse gets it, it is smooth, and dry as a strip of blanket, but the minute it finds any moisture, it soaks it up like a piece of blotting paper. Cotton wool dressings soak up moisture too, but the limp close fibres of the cotton if too wet become a hard sodden mass; whereas the more moisture the sphagnum moss can soak up, the *more* resilient and spongy and soft it becomes. This extraordinary natural absorbent will take up as much as twenty times its own weight of liquid, and still keep its spongy porous character that it held on the mountain.

On the mountain! – This is how it is brought down – far away the men haul it out and lay it loosely upon a rock, or upon the sloping hillside to drain a little. Then it is piled into panniers on the backs of ponies, or, stacked high on the strong wooden sledges that the mountain people also use to bring down their harvest of peat and bracken.

Last time I saw it brought down it was from the hill at the back of Snowdon. On ponies, down it came, down past the rocks, shining wet silver and jetty black, down past the little tinkling waterfall (that runs no less clear than the water that will presently splash from a hospital tap!), down past the little cairns, where the small mountain sheep stop cropping, and stand to watch, and stamp their little front feet at the ponies.

Up to London

Down past Ty-ucha cottage, where they reach the mountain trackway – the little pack trains falls into single file along it – and they make quick going after that down to the valley. Even as they come down, the moss is being shaken, and is packing itself tighter, and the water is dripping out, so that it is much drier already by the time it is packed tight into sacks and railed up to London. ... *Railed up to London! and the moss has left the hillside for ever!*

The dressing of the moss consists of sorting, picking and clearing. There is very little to remove. A small heath twig may have caught in it, or a green and shining rush, but it is the property of sphagnum moss to pervade its space, and so few weeds can grow in it.

It shrinks in drying, and sometimes it is compressed in smooth, whitey-grey layers like very thick, smooth blotting paper, or it may be packed up in gauze bags, or bales of it may be treated with special antiseptics, before it is again dried, and prepared for special purposes.

But through the smell of chemicals, and the white sealed wrappings of the chemists, it is *still* the iodine-scented, pale-green moss of the moors, that has heard the cry of the curlew and felt the trailing, cool freshness of the mountain mist.

Wednesday, 6 February 1935

Village magicians

The country chemist holds a position all his own in the life of the countryside. He must be a man of infinite resource and sagacity. From centuries of training, we hold the chemist direct descendant of the Magical Medicine Man. Not only simple country minds, we *all* feel it. From our early childish wonder of his big coloured bottles (that hold the strange inverted worlds imprisoned!) our adult awe continues quite naturally.

On a cold, dark winter evening when the chemist's shop is brightly lit up; and the queer, intriguing aromatic smell wafts out across the muddy street, who can deny we feel the same childish awe for one who is still slightly tinged with magic? We know, past reason, we are entering magic. We pass in into the wash of coloured light where bottles, phials, instruments, all swim together, in a warm multi-coloured haze.

Mysterious Passports

He asks us for our passport from the doctor and we fumble and give him a little slip of paper with queer magic signs on it. ... *We* do not know what it means, but *he* does. ... He looks at it and disappears. We wait… Sometimes through the unknown air behind the barrier we hear a query: 'In liquid form?' or the chill tremble of running water threading cords of silver through the coloured dusk. ... We wait … in a coloured fragrant void while glass touches glass – as small stars clink. ...

The chemist restores us, burning a little flame, making neat passes over a small white packet between his fingers, and – somehow, we find ourselves out in the street again, holding a white packet with two vivid scarlet seals. We walk quietly home – we are children again who have 'been to the chemist.'

In vain in the country he disarms us with familiar farm things, strewn upon the pavement, fills his counter with cheerful everyday needs to reassure us. We *still* feel that *our* chemist 'knows more than any *ordinary* chemist!' We are very proud of him!...

Actually, in the country world, your chemist needs to have a pretty good first aid knowledge, and as a rule works in with the local general practitioner. To the country mind, it is still rather a 'proceeding' that hall-marks you as 'really ill' to visit the doctor, but it's non-committal any market day just to 'look in at the chemist.'

Your G.P. must of necessity have definite surgery hours, and be often inaccessible for long periods, while away on his visits.

In All Emergencies

But the Chemist is always reassuringly *there*, and is expected to cope with all unexpected emergencies.

The croupy baby, the fainting lady. A sudden onslaught of rheumatics, or a common cold. He may be called upon to poultice a gathered finger, dope a gum-boil, cure chilblains (or rats), or asked to mix up something that will rectify indiscretion and bring you home to the missus without comment. (The morning-after-the-night-before of a 'Root' dinner, or some such gathering, your chemist is busy early!)

His is the 'Magic Domestic.' We consult him for lesser things. Fruit bottling, bread rising, animal dosing. He must clear our wines, clean our brass preserving pans, take stains out of our linen, and off our fingers. He must set our marmalade, and unstick our stoppers. He must restore our nerves and our hair. Hats off to our Country Chemist! a man of infinite resource and sagacity...

What Sally Says

I lay down my pen for a moment's consultation with Sally on our chemist's great utility.

'If it's the things the chemist gets asked for, Miss Dorothy, you'd be surprised! Lots of folks still ask him for things to work spells with. Nothing bad, you know, but *queer*; quicksilver and dried stuffs. It's really remarkable, Miss Dorothy, what some folks will believe! You want to consult him and see. ...'

'All right, I will.'

For a west wind blows fresh outside, and the three miles across the valley to the chemist run along a river path, and there's a magic runs through the rain-wet grass which is sovereign cure for writer's cramp!

As I collect my shoes in the hall I call up the staircase. 'Anything you want fetching, Sally?'

'Only a pennyworth of sulphur, Miss Dorothy. I always keep a lump in my bed against cramp – No, that isn't magic! It really works...'

Tuesday, 5 March 1935

A lesson in ploughing

All cornes fayre and cleane
That groweth on ridges out of the reane.

(Old English Lines)

They are ploughing the headlands down by the river. ... The plough jerks slowly through the uneven ground and the two horses stagger and swerve as the swivel-tree swings unevenly from side to side against their unsteady draught. The ploughman, well up between the handles of the plough, presses downwards, raising the plunging plough-head up out of the deep, or with a heave and a throw, half lifts her back on to the furrow line, hauling her back for a fresh start.

'Whoa, Boxer! back a bit, Florrie! Hey, hey, H'up – go on now,'
...

This uneven jerky draught on the headland is the most trying of all for a young horse. The other end of the field lies well enough – it is level, but this pesky piece by the river always cuts up heavily. The lay of the land is downwards so that the low furrows lie soggy with winter rain and in places tree roots run-in unevenly, underground.

What Are Headlands?
The ploughing of the headland comes last, after all the field is finished. It is the gathering up across the ridges and reans from the first to the last. After all the work is done, and the plough has passed steadily up and down the long furrows, then at the last, the plough runs parallel cuts, straight across the round ends of the turnings to the end. Ploughing the headlands is so well known, to come inevitably at the last of the work, that the country people, speaking of an old chap who is nearing his end, say, 'He is ploughing the headlands.'

The ploughman's lunch. —
> *'In borde cloths bright,*
> *Whyte bred they brought*
> *Chese & chyckens cheerily dyght.'*

It is the end of winter's ploughing. In the country we are too happy to die in the summer. Only during the winter's cold and rain, or before the almost unbearably sweet promise of young spring an old countryman can feel tired enough to die happily.

In full summer, when the corn is up, it is nearly always suddenly and unexpectedly that the old people go.

'The hale old do fall as elum boughs' is how the country people describe a sudden death in full summer, (for elm trees have this unexpected treachery, that they will drop their great boughs without any warning, breaking in full weight of leaf) but, for an old chap working steadily to the last, of him we say 'He is ploughing his headlands – steady – bless him.'

Following the plough. Sowing kidney beans in Essex.

How do they space out the ploughing of a field? It is a very, very old skill called 'feering a field.' The ordinary plough can only trench one way – laying a single slicing cut over to the right hand side. Though there are ploughs made called 'turn board ploughs' that can lay a slice to the left *or* the right, by turning the moulding board across, yet, even with a 'turn plough' the horses must stop, and walk around at the end of each furrow. So a field is measured out carefully beforehand, *so as to give the most straight furrows with the easiest turning.*

Roughly they work out sections, about 8 or 10ft across in pairs, so that each set is 16, or 20, in some places up to 30 foot across. The distance depends on the size of the field (and sometimes on the draining, etc.). At the end of each division they set up a mark against the hedge, and the ploughman cuts one dead straight furrow – from end to end – guiding to each mark (even as a ship steers to some point ahead). *This is feering the land for the plough.*

It used to be some small ceremony – maybe an owner Knight of the Manor would come down to his field, and stand, setting his sword to be the feering pole of the first furrow (and maybe they'd drink to his safe return from the Wars before the corn covered it?). Or on some monastery lands, a loved abbot would smile and hold his staff (and maybe they'd pray that they might live lives as straight and unswerving as the furrow).

Nowadays we have fewer ceremonies, but the Boss himself usually goes down for the 'first feering' and the first day the ploughman 'breaks the land,' he usually pours libation to the Gods of good Barley Corn – (though nowadays he pours it down his own throat as likely to do most good!).

Cop, Ridge and Rean

Once the feering is set, and the plough share follows up and down, down and up – piling the slices inwards to the centre furrow, which is slightly raised and called the 'cop'.

It looks as if the ploughman keeps going straight up and down – but really he is going a round journey, up one straight side, across the top (that is the headland), and straight down the other side – up and down, round and round each 'ridge.' Till he has finished that feering – then the plough moves right across and starts again from the middle of the next. The place where two feerings meet, the slices lie *away* from each other – that is the rean.

Rean was an old name for a gutter or stream, and the reans used to be cut deeper of old – perhaps to try and drain the land.

An Acre's a Day

The oldest plough ridges in England, mark the 8 ox plough – that divided the very land itself. Did you know that an acre was as much as one man and eight oxen could plough in one day? And that what they could plough in one year was 'a hide' – the measurement of Domesday Book?

Plough Monday was the first Monday that the plough went '*out*' after the Christmas holiday, and in places the ploughboys still drag around an old plough share, and threaten to plough up the mud before your doorstep if you do not give them something towards their night's frolic.

'*In*' plough evening has no definite date! It is the day they finish ploughing the last headland – before the sowing begins. But – it is an evening that means much in the country. It has no ceremony, no calendar date, but *that* evening the pewter mugs still ring good wishes to 'all cornes fayre and cleane, that groweth on ridges out of the reane.'

In England now – as heartily now as ever of old.

Tuesday, 19 March 1935

Elevenses I have known

'All right, if it's ready, I'll take it along.'
'Won't spill? All right, I'll lift it carefully over the fences. Is the sugar in? O I see! put it on top in case it splashes. ...'

It's 10.30, the end of the first yoking, and I'm entrusted with Bill's basket of elevenses. I have to go two fields down, and one field up, and then sideways over the fence, and Bill is rolling (with young Bill) in the next field. (No, not personal gymnastics; he's got two horses and the field roller and is going up and down rolling the land.)

The spring sunshine filters down through the bare branches, and the hedges have that fresh bronze of young green over them. Barracause, we call it – bread and cheese. The little green buds are good, clapped between thick crumbly bread and yellow, soft cheese in a sandwich. They used to make a pudding from the hawthorn buds in the spring, like a roly poly, only with shreds of boiled bacon, and the hawthorn buds (or may be watercress) where the roly poly's jam would be. Spring pudding, watercress for tea, and camomile when you went to bed was supposed to be good for all children-in-spring.

But here's the first stile, easy, over – I peer into the basket, all safe? My Bill's tea looks good, it's in a glass bottle, yellow and creamy-looking, with a bit of flannel wrapped round it to keep it hot. There's another bottle, too, that looks as if it were put in for me – hope so. I want my elevenses, too!

In the Cottage

You people in town who just have your tea and biscuits, or your coffee and dominoes, don't know how much more our elevenses mean to us in the country.

In the cottages or farms it used to be beer or buttermilk; it's nearly always tea now. In the fields you get it taken out to you with a slice of bread and butter (or cheese).

In the cottage you want it just as much. For see, here's the morning – 6.30 or 7, your man gets off to work, and if the boys don't get back to dinner, you are cutting and packing their dinner basket while they're eating their breakfast.

By the time they're off 7.30 or 8, there's the children's breakfast. That means unpacking two or three energetic youngsters out of their beds and packing their breakfast into them, and then repacking them into their coats and caps for school. Mostly *they* want elevenses to take, too (and incidentally that half pint of milk at school has saved many a minute in the hurried morning).

Well-Earned Snacks

By the time you've collected the last of their belongings, the school bell is ringing for 9 o'clock. Then if you've got a baby you fetch him down next, and feed and wash him (and the woman who can get through that job inside an hour hasn't been born). By the time my Lord Baby is digesting himself, full of peace and plenty, in the sun, it's time to make the beds and clear upstairs, and that takes half an hour good (maybe more), so by then when you get down to the kitchen and put the kettle on for washing up it can boil a cup of tea at the same time – and, my word, you've earned it.

Praise household elevenses! We usually have a big slice of solid cake, or a slice of bread and jam with our elevenses in the country.

Here is the second stile – tea still intact? Yes, and still hot, not a drop spilt, sugar still dry, right o, Bill, your elevenses are coming quite safe.

If there's any general development of recent years that's added to the Peace of Nations – it's elevenses. It's not so modern, either. The old oak livery cupboards of early centuries were really the old equivalent of our modern snack bars. Bread and cheese and drinks

Hikers!

waited handy in those oak cupboards for a snack between times. I expect if their heavy iron hinges could squeak they'd tell us a lot of cheerful elevenses, for in the fabulous good old days there was only one real meal a day, one real good feast for everybody about the place in the great hall.

Here's the last stile, and there's Bill, with his team, just nearing the end of the row. I hail! so he'll know to stop his horses when he reaches the end of that line, and not start going down another ridge. I'll not have his tea chill after carrying it so carefully for him. He's seen us coming and will reach the end of his row by the time the elevenses reach him. ...

Other Folks' Elevenses

Elevenses I have known… they'd be varied! Mostly pleasant.

In Scotland they'll give you milk and whisky in the spring. (In winter? there may be less milk to spare.)

Cape Town makes delicious coffee, and has enormous cream cakes about four inches across. (In any other climate they'd incapacitate you from lunch.)

Jo'burg seems to have tea quite as frequently as coffee, but perhaps that was my luck.

On a Boer farm you got huge mugs of black, black coffee, strange and strong, but likeable, and brownish honey in it. 'Out' you get a piece of biltong (sun dried meat, that tastes like firewood soaked in meat extract with pepper on it; looks queer, but quite good), and a swig out of the canvas water-bag, icy cold.

North of the line 'elevenses' seem to be Turkish coffee, thick, with rose-water and a big glass of ice water to rinse it down.

Hikers' Tea

Here's a word to summer hikers: have you ever tried fresh-plucked lime blossom for your elevenses tea? A handful to a pot – it's as delicate and fragrant as finest China tea and needs no sugar or milk (though a squeeze of lemon juice improves it). Also the tiny green shoots at the end of blackberry brambles make a pleasant refreshing tea, if ever you're stuck out of doors (don't let them stew too long, or they'll be bitter).

But here you are Bill, here's your elevenses for to-day! I've carried it awfully carefully and don't think it's spilt a drop.

Tuesday, 26 March 1935

England, home and mud

I thought I had eaten everything eatable in England except black puddings – but I had not! This was something new, very new, and by my luck the first ones, out of the first catch, out of the first run, out of the first high tide, out of the first month of Spring, when the Elvers are running!

And they looked perfectly awful!

******

Elvers are the very, very, small eels, when they are still in the shoal state, and looking exactly like transparent gelatinous spaghetti. They get them all round the coast up the river estuaries, but they are perhaps a speciality of the long dykes and rhines in the green willow banded marshes of Somerset.

On the roof of every shed, at the back of every little house that tilted its floodgates down to the waters, the big square white elver nets were flapping dry in the morning breeze, and the lamps were trimmed and there was a pan of elvers, caught the night before.

They are thought a real delicacy around here. 'And you have never seen them before?' I was asked.

'Dad, he always gets them first thing, and mother (she is a real marsh woman!), she has an eye for their coming up, as quick as Dad! You can't get them very often, only on the high tides, and only in the Spring – these were got (the first lot!) last night; well, early this morning really – and to think you have never had any!

'They send some up to London, but of course it isn't everybody that likes them…'

'Carry them? Well, you could; but if you are not in a hurry, won't you come in and sit down? and I will cook you some – now.'

'Yes, I would like to.'

Country Hospitality

And she smiled a welcome as genuine as the sunshine that was warming my back, caking the thick mud on my boots, and making me jolly hungry.

The English countrywoman always has time to be hospitable, and elvers in the marshes are an institution, and a tradition and no public spirited marsh housewife would let you miss the delicacy of the season; elvers are all as 'choice' as whitebait in these parts.

They dip them out of the rhines in square white calico nets, or rather scoops (for the elvers are so thick, that in the middle of a heavy shoal you can bail them in bucketfuls). At night, when the tide is running, and the shoals are sweeping up stream, a lantern is dropped down on the bank to the water level, behind the net, and the mass pours into it and – elvers for supper!

Scientific Surprise Packets

They are frying now on the stove, draping the fork like spaghetti – (limp white spaghetti; still, courage! try anything once!). And – they smell quite appetising! Though they look – queer!

Eels are surely one of the scientific surprise packets. For hundreds of years it was known that elvers came swimming up all rivers in Spring, and penetrated down marshes, across wet fields, over dykes far inland. Naturally it was supposed they bred in the seas and estuaries, like every other fish – *but they don't.*

Eel catchers knew there were different sorts of eels, but could find out very little about their mysterious comings and goings. Quite recently, within the last thirty years, scientists have been studying the eels' home-life, but it was not till 1904 that Dr. Johannes Schmidt really found out the extraordinary life history of these eccentric eel travellers.

Apparently there is only one place in all the world where eels breed, and that is one remote spot in the far west of the Atlantic by the Bermudas, and *every eel in the world goes three or four thousand miles to the warm blue Bermuda seas eel breeding station!* There, all the mother eels die, and the larva (which then is a tiny flat leaf-shaped thing) comes up from about twenty-five fathoms and starts off across the warm western water on its three thousand mile swim back to England, home and cold *mud.*

There are two varieties, one which grows quicker than the other, turns left, and gets to America; the other grows more slowly and takes longer to reach Europe and the Mediterranean ditches.

It is still only about an inch long, because it takes three years for the English eel to develop from the egg to the wriggling spaghetti stage, but the American eel can do it and strike up for home and mud in one year.

Anyhow, all those swarms and swarms of live spaghetti-like elvers have come from far across the world, from the eels' ancestral breeding ground. So when you see a tiny wriggling piece of silverish macaroni, about four inches long, slithering through the soft mud, please realise it is four years old probably and an experienced traveller.

Yellows and Silvers

The differences in a full grown eel (that eel catchers had seen for so long) were explained, partly. Eels that are still growing are the yellowish ones. Their eyes are small, their lips are thick, and they have blunt little fins either side of their rather rounded heads. The fishermen call them yellow eels or suckers (or various names locally).

At the end of five or six years when full grown they stop eating, the head becomes pointed, the mouth shrivels smaller, the eye gets bigger, and they turn the black and silvery colour of 'silver eels.'

Then at the end of that summer or *as soon as they can* (it is still a problem what happens to shut up eels that cannot get away) they turn round and migrate back, all those thousands of miles back, to their breeding place. ...

******

The sizzling frying pan is full of crisp brownness. They are strewed with chopped parsley, and in every way they cook them very like whitebait at Greenwich. They are served with vinegar, or a squeeze of lemon juice, and bread and butter, and are really a very appetising dish.

But, if you had told me beforehand they were edible I would never have believed you. Astonishing place, England! Always something new! and this dish is as old as King Alfred's cakes – probably!

Tuesday, 2 April 1935

Jubilee in the green world

Jubilee dawn in the country.

A cool wind blows in through the open window, swaying the muslin curtain and bringing a scent of dew wet woods...

Cautiously I cat-foot downstairs, shoes, string held in hand, carefully avoiding stairs three and eight (known to be creakers), but stair number seven croaks instead – and a sleepy voice asks: 'Is that you?' (Idiot questions people do ask at 6 a.m.)

'You go to sleep again.' I reply firmly, sitting on the mat and pulling on my shoes.

'It is Jubilee Day and I will bring you up a cup of tea to bed when I get back'...

I just looked into the larder in passing. Pretty full larder, visitors for Jubilee.

There are people who would not eat half a custard pie at 6 a.m. It is not I! I also took a sausage in my other hand.

Noisy Nesters

The heavy kitchen door latch gave a raucous squalk as I raised it, and the noise startled two starlings nesting in a hole in the porch roof, so that Mr. Starling jumped out and accidentally swallowed what he was carrying (I heard Mrs. Starling swear overhead). Starlings are awfully noisy nesters.

It was peaceable sitting in the porch... sun warm... not a breath of wind, not the faintest sign of Jubilee about yet, and it might be any other morning... very, very, peaceful.

From a cottage comes the sound of snapping dry sticks and blue smoke begins to weave out of the chimney pot, and a pump handle creaks, filling the kettle.

Thoughtfully I poke the sausage tail through the pine-knot hole into the starling's larder and paddle off down the wet garden path between the gooseberry bushes.

For Robin

The resident robin appears and accompanies me hopefully, as far as the damp handle of the garden fork left sticking up among the cabbages. He flicks on to this facing first this way, and that, and 'chip,' 'chipping' as I pass, so that I have to stop and turn over a couple of forkfuls for him.

Then I cross through the little wicket gate into the wood. The wet bushes shower drops into my shoes and over my head as I push the gate open, and a dripping wet cherry tree shakes drippings down my neck, so that I give a little gasp at the cold.

Beyond, where the path opens, the sunshine lies on paddock grass, already yellow with buttercups, where the tracks of the cows passing out through the gate to be milked have shaken green tracks across the dew whitened grass, as if one had trailed giant fingers over the meadow.

All gold in the sunlight outside, but within the wood all is still, shadowy blue dawn. All over the sloping green banks are great soft splodges of wet primroses, almost spongy wet and glistening white in the dimness. In beyond, under the low boughs, lie drifts of dull bluebells, soft, deep blue, as if the quiet of a summer night still lay sleeping in the woods… and drifting over the blue a milky way of the ghost stars of frail white wood-anemones…

Noiselessly an owl goes through the green twilight, the small shadows of the wood rippling and patterning over his downy back. Noiseless as a ghost he goes, and the scent of violets lies heavy in blue pools in the still air… The wood is still asleep.

Suddenly! A magpie tilts and rocks and crackles through the fence like a feathered alarm clock exploding the sleepiness, like a black-and-white nursemaid chattering and arousing the sleeping wood to wakefulness! And ludicrously! completing the fairy tale, out bundle two baby bunnies, their brown fur matted together into little points with dew and the pair of them lop off hurriedly down the path before me, bob under the hedge and join the nibbling family at breakfast in the paddock, exactly like two baby late-for-breakfast culprits.

A second magpie trails after the first as I go through the little wicket out on to the wet green grass. There is a new sweetness in the meadow, for the cowslips are out, pale lemon gold, shaking their heads gently to the spring air.

Old Man Trout

At the foot of the meadow runs the small river and beyond, down the valley, a cuckoo is calling – calling – calling – calling, through the mists behind a white hawthorn bush... It is very peaceful.

Deep in a pool under the bank a fish rises, plops and sinks down again... My Grand-daddy tried to catch that trout, his son tried to catch that trout. I reckon all the men of our family have always tried to catch him. He is a sort of institution. I believe if any of them did catch him now accidentally, they would put him back – it would be so awful not to have him hanging round...

Now a second cuckoo is calling, faintly; faintly;... far off at the other end of the valley. The two soft insistent notes catch up, and pass, and interlock, with the cuckoo in the nearer meadow, so that the grey rounded notes fall as loosened pearls on the smooth string of the silver river water...

Behind, the village on the hill is waking, the cocks are giving off a regular fanfare...

Sitting here in the sunshine it is very, very still... all the people who would have gone to work by this time are still in bed.

The day unfolds, without the sound of hooters from the valley; nor the church bells from the hill.

Our Lords and Ladies

The river runs on, the ants toil ceaselessly up and down, a frog slides down through the water. I see him go down, down between the green stems.

On the tiny island the yellow kingcups with their purple-stained stems shed their gold, unsung, to the silver minnows warming their tails in the shallows, or nod to their own gold reflections in the stream. The only Lords and Ladies we have stand green-hooded and hidden under the steep green banks.

To be alive, awake on a May morning is the Jubilee of the green world.

As I stand up a lean old water-rat comes out of a hole in the bank and breasts the stream... The current makes it stand up in a tiny frill around his neck, and the wash lays his whiskers back over his wet shoulders – he is looking for breakfast – and as I turn to go the last piece of crust, gold of a vanished custard pie, goes bobbing down the stream to meet him.

Tuesday, 7 May 1935
[King George V's silver jubilee was celebrated on 6 May 1935.]

The perfect winkle eater

I merely quote wot the nobleman said to the fractious pennywinkle ven he wouldn't come out of his shell by means of a pin. – Sam Weller

Unbend the pins, replace the pepper.

On May 14 begins the close season for Winkles! To-day, vagrant between the tides, willy winkle is liable to be picked up and popped off in mid-career.

To-morrow, safe under the majestic arm of the law, the little winkle may pass his way in safety – winkle home to mother, in fact (though a winkle has hardly any home life).

No Written Recipes
The historical succulent lore of the winkle is purely traditional. Nowhere is it confirmed in writing. It is entirely oral and edible.

You will not find winkles mentioned in cookery books, even the gentle Mrs. Beeton herself 'preserves an elegant reticence.'

As they say, 'anyone will *tell* you how to prepare winkles' – but you will not find it written down. Traditionally, therefore, for centuries the tradition of the winkle must have been handed down, as you might say, from father to son – or a wife might, so to speak, 'marry into winkles.'

Now: if they were just a few unexpected edible shellfish, you could understand this, but with winkles *thousands of tons are consumed yearly – millions of winkles are eaten daily* and yet, to put it crudely, you would never think of eating a winkle if somebody else did not put you up to it.

Injustice to the Winkle!
The tradition of winkles seems to be a family matter. This seems unfair! For other snails are noteworthy!

In several parts of England live colonies of the huge great edible snails, traditionally supposed to have been introduced as delicacies by the Romans; and country people use the small garden snails as tonic food for consumption. In Soho you may order snails (imported) to be served with silver prongs and garlic.

Since Cæsar, every enterprising visitor into England has always eaten our shellfish, our oysters, cockles, mussels. And lobsters, crabs, are sauté, paté, fried or piéd, and have a dozen buttery introductions – limpets are traditional in the Isle of Man; crayfish were probably eaten by medieval monks.

Even the blatant whelk may be bewreathed with parsley, but – nothing is said about winkles. They are just 'consumed.'

Also their spasmodic distribution is intriguing. London eats tons, so does Blackpool, Chester eats but few. At Friskington-cum-Salt the winkle statistics may be high, and yet at an adjacent hamlet, the winkle will be practically unknown.

Ditto with fishmongers. Some fishmongers always 'keep them in stock,' others 'do not get asked,' and a few 'would not have a winkle in the place.'

Now, what undercurrent of traditional personality, what subtle national ancestry of our mixed island race, accounts for this anthropologically eccentric distribution of – the winkle eater?

Perhaps the intriguing answer is psychological and based on the adult ability to consume winkles? Because you must not give babies winkles – they swallow them. Even in my infancy in the North, Mayalice Adamans, who would give me anything from shrimps to chips ('if you promise not to be sick'), barred winkles; so, perhaps there is still the childish glamour of the unobtainable?

Or is it the meditative and philosophical air they induce? There is a sort of 'she loves me; she loves me not' detachment about winkles. All winkle-eaters grow retrospective. I remember Our-Old-Tom. He was a perfect winkle eater. He was night watchman where they were mending the road that ran along the embankment by the canal.

He used to sit there by his little sentry-box shelter. He had a big red coke fire bucket, punched full of holes, in front of him and a bit of folded blanket, brown, over his knees, and his hot mug of tea keeping warm beside him 'to his hand,' and a little enamel bowl full of winkles. And he would turn up the little tab end at the bottom of his waistcoat, under the last button, and pull out a long pin and take a winkle... And then he would chuck the empty shell neatly over his shoulder into the canal with a tiny plop.

He did it quite slowly and he always paused. ... (I can see him now, red in the firelight, head aslant, his huge hand just up a bit and held still half-open – curved like a hoary brown shell. ...)

He always paused; just that second, till he heard that tiny plop, before he bent and picked up the next winkle...

His old woman had put him a 'reet proper breakfast' in a basin with a saucer on top all tied up neatly, and he had a basket with a bottle in it. But, as he said, 'winkles they *do* pass the time along very pleasantly One pint I have regular, and when you are so old you can set this seat without your legs dangle you and me will share a quart...'

Winkle-eaters like Our-Old-Tom are so reassuring; they never put you off with vague dates. They have leisure to think out what they mean beforehand.

They have the punctuated outlook on life and you can pin them to the point. ...

Y-e-s, there is something to be said for winkles – but a lot more can be thought. ...

They cost about fourpence a pint. Could you buy an education in philosophy for less?

Tuesday, 14 May 1935

With the once-upon-a times

Once upon a time in a tiny hut in a green forest there lived a charcoal burner who…

(Old Fairy Story)

Well is this series called 'In England Now,' for time and time again I find old jobs done in new ways, and new jobs proving as old as the hills. …

So old, and so constant, is small green England, so unchanging, that many a time between a whiff of wood smoke, and the crackle of a faded yellow parchment, I've gone back far away, dreaming down the old centuries, the lost years, passing by, soft as moths on a summer night… Old… so old and gentle are the ghosts of the old workers who made England. …

Then; Biff! – as if a cockchafer steering his taut-line flight through the dusk had hit me on the nose! I am awake! and back, all dizzy from old dreams and clutching at the fact that it's *to-day* – nearly to-morrow – in England now!

Facts, then, facts before fairy tales.

12th or 20th Century?

In England *now*, within 50 miles of London, lives a charcoal burner, dwelling in a little hut in a green wood full of bluebells complete with nightingale. (With water nymphs in moonlight pools, and magic frog who gives him three guesses thrown in.)

That's *facts*, and he drives a car, and sits in his hut of nights listening to the wireless. There now, do you see why I keep puzzling, whether this is the 12th century or the 20th in England now?

Quite quietly there he is, working in a hollow between the trees, by a quiet lake in a green wood. Four or five hearths smoking away;

[281]

logs piled up, brushwood and windscreens, straw thatch and tinder, log rake and besom broom, and a little wooden hut among the bracken fronds. *And what he doesn't know about charcoal burning isn't knowledge.*

Long Job to Learn

He is a charcoal burner, and his father was a charcoal burner, and when he'd been at it all his life, and thought he'd learnt all there was to know, there came an old chap of about eighty, and he taught him something new.

It's a skilled job charcoal burning. What's more, it's an 'experienced' job. That is, you can't hurry your knowledge, nor increase it by intensive methods. You've got to acquire it slowly. Only experience and knack (which is one part instinct and one part skill) make the charcoal-burner's job inimitable.

Any artist will tell you it takes seven years to learn to draw. And this applies to very many of our English country trades, the workers *are artists* in their craft and only people who know them well realise what consummate artists they are.

Method? They will willingly teach you anything that can be taught in *words* – but it's the doing wherein lies the skill. See; a hearth is built so – sink a little pit in the earth, fuel here and the logs are piled sloping up about a wooden centre set open so (such a centre as one fixes in a stack). It's a wood fire (such as one builds a hundred times in camp). But with this fire *slow*, even heat is wanted, and the weight of the logs must lie so, and the fire must breathe so – this large heavy log go here, that thin one fit there…

Not Mechanically Possible

Thus, the meeting place between the unscheduled growth of life and heat, must be a living skill, impossible of mechanical measurement.

To seal up and calcify wood in a steel furnace would not produce the same quality of charcoal. No, if you cut the wood till it was all level sized, as sticks in a matchbox, there'd still be Nature's incalculable changes of weight, of density, change of sap in the wood, *of life itself.* That subtle unconscious adjustment of air space here, and dry log there, a foreseeing of the inward growth of the fire on the hearth, which he follows in his own brain, in fact, the element of life itself which defeats mechanical jurisdiction.

What is charcoal used for? Well, the charcoal burners follow various trades all over England.

In Kent, they still use some for hop drying, in the North for the haver ovens, on the waterless downs I've known them burn a hearth or two for a rain water filter. Then charcoal is used for welding, fine wireless sets, and aeroplane parts – jewellery soldering – dentifrice – biscuits – gunpowder – distilling. Artists use it to draw with (that's mostly imported vine charcoal, more's the pity). Butchers and florists use it. Great sack loads are sometimes ordered by water boards.

Water Nymph's Secret
Nearly a week the hearths burn.... But while each hearth burns it is a personality to the charcoal burner who has fashioned it. A tractable personality, to be calculated with, and humoured and managed.

'If I damp you down now will you stay quiet and let me get to sleep?'

And then, over the hearths, to the rising mist of blue, the nightingale sings, and the smoke of the watcher's pipe goes up, quietly, quietly, to the trees, and the centuries drift back, and back, through the warm summer night....

What of the water nymphs? Oh! there's a road house close down the highway. And the magic frog? Oh! *he* got into the water pipe and kept them guessing!

Tuesday, 28 May 1935

Before you're up

The valley field lies below my window; beyond, runs the river; above, the slope of the hill meadow cuts off the view. In the dawning, the night mist fills the valley and nobody knows what goes on in the fields, for only the tops of the trees stand up above the whiteness. When the sun is fully up, the mist slides back into the river, and the meadow is left empty for humans again.

The first human that goes into it calls 'C'up, C'up, C'up' and the horse shambles sleepily towards him, and they go back to the farm together, the man leading the way. After that, the other animals begin moving about the meadow. The sheep start first – only the ewes, with late lambs, are down from the hills now. The ewes, close shorn, look thin and small beside their large, woolly ex-lambs.

It's silly poets who lay on about the 'gently nibbling sheep.' A sheep nibbles daintily sometimes, the delicate brown tassels of the rushes, they will nibble those off one by one; the aromatic wild thyme, they will nibble at that as if was sweet-meats – but when there is a good full morning bite of grass, catch them nibble!

Sharp, close-biting teeth – 'C'rusp, C'rusp, C'rusp,' they bite hard at it. Whiles an old ewe will lift her head, and look at you, with her busy mouth full, and the grass ends of her latest bite sticking out in green whiskers at the corners; and by the quick way those green ends spin around and slide in you can tell the pace she is eating....

'Nibble?'... 'B-a-a-a-a-a-a-a!'....

A lot of gawky, black rooks are stalking about the field, stabbing at the green just beyond their splay feet. Every now and then a rook will tilt his head sideways, and peer up at the sky, looking for all the world as if he was sizing up the weather. Probably on the watch-out for the other rooks, or hawks, for we get a lot of hawks on the mountainside.

The starlings, glossy, greasy-looking birds, are strutting and jerking about among the sheep. At intervals, a pair of starlings return to the nest overhead, their last-hatched brood really ought to be independent by now; but there's still racket enough for a dozen in the starling's attic.

The big, gentle, young red bull, the pride of the grazing, is up and awake first among the herd. He goes around, giving them a friendly bunt with his head, exactly like a clumsy little boy wanting someone to play with him.

Presently, a few house dogs that have been shut up and are now set loose go trotting out, and contrariwise the cats that have been shut out all night go trotting in. They all make for the back doors, and when the rugs have been shaken and put out they promptly sit on them and wait for the milk. Chimneys begin to smoke, children's voices are heard, and pumps and water taps thump and gurgle.

Now, out across the field, come two sheep dogs circling joyously, with that smooth, weaving motion that sheep dogs develop from weaving backwards and forwards behind a gently moving flock of sheep. They circle round their shepherd, who stops and has a look at his ewes and lambs in passing. Then he goes out through the field gate and starts off up the mountain. He has a twenty-mile round in front of him to-day.

See that bass slung over his shoulder? That's his dinner and tea, but the bottle is a 'dressing' as like as not, of sheep dope of some sort, because he'll count on scooping plenty of fresh drinking water up there. It's the field workers who take the bottles of cold tea.

The shut up hens are let out now (but the runner ducks won't be let out till after they've laid, so as they don't leave their eggs about in the hedges but safe at home). The hens shake and scatter like a glimmer of brown, and white, and black currant crumbs, on the big green grass tablecloth of the meadow. Billy Cock stretches on to his toes and crows! – flapping so wide that the white feather-sleeves under his black coat show… and from here I can see our Bill down in the farmyard flap his coat off and his rolled-up shirt sleeves white, as he, too, stretches before he souses his red head under the water tap – (Bill Man and Bill Cock look so alike from here!).

What time the humans begin to wake up is really morning.

Along the road beyond the river the long distance lorries swing past. Some miners went to work, the sunlight catching their tin pails. About seven go the café and shop workers, who have to get the places ready before the other workers come.

And So Good Morning

About eight the office workers are going along, and because it looks like rain they carry umbrellas (the other workers went without them).

There's a pause then.

The animals have had their breakfast – most children are having theirs, and only single solitary figures scurry along the road, mostly with bundles.

At 8.30 go the school teachers, on cycles, each with a little packet of books on behind, and about 9 go the school children comfortably in buses, and then it has stopped being morning and it's awfully late because everybody's up and working – (only me!).

Good morning, quickly, to you! – Good Morning!

Tuesday, 30 July 1935

Spell of the sand

There are hundreds of miles of sand dunes around England and many are almost unknown. One holds our first tiny English church, barely 10 feet square, embedded for years deep in the shifting sands. Some sand dunes are shifting away out to sea, others are piling up inland, overtaking and burying small villages, so that here and there a derelict chimney pot stands out among the grass. The dunes hold a spell of their own – they are strange lands, neither earth nor sea.

A wide, free, open sand dune can be the emptiest place on earth. It is well-nigh impossible to cross an extensive dune except on foot. Lumbering and broad-wheeled sand carts may work their way slowly over.

Cut grass and carried timber may make a road for a time. Or wire netting laid down, or trails of tar may hold a track for a while, but one night's gale or one season's quiet persistence will sweep them away and the wind and the sand will obliterate all tracks and leave the sand dune empty again.

Along by the sea, the hard sand may make good going for a horse, or smooth running for a passing cyclist, but the motor-car is frustrated. The motor, all pervading elsewhere, may puff and pant down the last inch of a weed-held sandy track that peters out among the mountainous dunes, but there, at the rim of the golf-course, by the fringe of the shingle, communication ends, the car stops helplessly, and the seagulls swoop ahead laughing. Thus there are miles and miles alone, and withheld, for ever.

I have spent weeks in a half-buried hut on a derelict sand dune, absolutely alone, seeing no one, hearing nothing but the cry of the gulls, or the occasional cry of a rabbit to a hawk or weasel, or a clamour of oyster catchers along the shore.

The hut in the dunes where DH lived for three months.

Yes, this solitude is to be found in England now! Think of it! in contrast with the crowded beaches of Southend, Brighton and Blackpool! Where a stream of fresh water runs out to sea, or a small well bubbles up, camping on a sand dune is just about perfect, otherwise you must camp without washing, except in the sea – (who cares?).

Rain on sand dunes complicates camp life badly, for it rains sand and water simultaneously. Also a sudden wind will bury camp and kit completely within half an hour and obliterate footprints and leave you as lost and derelict as Crusoe.

Because these sand dunes are so empty, do not think they are lifeless or have no industries of their own. According to the variety of the sand dune, very much goes on. On many of the coastal dunes the long level lines of sand have their own industries – of cockle gathering, bait digging and all manner of small fisheries, and across some the weed carts and the sand carts trail their heavy loads back to the mainland.

Where the marrum grass grows – in some places they still cut it, set it to 'win' in shining cones, and then harvest it and take it back and make from it mats to cover hayricks, or long narrow strips to lie between strawberry plants, or sometimes the strong green swathes are twisted into sturdy, short besoms that are used for sweeping or for whitewashing or scouring the shellfish before they are sent in their barrels to market.

Where the short grass covers the dunes, or the low marshes stretch out to sea, the dunes are used for sheep grazing.

On many of the southern dunes there is samphire, which is still pickled, and in the winter wild fowling takes many out across the dunes, over the sandy marshes, on the wild dark nights.

Only for Peace Lovers

Many of our sand dunes are now preserved as bird sanctuaries, others are rabbit warrens (horrible with steel traps in the autumn.)

Some of the smaller dunes are built over with summer bungalows, little communities living happily, between an oil stove and a boat on the beach, through the hot summer days, and leaving a shut-up empty shack to rattle in the winds of winter.

Only, people with weak hearts or semi-invalids should not attempt the sand dunes, for the loose dry sand is the most tiring walking in the world. Only if they are content to stay still in some sheltered spot, should they attempt to penetrate the fastness of the sand dune. The sand dune is for strong lovers of peace!

Tuesday, 13 August 1935

Catching a crab

I'd set the alarm clock for 3 a.m.... 'Whirr...rr...!'

In the silence afterwards the clock of the little red church across the water said 'Three' quietly. I rolled over and looked at the stars... and wished I needn't get up... then pulled on gum boots and a sweater.

Night mist fogged the lamp across the little Hard, and the water slid in long washes to and fro. The running tide sucked and gurgled going out fast... Then I heard the low, hollow sound of rowlocks....

The crab boat swung at her moorings. She was squat and broad and strong. Of old, hundredweights of iron ballast held her steady. Now a small engine is fitted amidships. It squats down low between the wide floor boards, looking like an enterprising hermit crab in the centre of a wide and solid scallop shell.

The tide was running out steadily, smoothing out our wake in oily silver swathes. Gulls, still dark against the greying skies, slid down to break a sheet of molten light. The faint new moon was sunk, and the stars dim. The mist lay low over lost landfalls.

We slid past a sleeping bell buoy, hung silent over a painted buoy below. The mackerel fleet were away, south by south-west. The captain had got his pipe going, and leant back, arms folded. In all the level, empty grey world, the dawn and the silence, held that Peace that enfolds those who escape in boats (even if they only manage to do it sideways in somebody else's crab boat like me!).

There was a pad of bait in the boat; it had been making its presence felt. Now it was got out and sliced up. It was (had been!) gurnet. The plebeian crab likes his fish salad fresh; the aristocratic lobster prefers it gamey – (*very!*).

The sea world was awake over the bar, and the cross current tide broke going down Channel, so that the drift dragged like uneven silk against the rudder...

The round, red sun was come up through the mist when we reached the grounds.

The grounds are rocky bottom. It was on a tossing criss-cross sea we picked up the line of floats that marked the pots.

Six cork floats to each line streaming out down the tide. The line taut between each float, and from the last float the line went plunging down, down below to the pot....

Work Begins
Then came hard work. The boat swung alongside, steered skilfully, close enough to get the short boathook under the line.

'Hoy!'

Engine switched off and the way carried us forward so that the haul came perpendicularly over the pot below... Haul – and up she comes. Haul – hand over hand, hand over hand, and Ho! heave – in board.

The pots are heavy, thick, strong wicker and four bricks tethered, or iron, to weight them down. Some come up empty, from some came the hopeful rattle of hard shell, and the reddish crabs clattered sideways; or a splash of spray, and there were the gunmetal blue and emerald lobsters with scarlet feelers.

Crabs have a period of soft shell, and it's long after the crab has regained the outer appearance before he regains his weight. Only the fine, heavy fellows, the really worthy crabs, went into the catch basket. The others, having had a free fish lunch on the bait supplied, were flung back.

And herewith let me comment on the deportment of crab.

Captive but uncowed, they squat, firm hooked to the wicker, and continue to stuff themselves with bait to the very last! In fact, one fierce old crab attempted to grab a piece to take with him into the basket, and several rejects hooked a souvenir to take back into the sea with them.

The bait is secured thus in a lobster pot. The bait stick (some had been sharpened on the way out) is wedged between two specially sprung withies on the outer side and the point thrust into the thicker, inturned section in the middle. The bait is slung inwards towards this centre section to encourage enterprise down the hole – and discourage hooking it out through the bars.

The bait varies, as each pot was emptied it was rebaited and flung back, splash! The line paid out, the floats again took up their work, and the boat turned and went on to the next pot.

Sorting the Catch

Up and down, backwards and forwards we cruised, turn; haul; and splash back! – forty or fifty pots – in fair weather plain, heavy work, in foul weather each pot a separate strategy and a fierce bit of fighting to get her in board.

CATCHING A CRAB

The first part of the hauling, grooving over the stern, the last part trundling over the heavy iron roller, the water spurting from the wet line in a little sickle-shaped curve.

The lobsters are sorted separately and the pot is rebaited and flung back, splash! The crabs fill a deep pad. Crabs, lobsters, and a make weight of whelks – that's the last pot – let her go – and homeward bound.

A hunch of bread and cheese across the turning of the tide, then work to sort catch – and clear ship, in the quieter water over the bar....

It's broad daylight now and hot sun. All the gulls who have followed the crab boat have left her, and gone back to watch the bobbing floats, till the tide brings the fishers again tomorrow....

The gulls back to the sea. ...

The crabs to the market....

The fishermen to bed....

    and...me?

Well have you ever tried walking home over a sun-bathing beach, in gumboots and thick sweater at 12 noon?

And do you like dressed crab for tea?

Friday, 23 August 1935

The hundred things on my shopping list

This little pig went to market, this little pig stayed at home, this little pig got some fine ros' beef, this little pig had none, this little pig cried wee, wee, wee all the way home.

Oh wise pig, who went to market!…

The one who got 'ros' beef' obviously ate market ordinary dinner, in the small cook-house at the end of the market hall! (Roast beef, new potatoes, and choice of veg, one shilling.)

The littlest pig who squeaked wee, wee, wee with excitement was hurrying back with a basketful of good bargains… (same as me!).

It's not absurd to make a nursery rhyme of a market. There's something like a schoolroom tea-party about a country market of the right sort – very earnest, and to be taken seriously, but a warm friendly atmosphere and lots of fun. I do wish country visitors would *all* trot off and explore their country markets, and enjoy them, because nowadays in the country markets of England you still will find the very freshest, nicest, and in every way the best things we grow or make.

Goodness and Sadness

You will get them fresh, that day, out of the field or dairy, from the very people who grow them, or the very cooks who make them.

Alas! there are sad, forsaken market places where the country folk have been displaced by wholesale dump stalls of ready-made goods. It's heartbreaking to find the last of the country folk shoved away in some forgotten corner of an echoing market hall, that used to be their own, but where the good old pannier markets are still going strong, oh there are the good times, and the big baskets!

Every sort of basket.

Come and see. Here are the goods I found in one small market town last week. Northern markets would have different things, but this was in the warm, rich West country.

So first thing was the cream. Deep bowls of clowted cream, yellow crust top, ('most yellow as butter) and underneath soft fluffy white, and everyone had a little bit to say about just the exactly different way they made it. Some favoured shallow dishes, some 'belonged to use the deep panshons.' ...

Butter, every shade of gold and cream – rolls of it, white wrapped in cloth-lined baskets, circles imprinted with patterns squatting on cabbage leaves, cream cheeses, milk cheeses; eggs, duck-eggs, white and green; custards, lemon-curd, yellow as marigolds, and rich; honey in the comb, in neat sections, honey on the rack (long, crackling foot-long sections of honey), skelp honey (crumpled and brittle, in deep bowls) – honey in jars....

Great bunches of flowers, phlox, stocks, sun-flowers, sheaves of gladioli, bunches of late country roses; jam jars full of honeysuckle; vegetables, in piles or lying about among the flowers on the stalls even as they had done in the garden; big vegetable marrows, cabbages, kidney beans, green and crisp, with some of the biggest beans snapped across to show the seed still juicy, unfilled, a sign that they are fresh and young, for all their size.

Onions plaited on strings; onions, gold-papered, silver-streaked, in rough baskets; little neat pickling onions, green onions for salad.

Bunches of sage, thyme, and parsley, bunches of tarragon for vinegar; green peas, in crates; beans, soft white-lined; new potatoes, young turnips; carrots old and young; cucumbers, slick and straight, or recalcitrantly curled.

A little water-cress (somebody always wants that); boiled 'betrute'; lettuce (cos and cob); samphire, from the stones; mazzard cherries (that of old were used in the cyder); ducks with sage button-holes; chickens, with their livers under their wings; boiling fowls, with suggestive onion alongside – giblets on plates, for soup, 'scratchings,' crisp and yellow (from rendering the pork fat or flead).

Fat Little Thieves

Mint, and bottles of made mint-sauce; pickled walnuts; mixed pickles, dressed horse-radish. Jams, and jams, and jams, (specially) raspberry and strawberry, and currants – red, white and black.

Wind-fall apples, and wind-fall plums (sold for making other jams 'jelly'). Young rabbits, fat from stealing the corn. Blackberries (the earliest). Bilberries (whorts they call them down West). Damsons. Apple pies – pork pies.

One very country dish, a big bowl of wheat, dark, in rich brown gravy. It's the same filling that makes the glossy, thick black-puddings. (This always seems an Eskimo dish – perhaps the Norse folk left it behind.)

Pasties, large and small – all-meat pasties, meat and potato pasties, splits, saffron cakes. Bread of all shapes and sizes (straight from under the bake-pot). Brawn, glassy shiny. Jars of mustard-sauce.

All Lovely

The cooked meat stalls, where the great joints of pork and beef and legs of mutton and ham are cut, and the bowls of butter and the fresh bread – *they will cut you a sandwich while you wait, and pop a fruit pie into a paper bag to carry along!*

Jars of potted meat, dishes of potted fish; shelled shrimps in a matrix of melted butter. A pot-stall, for pans and dishes and tea-pots, cider jugs and wash-basins.

A little stationery stall, for labels and note-books.

Downstairs, meat stalls and fish stalls, with gurnet, mackerel (and the rainbow still on them), plaice, soles, dabs, dried fish, crabs, lobsters, and prawns....

The basket stall (where you'll have to buy the biggest basket).

And don't forget to stroke the market cat before you leave!

And cry 'Wee-wee-wee' 'In England now!' 'Wee-wee-wee,' all the way home!

Tuesday, 3 September 1935

Hold-up by ploughboys

Plough Monday, the first after Twelfth Night be past,
Biddeth out with the plough! The worst husband is last.

That was from the country between Essex and Suffolk in 1571, but Plough Monday was held variously all over England and still *is*.

In some places it marked the return to the field after the Christmas holidays; in other places, farther south-west, it sometimes came a little later and celebrated the lifting of the plough after the early ploughing was all finished.

Accordingly the date varied from the first Monday after Christmas to the first or second in the New Year, for, being a compromise between the delay of weather conditions and the urgency of boy appetites, Plough Monday is a movable feast.

It has its greatest force and reason in the old 'statice' or 'hiring' days, when the farm lads were contracted for much longer periods.

Business and Feasting
Plough Monday feast did give these farm apprentices (i.e., the ploughboys) a chance to meet and compare notes with each other. Often in those days, when farms were much more isolated, and the men and boys 'lived-in' or close to their work, this was really important. It meant that no one farmer could get away with some bad conditions, under-payment, etc., by saying 'it was the same all around the district,' and 'every other ploughboy had to put up with it,' because, on Plough Monday, *all* the ploughboys in all the district, could get together and compare notes. Sometimes two lads on adjacent farms would arrange to swop places, next hiring day, to mutual advantage.

This customarily enforced holiday was so general everywhere, that every farmer had to let his lads off, on Plough Nights, two nights, one for the collecting and one for eating the feast.

The Plough Feast had advantages for the farmer, too; for a wise man, understanding boy nature and liking his lad would say: 'Look you out for a likely young chap to come and work with you next spring,' knowing that if the lad had his own say in the choosing of a comrade, the two were likely to work better together.

In olden days the ploughboys used to drag round a plough with them, and if the farmer did not hand out handsomely towards their supper, they would drag it backwards and forwards in front of his mean doorstep as a testimony against him, a vengeance that would mean his going muddy-footed in-and-out of the house for weeks and have all his womenfolk on to him for the mess!

Nowadays, they just drag round any piece of old metal, and scratch up the gravel a little before your door – as a mark to show they've been, and other parties in the troupe won't come to the same house twice.

Fancy Dress Essential

In Leicestershire they still come round regularly. All the ploughboys get together, disguise themselves with burnt cork, put straw wigs under their hats (anything to prevent their own employers recognising them!), and come along round to all the farms and houses in the village, collecting for 'The Ploughboys' Night.' At houses they begged money. At farms perhaps they'd ask for 'a pork-pie,' at another 'some of the old lady's cake'; at another farm perhaps a fat goose would vanish and some potatoes be missing.

Diligently from dusk till closing time they went round. You all gave them something. They duly scratched the gravel before your door till, amid much laughter and goodwill, the customary collection was made. Sometimes reproof was meted out with some humour.

Hot Humour

I remember in our village (near Leicester) one notoriously mean taskmaster was bearded at his far outside kitchen door at supper-time. The ploughboys in chorus acted very propitiatingly. The spokesmen, very timid, asked diffidently, 'We know, sir; you'd not give us naught, but thought it wouldn't break you *to spare us the mustard for the ham?'*

And while the irate farmer was laying about their shoulders with his spud, the rearguard nipped round through the front window and hooked the ham off his own supper-table!

'It was a fine ham. He'd not cut more than a slice, but' – (as the ringleader confided to me next day, laughing among the straw in the stable) '*us left the old boy his mustard right enough, since he seemed unwilling like to give us any!'*

Mother H's Job

Next day, all the goods they'd collected, and the money, were left in the hands of the local innkeeper's wife, with instructions to sort and cook them a good supper the following evening. And as old Mother H— was a capable soul with a liking for boys, she'd average up the queer collection, buy in the needful, and cook them a really good supper. It used to be a jolly good night's feast. The boys had the room entirely to themselves, and always kept half a crown out for Sally the waitress, because she never would own up quite how much they'd any of them eaten.

Ploughboy Night still continues, but the ploughboys who came with laugh and jest to our door are plough*boys* no longer. Some of you went to the war (and returned, incredibly older, to drive new motor cultivators) – some of you never came back – some of you own farms yourselves now – but – tell me? all you ploughboys – have you forgotten Ploughboy Monday? *No,* and you never will.

Wednesday, 8 January 1936

Town mouse or country.
Which has the best of it?

It's interesting to contrast the country child with the town child at the end of the Christmas holidays. Town children have been to the country for Christmas, country children have been up to Town for the pantomimes.

Whether town child or country child gets the best of life is controversial. The town child has more opportunities, the country child more advantages. The town child has quicker wits, the country child thinks more carefully. Town children learn sooner to depend on other people (if they get lost they take it for granted they will be found). This 'ask a policeman' attitude makes the town child *seem* to have more initiative, but often the country child is more carefully weighing up its greater difficulties, and making up for initiative in self-reliance.

'Entertaining' and 'Doing'
Here's an important difference: The town child is more used to 'being entertained'. In the country we 'do these things for ourselves!'

For instance, if you've ever tried to jump through your hoop and land on a pig – well, I mean the circus has nothing to it! And we have our own horses and our own donkeys, and a great advantage in the country – we can make as much noise as we like – almost always, and nearly anywhere.

Then again, town children are made to go for walks, which must be mouldy, and in the town you wear gloves, or 'take things to play with,' according to whether you are going in the park or not.

In the country you don't '*go for walks*,' you just '*go off*,' and you only wear gloves if your hands are cold, and you come back having had incredible adventures (which you're usually told you oughtn't to

Morning in the village.

have had, but you've had them then, so it doesn't matter). Actually the régime of a country child has not varied so much as the town child's. I am thinking of the *real* country. In remote villages, isolated farms or rectories, and so on, their life is very much the same as their grandmother's was, plus a little extra freedom and rather more schooling. This real country life I know very well.

About a quarter to seven is 'getting up time' (earlier than in town). The country child doesn't have a hot bath in the morning nearly so usually as the town child, for very few country houses have the same bathing facilities, and the jug of cold spring water and basin are still most usual in the country bedroom. The country child has a good, cold splash and them tumbles into warm clothes and scatters downstairs to the kitchen where the newly-lighted fire is roaring up the chimney. Usually the men folk have had some breakfast, and the simplest, most favourite child's dish is bread, fried in the gold bacon fat still left in the pan.

Country children usually have breakfast on the table by the kitchen window, tea, not coffee, plenty of milk, and then the boots and gloves warming in the kitchen fender are put on, school books and lunch are collected, and they're on the road soon after eight for nine o'clock school, for in spite of buses and bikes the real country child often has a long walk.

They Don't Forget

At noon, when the town child is having 'school dinner,' or come home to steamed fish or grilled chop, the country child only gets a cold snack, though usually they can get hot cocoa, or a vacuum flask of soup, or 'something hot' at the school.

Country children start back earlier from school say, by three o'clock, and often (this makes me label them as reliable) have errands and messages to deliver, or things to bring back, *and they very seldom forget.*

In summer it's 'play-time' on the way home, and most country children are well scolded for 'dilly-dally dawdling' and not getting home and 'being late for their tea.' 'And they should think of the little ones, and not let them go hungry so long,' etc., etc. But healthy hunger brings them home pretty quick in the cold winter, and then they have dinner.

This, the big difference in the régime of the country and town child, is, I think, an advantage to the country. The town child having to go back to school directly after a big dinner (or romping it off without a proper rest) is at a disadvantage compared with the country child, who comes home, is told to take his wet things off, change his boots, wash his hands and face, and then sits down to a really satisfying meal.

Homework and Odd Jobs

The steamed fish and the delicate fare may be lacking, but the big slices of cold meat, the gravy and potatoes and the puddings that have been cooking so gently, can be eaten slowly, and afterwards legs are tired enough to keep them quiet for a little. Then, in the evening, homework, jobs about the house (for country children have very definite jobs to do), and then, milk, cocoa, and bed, in a room usually quite as cold and as draughty as being out of doors!

In diet, the country child has less variety. 'Fruit' in winter means 'apples'! Oranges are still only Christmas, and the idea of squeezed fruit juice would be thought purely medicinal. If the healthy country child feels a need for vitamins, it's perfectly capable of helping itself to a slice of raw turnip and digesting same.

Still, country food is good, is wholesome, and very pleasant. So – it's difficult to know which gets the best childhood!

Tuesday, 14 January 1936